MW00387556

Nantucket Publishing

[signature]

Unshackled

The names and descriptions of many of the people
in this book have been changed to protect their
identities, and some of the events have been altered.

Also by Harold Morris

TWICE PARDONED
BEYOND THE BARRIERS

Harold Morris

Unshackled

Published by: Nantucket Publishing
602 S.W. Ward Blvd.
Wilson, N.C. 27893

ISBN Number 0-9662718-0-7

Library of Congress Catalogue Card Number: 98-90159

Manufactured in the United States of America

Book Design, Ruth Moore

Editing, Cheves Robinson

Exclusive Distributor To The Trade:

NANTUCKET PUBLISHING
Wilson, N.C.

For ordering information, please see the final page of this book.

For Edwin Tucker

Thanks for your friendship, encouragement, and loyalty.

Unshackled

Acknowledgements

I would like to thank Cheves Robinson for his help
with this book. When asked, he gave me the truth.
The mistakes are all mine.

PART I
1938-1969

One

Georgetown, South Carolina, was a small, friendly town of 10,000 people on the Atlantic coast. As a child, I was fascinated that many of the stores along Front Street were built over the water, and fishing boats could ease right up to the rear of the buildings to unload the day's catch. I never thought life could be better than it was in Georgetown during my early years.

My father worked at the International Paper company's mill, one of the largest of its kind in the world. He was a middle-aged widower with seven children when he met and married my mother, who was twenty-one years younger. Four more of us came along after they were married; I was second-to-last.

Life in Georgetown was tough with so many mouths to feed, and my father longed to return to the farming life he had known as a boy. By the time I was in the third grade, Dad finally left his job at the mill and moved us to the country. We settled on a farm at Pleasant Hill, South Carolina, about forty miles from Georgetown. It was a sparsely populated community with fields as far as the eye could see. The pace was so slow and the community so small, there wasn't even a traffic light.

Times were hard, and it was difficult to make a living off the land. As sharecroppers we were so poor that poor people called us poor. There was a black family who lived on the road leading to our house. They lived off odd jobs their father could get. One day, Jeremiah, who was about my age, said, "Harold, y'all poor." A friend asked me one day if we had running water. I said, "Yeah, if you can catch it before it runs down the hill." All we had was an old pump that had to be primed before you could get water out of it. At school one day, I told a friend that our bathroom had caught on fire.

He said, "Did your house burn down?!"

I said, "No, we put it out before it got to the house."

He burst out in laughter. We often didn't know where our next meal was coming from, and to help ends meet Mom took a job at the International Paper company's container division back in Georgetown. A neighbor provided the transportation.

Looking back, I don't know how my mother managed to meet the needs of the whole family, help with the chores on the farm, and work in Georgetown, too. She seemed tireless, and I always thought she was the sweetest woman on earth. A gentle lady who always looked for the best in people, she was loved and respected by everyone who knew her. Even tempered and generous, she never turned a stranger away without giving him a hot meal.

On rare occasions when she had the time, she attended church services. Once or twice my father went with her, and I even went a few times to see my friends, to meet girls, or to attend social functions. I was interested in having fun when I got away from the farm - nothing else.

Although my father had little use for church activities, he was a good man who expected goodness in return, an honest man who demanded honesty from his family and from those with whom he did business. He loved to tell salty stories, and my friends often came to hear the earthy experiences of his boyhood and the outlandish yarns born of his imagination. He also had a huge storehouse of off-color jokes. In spite of his raunchy language, his engaging personality seemed to win over anyone who knew him.

Because my father had lots of common sense and could hold his own in a conversation, people assumed he had been well educated. No one ever guessed that he couldn't write his own name and that he hadn't been to school a day in his life. Because he was so honest, Dad never tried to hide his lack of education. He loved to joke about going to school two days in his entire life - one day to sign up and the next day to tell them he wouldn't be back. But whenever the conversation was turned to education, I changed the subject. Although I was proud of my father in many ways, his illiteracy humiliated me.

Nevertheless, I hated school, and I'd never have gone a single day of my life if my father had not insisted. "You'd better make good grades," he warned me. "I don't want you to end up like me." He desperately wanted me to have an education, but paradoxically, he did not know how to encourage me. Many times he kept me out of school to work on the farm. If I wanted to play a game of baseball in the afternoon, I had to stay home from school in the morning to finish my chores. Work always came first.

Every day after school, every weekend, every summer, I worked on the farm until dark - and sometimes long after dark - cropping tobacco, picking cotton, and feeding the animals. I plowed with mules until we could afford a tractor. There was little else in our life outside the farm.

It was at this time in my life that I received my first real lesson in racial prejudice. When I was about fourteen years old, I was plowing a mule one day. The sun was blazing hot overhead. My father was following about twenty yards behind, dropping seeds into the furrow.

A bus with a Winyah High Gators banner drove by, and distracted for just a moment, I let the mule go off line in the hardscrabble I was plowing.

"You idiot!" my father shouted, "D'you know what a straight line means?"

I reined the mule in and stopped for a moment to take a drink from my jug. A skinny black boy about my age, Jeremiah, struggled down the road towards me, obviously suffering from the oppressive heat. Jeremiah lived along the dirt road that went to my house, and when I wasn't working in the fields we often played together. As he approached, Jeremiah watched me with pleading eyes. After I finished, I handed the jug to him. But as he started to drink, my daddy suddenly jerked the jug away from him.

"Ain't you got no sense at all?" he growled at me. "And you!" he glared at Jeremiah, "Somebody sure better learn you your place, boy!

Now, git!"

My father watched him go, smiling with dumb cracker pride.

"See, you can't reason with 'em," he explained to me, "because they can't think like we can. So, you gotta tell 'em."

He looked solemn, like a father passing on one of life's great lessons, and I nodded, taking it in like the Gospel. He ruffled my hair with his hand.

"Now get back to work," he said, "and be glad you ain't no nigger."

Good times were few, other than an occasional swim in the lake or a movie in Hemingway, a very small town about thirteen miles away, or the annual trip to Hemingway when the fair came to town. We couldn't afford a television set, and keeping the chores caught up left little time to cultivate friendships. Our nearest neighbor lived quite a distance away, so my brother Carl, who was a year and ten months older than I, was my best friend.

There was one thing my father enjoyed more than working the farm and that was hunting. I hated the overnight hunting trips because my dad couldn't understand how much the killing bothered me. I simply could not kill an animal. Whenever my dad positioned me on a deer stand I desperately hoped a deer wouldn't come. I knew I could never pull the trigger. As I grew older, I refused to go along on the hunting trips.

Often on these trips he drank heavily, and many times I saw him pass out in a drunken stupor. One day he returned from a trip feeling ill after skinning a deer. Flinging his beer can across the yard, he declared he would never take another drink. As far as I know, he never drank again.

Although the people in the community admired this kind of determination and fortitude in my father, at home his strong will made him hard, domineering, and determined to have his own way. I loved him deeply, but I did not know how to express that love and neither did he. Our inability to communicate was complicated by the great gap between our ages - he was forty-six when I was born. He could not understand why I disliked school and why I hated hunting and killing animals. Because we never understood each other, we never developed a close relationship.

Because my father was so unbending about what he wanted, he demanded obedience. And when we didn't obey, his discipline was both swift and harsh. Using a board or a belt or his fist, he would beat me. "You're no good!" he would rage at me. "You'll never amount to anything!"

No matter how bruised or battered I was after a beating, the verbal abuse was more painful. I told myself he didn't really mean it, but his words etched themselves upon my soul and I could not forget them.

My dad was not the only one who berated me like that. At school my teachers and coaches reinforced what my father was screaming at me when I was home. "You're no good, Morris," they would say. "You'll end up being a no account."

I didn't want to believe them. High-strung, angry, and aggressive, I was determined to prove all of them wrong, bent on showing everybody that Harold Morris was worth something. To me there was only one way to do it, and that was to become a great athlete. I wanted to be like my idol, Mickey Mantle of the New York Yankees.

My brother Carl also loved baseball. Strong and athletic, he was a left-handed pitcher. He spent hours pitching to me, and that practice worked to my advantage.

Although Pleasant Hill was one of the smallest schools in the state, we had a baseball and a basketball team. Since the students were from farm families who valued hard work as highly as my father did, chores always came ahead of sports. One day when I was in seventh grade, the high school baseball coach called me out of class. His catcher had to help harvest his father's tobacco crop, and the coach wondered if I could serve as a substitute.

The catcher's gear weighed more than I did, but I caught a great game, called the signals, and I even got two hits. The local newspaper carried a story calling me the hitting star of the game! Carl had pitched a one-hitter, and we won thirteen-zip. For the rest of the season, and for the next year as well, I caught for Carl whenever he pitched. By the time I was a freshman, I was the starting catcher.

All during that time, I longed to play sports at a more competitive level. Often as I plowed the fields, I'd see a school bus with "Big Red Winyah Gators" painted on the side. It was carrying Winyah's athletic teams to games. Winyah High School in Georgetown had a great sports tradition. The teams wore beautiful red and white uniforms, and the newspapers gave their games generous coverage.

One autumn day, I stopped the tractor and watched the bus fade into the distance. The sun was setting through the trees, and only the wind and earth heard my dream. I'd give anything to be a Winyah Gator - to dress in one of those red and white uniforms. If only I could play at Winyah High!

When I wasn't working in the fields I was bouncing a basketball in the dirt outside the small shack where we lived. I'd nailed a rusty bike tire rim to a tree, and at the base of the tree I'd set a pine board at an angle to the ground. The ball would sail through the rim, bounce off the tree, the pine board, and the ground before rolling right back to my feet.

I would play imaginary games. I would say to myself, "Tie game," and I'd dribble the ball at the free throw line I'd etched in the dirt with the toe of my shoe. "This ... is for the win and the state championship."

I'd arc the ball through the rim. "He scores!" I'd shout. "The crowd goes wild!" And I'd jump around with my arms over my head as I made the sounds of the overjoyed crowd. To me, my dream had come true. I was a Winyah Gator, and I was the star.

This all came to an end when my daddy hollered, "Get your dumb behind in this house! Right now! It's time for supper, boy."

As I walked into the house, chastened, he would push me through the door. But nothing, nothing on earth could take away my dream of becoming a Winyah Gator. And one day that dream became a reality.

Two

The headlights of the police car flashed across a solitary figure crouched on the sidewalk. The police car slowed, turned around in the middle of the empty street, and pulled to the curb. The woman sobbed helplessly, unable to stand any longer. Her face was slick with tears as the officers lifted her into the patrol car. The contractions were coming fast, she said. Before they could get her the rest of the way to the hospital she warned them her time had come, and Marcus Eugene Odomes was born July 26, 1946, in the back seat of a patrol car at 1:26 in the morning.

Growing up in Harlem, Marcus was never allowed out of his mother's sight. He was her one treasure, and she guarded him jealously. His mother worked as the maid for a wealthy white family, and he accompanied her every morning to the house where they lived. He spent almost as much of his day in that house as he did in the small apartment he and his mother called home. Marcus couldn't help but notice the difference in the way he and his mother lived and the way that the whites who his mother worked for lived. He particularly noticed how many toys the white boys had to play with - they had a whole steamer trunk filled to the top with toys they *didn't* play with anymore. One day Martha saw Marcus playing on the floor of the kitchen with one of these toys, and she asked him where he got it. He said that one of the little white boys had given it to him. She told him to return it. He didn't want to. She insisted. He blubbered. She snatched the toy away from him and returned it to the toy box. She thanked the boys for their generosity, but said that Marcus had accepted the toy without asking her. The two little white boys didn't know what she was talking about. They said that they hadn't given Marcus a toy to play with. They said he must have gotten it out of the bin himself.

She returned to the kitchen furious at Marcus for trying to steal the toy and furious at what she felt was the implication behind stealing the toy: that she wasn't doing a good enough job providing for her own child. But when she got to the kitchen she couldn't find him. She finally found him hiding out in the pantry. "You'd *better* hide," she seethed, almost unable to speak. "Because when I get you home I'm gon' tear you up." And she did. Her frustration at his ingratitude poured out of her and all over him. She slapped him so hard she hurt her thin hands.

When it was over, when she had no strength left, they were both crying and sad and angry. Neither could speak. But there was nothing to be said. He had stolen, and he had been caught. He had dishonored himself, and he had dishonored her. She thought that was clear. But Marcus didn't see it that way. He saw the way the whites lived. He heard the little white boys calling his mother by her first name and ordering her to do things for them that he had to do for himself at home: "Martha, fix me some chocolate milk, please." Or, "Martha, I can't find my blue jacket. What did you do with my blue jacket?" They spoke to her as if they were both adults and she was a child. They did not speak to him at all, and all of it made him angry.

They had everything in the world, he thought, and they didn't even seem to appreciate it. They had toys that they didn't play with - toys that he wasn't even allowed to *touch*. And so he took one. He knew it was the wrong thing to do in his mind, but in his heart it *felt* like the right thing to do. And then he was punished because he wanted one small toy from all of the toys heaped in the giant toy box. He didn't see how it was fair.

Her employer offered to give Martha the clothes her children couldn't wear any longer. Martha tried to refuse this generosity, but in the end she took the clothes and then gave them to charity. She remembered how she hated wearing "hand-me-downs" as a child, and she would not have her son looking or feeling like he was second rate for any reason. She was determined to support him on her own, but the almost constant work weighed on her heavily. Because she could not afford to be sick, she had to work through her illnesses and consequently stayed sick much of the time.

She was always worn out from her work and rarely ventured out after dark. She did not see many men. But she tried not to resent her child because of it. She was determined that Marcus should never feel for even one second that he was not wanted, as she had sometimes felt as a child. She was determined not to be a harsh disciplinarian like her father was, but after a time she found that this was the only way to control the child. Marcus lived by a very regimented schedule - up at a certain hour and in bed at a certain hour - and, when he was old enough, the schedule included helping his mother with the evening wash. Marcus didn't want to wash other people's clothes and one time asked his mother why white people didn't do their own wash. His mother responded curtly, "You better be glad they don't. This job puts food in your mouth and clothes on your back." And that was all that she had to say on the matter.

Marcus didn't have any friends - didn't have a chance to make any friends - until he went off to kindergarten. His mother knew that he was the son of a college man, so she expected him to do well in school and she hoped that perhaps he would go to college one day. Every morning she dropped him off at kindergarten where she asked the teacher, a stout black woman in her forties, how Marcus was progressing. The teacher said Marcus was one of her brightest students, but sometimes he liked to "act out" and get all of the attention. His mother had the same problem when she was younger, and she told his teacher that Marcus "came by that honest".

Marcus acted out often to get the attention he needed. He didn't even mind being sent to stand in the corner because he knew that all of his schoolmates were more interested in what he was doing in the corner than they were in what they were being taught.

Outside of his misbehaving, Marcus was a very charismatic young boy who made friends easily. It was in kindergarten that he first became a leader. He enjoyed the sense of importance he got from being the boy the other young boys wanted to sit next to. Marcus looked forward to going to school and being with his friends, because at home his mother did not put up with the kind of "nonsense" that he got away with at school, nor did she give him the kind of attention that he got from his friends.

He did not look forward to weekends, however, because most Saturdays he had to stay at home and work with his mother. It was on one of these Saturdays, when he was feeling especially put out about having to work, that he finally decided to ask her why he didn't have a father - a father who supported them with his work. Up until this time he knew or sensed that his mother didn't want to talk about his father. At first she was angry, but then she decided that he deserved some kind of answer. For a moment she thought about telling him that his father was dead, but she didn't. She sat him down and told him the truth.

At seven years of age he found out about how his father, a college student, got his mother pregnant and then abandoned her. She told him about how she left home without a word to her parents and came to New York City to find him at school and to tell him that they had a baby on the way, and she told Marcus how his father wouldn't believe her and how he turned her away. She looked down into Marcus' eyes and without a trace of anger in her voice - only resignation - she told him, "And that's why you don't have a father. And that's also why you have to help me work on Saturdays instead of going to the park to play with your friends. Because I was in love with a man who wasn't in love with me."

Marcus saw that his mother was close to tears.

"It's all right, Mama," he said, "I love you."

"I know you do, baby."

"When I grow up *I'm* gonna marry you."

And that just made her cry harder.

From that point on, whenever Marcus heard stories from his friends about their older brothers making big rolls of cash dealing drugs on the street corners he thought about doing the same thing and giving the money to his mother or using the money to buy her a car or even a house. From everything that he had seen and heard, living the honest life was hard and tiring work, and it was impossible to get ahead doing it. This lesson was brought home to him when his mother became seriously ill for the first time. She took a day off from work - the first day off Marcus could remember - and she went down to the free clinic.

When Marcus got home from school, she told him the trip to the clinic was a waste of her time. She said that the doctors down there didn't know any more than she did. "You'd have to be bleeding out the eyes for them to take a good look at you down there," she ranted. "I *know* there's something wrong with me! I don't need a medical degree to know *that*. And then I go down there, and they tell me that there's no *reason* for me to feel bad and to go on home and get some *rest!* I'm not a *child*. They treat me like I don't know *my own mind*."

Marcus watched as his mother became sicker and sicker and missed more and more work just to go down to the free clinic to be turned away and told that there was nothing seriously wrong with her. Money got even tighter, and Marcus told his mother that he wanted to get a job. She resisted the idea of her thirteen-year-old son working outside the home. Nevertheless, Marcus set out with high hopes but soon found that jobs were scarce and many merchants didn't even want him in their stores. When he told the store owners about his sick mother he saw that they didn't believe him for some reason. He didn't know why they wouldn't believe him, but it made him angry.

Then one day he heard that the drug dealers on the corners had started using young boys to make their deliveries for them. Marcus knew he could make money walking brown paper bags from one side of the street to the other after school and before his mother got home. He wanted to start right away, but the dealer wanted to make him a "lookout" before trusting him with moving the merchandise. Marcus was paid to stand around and look for cops. After the first day, he told his mother he had gotten a job sweeping floors at a local hardware store. At first she was angry, but then she was very proud of him.

As soon as his mother was well enough, she made a point of going down to the hardware store to thank the man for hiring him. The man told her that he never hired her son. Once again, Marcus had made her feel foolish. As she waited at home for him to return that evening, her anger grew and grew.

When Marcus came through the front door he found his mother scowling at him. Before he could say anything she spoke.

"I went down to the hardware store today . . ."

Marcus didn't move - he just stood there with his hand on the door-knob. He didn't know whether to take off running or to stand there and risk a beating.

"You want to tell me where you been getting that money?"

"No."

"Why not? What have you been doing?"

"Nothing really."

Marcus pulled some bills out of his pocket and put the crumpled up wad on the table where his mother was sitting. She looked at the money suspiciously. Then she looked at him, obviously waiting for him to continue.

"Ain't nobody going to pay you for doing nothing, Marcus."

"All I do is stand there and watch up and down the street. That's all."

"A *lookout?* For *who?*"

"Floyd's big brother's friend."

"Who?"

"Little Nero."

"Get that filthy money off my table and out of my house. And you tell him that you can't work for him."

"You don't know -"

"I know. Take the money back."

"When I get to be a runner I'll make almost as much money after school as you do all day long."

"You take that filthy money off my table *this instant.*"

Marcus gave her back a stare and stayed rooted to the spot. She stood, slowly came around the table, and advanced on him. Marcus suddenly found himself backing up until he was standing in her shad-ow, pressed up against the door.

"You are still a *child*."

"*I am not!*"

"Just because you get paid like a man don't make you a man. So *don't show your behind to me*, I'll beat you until you can't see straight and if you don't believe me now I'll *make* a believer out of you!"

Marcus went the very next day and quit. Suspicious, his boss wanted to know why he was quitting. Marcus fumbled around for an excuse, but the drug dealers quickly guessed the real answer and their taunts sent Marcus home in tears.

The next time she fell ill Martha knew it was serious. She skipped the clinic and went straight to the hospital. After a series of tests, she spent a sleepless night worrying. The news was grave: leukemia. The doctor said she had less than a year to live.

Three

Finally, my dad realized we couldn't survive sharecropping, and he decided it was time to give up farming and move back to Georgetown. It would take a while to sell the equipment, but Dad said I could stay in Georgetown with one of my brothers who had offered to help us. I could go to school at Winyah. I was thrilled! For me, moving from the sticks to a town of 10,000 was like going to New York City.

As much as I wanted to go to school at Winyah High, I was scared to death. It was a big school, and I was a bashful country boy. I didn't know how to "act", and I had a tremendous longing to be accepted and loved. In almost every area I felt inadequate - but in sports I knew I could be a winner. Natural athletic ability and my six-foot-two-inch, 180 pound frame gave me confidence and an advantage in sports. For the first time in my life, I knew I was good at something.

Winyah's football games were the biggest events in town, and the first game I ever saw dazzled me. Mesmerized, I marveled as the quarterback, wearing number 50, scored one touchdown after another. The fans cheered, whistled, and screamed their support and approval.

"I'm going to play football next year," I said to a friend.

He laughed, "You don't know anything about football!"

"Oh, yes I do," I lied. "I'm good - and next year, I'm going to play."

I didn't know what "first and ten" meant, but I knew this: I'd play football for Winyah High, and I'd wear number 50.

When I went out for football in my junior year I knew so little about the game that the coach asked me if I'd ever played before. I admitted that I hadn't.

"Boy, you are country!" he said. Everybody laughed, and the nickname "country" stayed with me all through high school and later years. I hated it. Later, when he was angry at me, he said, "You can take the boy out of the country, but you can't take the country out of the boy."

At our first scrimmage the coach assigned me to a defensive position until another player broke his arm during the first quarter of our first game. For the rest of the game - and for the season and throughout the next year - I played both defense and offense, rarely missing a down.

But I didn't limit myself to football. When I asked the basketball coach about trying out for the varsity team he laughed.

"All right," he finally said. "It's another month until practice starts, and some of the players come here at night to get in shape. You can work out with them, and then we'll see."

I was scared. What if I wasn't good enough after all? Although I hadn't learned the fundamentals of the game, I could shoot a basketball, and apparently I made a good impression. The coach not only picked me for varsity, but he also started me in the first game. I was the first sophomore ever to make the varsity.

Being one of the top players thrilled me, especially since our first game was against Pleasant Hill. I scored thirteen points. The game was more than a victory for our team; it established me as an athlete, and that recognition was my key to peer acceptance throughout high school. It gave my self-esteem a tremendous boost.

I loved all sports, but baseball was special. Bad grades cost me my position my sophomore year, and during my junior year I was suspended from the team for three games for being late to school. During one of those games a scout for the Cleveland Indians came and asked for me. The coach told him I'd been kicked off the team. Later, the coach could hardly wait to tell me I'd blown my big chance; the scout had decided I wasn't the kind of material he needed. I realized I'd missed the scout because I'd ignored the rules. My heart was broken. Time after time that happened in my life. I always seemed to mess up the big opportunity.

Nevertheless, the goals that I set upon entering Winyah High became a reality. During my senior year I served as captain of the basketball, baseball, and football teams. I felt an enormous sense of accomplishment when I was recognized as the best athlete not only in the school, but in the entire county, and when I was selected to the all-state basketball team. I particularly enjoyed the attention the girls gave me.

One especially beautiful girl, Katie, had captured my attention in my junior year. Her numerous beauty titles verified my opinion that she was absolutely gorgeous. The only child of wealthy, college-educated parents, Katie knew exactly where she was going in life. A straight-A student, very goal-oriented and emotionally sound, she was exactly the opposite of me, and I was ecstatic when she agreed to go steady with me. Although we loved each other, we agreed to break up when she graduated and went away to college.

I missed Katie, but I filled that void by going to parties with other girls, and I ran with a loose crowd of older guys. My two closest friends were a couple of years older than I. One boy had a fine character and a positive influence over me, but I was attracted to the wild ways of my other friend, and it was with him that I drank my first beer. Easily swayed by peer pressure, I submitted to the standards of the older crowd to gain acceptance.

Yet in spite of my athletic accomplishments and the approval of my friends, something was missing. I never truly saw myself as successful. Perhaps it was because the person who mattered the most to me could not understand me. Day after day my father tried to discourage me from participating in athletics.

"You're wasting your time," he would say to me. "You need to quit playing games all the time and do something worthwhile with your life. If you don't, you'll end up being a good-for-nothing!" Not having any background in sports, he could not appreciate my ability, and he steadfastly refused to attend any of my games.

During my senior year, the homecoming football game was father-son night. The players' fathers were to sit together at the fifty yard line, and at half-time they would be introduced along with their sons. I begged my dad to go.

"It's a very special night, and all of the fathers will be there," I said. "I'm captain of the team, and it would mean a lot to me if you would go."

Dad had never seen me play, but he finally agreed to attend the game. As I dressed I was beside myself with excitement. "Tonight my dad will be on the sidelines with the other fathers," I thought. "Tonight he'll see how well I play, and he'll be proud of me."

We won the game, and I was chosen the most valuable player. I could hardly wait to hear what he would say about my winning touchdown, but I didn't see him after the game. When I got home, my father told me he had left early. I swallowed hard and turned away.

"That's the biggest bunch of nonsense I've ever seen," he said. "Running around wearing all that junk. You looked like something from Mars. I couldn't tell one person from another!"

He hadn't even recognized me! He wasn't proud of me after all. He'd thought it looked ridiculous, and he'd walked out. Although I realized he didn't understand the game, I couldn't comprehend why he didn't want to be there to support me, to be proud of me - to love me.

Later that same year, another incident solidified my sense of isolation. I was chosen to play in the North-South Coaches' All-Star Basketball Game at the University of South Carolina, and I was elated. The celebrated event was a sell-out, and the field house was packed. I was chosen as one of the five starting players, and I played most of the game.

After the game, parents were hugging their sons and telling them how proud they were. I stood off to the side and tried to look inconspicuous, because none of my family or friends had come to see me play. I even had to thumb a ride to get to the game. I'd have given anything if someone had been cheering for me.

After the game, a former coach approached me with his arm around a man.

"Harold, I want you to meet Gene Amaker," he said. We shook

hands.

"You played a great game, son," Amaker said. "How'd you like to come play for me at State?"

I looked to my ex-coach who was beaming, "Gene's a college buddy of mine. He's an assistant coach at State."

I tried to appear unimpressed. I knew I didn't have the grades to go to college.

"Didn't he tell you?"

"Tell me what?" Amaker asked glancing at his friend.

"Man, I didn't go to school but two days in my life: one to sign up and the other to tell them I wasn't coming back," I said.

My ex-coach's smile faded quickly, "Harold, just listen to Gene."

As much as I wanted to play basketball at State, I knew I'd be lucky to graduate high school. I had no choice but to reject the offer as I had many other offers in basketball and football. Again I paid the price for not applying myself in the classroom.

As I left the locker room that night I heard the recruiter say, "Maybe he'll change his mind."

But my ex-coach quickly responded, "He's as hard-headed as they come. I don't know if he'll ever change."

I stopped in the doorway and smiled cockily, "Hey, man, who wants to change? I might end up like you!"

I knew I could not be a jock the rest of my life, and deep inside I really wanted to be a success. The truth was, I didn't know how. I had grown up without learning the importance of continuous goal setting and the importance of moving the target higher each time after a goal is reached. So, I had no plans for after my graduation, and the foundation for my future seemed to be in the fast-and-loose lifestyle I'd begun to enjoy with some of the older kids. At the time, drinking beer, chasing girls, and running with an older crowd seemed to me a good way to prove myself. In reality, that lifestyle was setting the pace for the days to come.

Four

Her first thought was of Marcus and what would happen to him after she'd died. Her next thought was of her parents. She called them from the hospital and gave them the news. They were heartbroken and told her they were coming to get her that day. Marcus and his mother packed their few belongings and moved back into the house in Philadelphia that she had slipped out of in the middle of a cool March night thirteen years before.

Marcus seemed to genuinely enjoy all of the attention - especially the attention he got from his grandfather. They got along very well in the midst of all of the other women. But even in the best times Marcus could never forget that his mother was slowly dying, and he regretted every hour of every day he spent in school and away from her. The disease spread quickly, and soon it was an effort for her to get out of bed and shuffle to the bathroom. The doctor administered prescription painkillers.

After eight months of agony the end seemed at hand. All of her brothers and sisters were called home to see her one last time. They arrived one by one and immediately went up to Martha's room. First there were smiles, then long faces, then tears.

On her deathbed, Martha asked her sister Florida, working as a nurse in Atlanta, to take Marcus with her and raise him. She told Florida she knew that it took a lot of energy to raise up a boy into a man, and she didn't think that her parents had it left in them. Florida, who was still single, agreed only because she could not bear to turn Martha down.

"I don't want him to mope around here for the rest of his life. I want him to start a new life in a new place after I'm gone," Martha said. "I want him to get an education like you did. I just know you'll raise him right. You and I were always of the same mind."

"Well, Atlanta ain't exactly New York City," Florida said, "but I expect he'll like it right well."

At the dinner table that night Florida told the family - out of earshot of Martha, who had her food brought to her in her room - that "those white clinic doctors" in New York City robbed Martha of her life. Florida got Marcus to recount the number of times that his mother went to the clinic complaining of feeling ill only to be sent away. Marcus said that his mom hadn't been well in a long time, "She was always feeling bad, tired, getting thinner and thinner. Anybody could see that."

"I know how they do black folks at them free clinics," Florida said taking up the fight. "Those devils don't care one way or the other about you. They just want to get you out the door and back into the street. Now, if you're white, that's different."

Martha died within the week, but before she did she asked to speak to Marcus for the last time.

"I'm so proud of you," she told him. "I don't know how you turned out so well, but I'm thankful that you did. Please respect Florida. Listen to her. Get an education like she did. You're so smart, I just know you're gonna be fine."

Marcus threw his arms around her neck, "I'm so scared, Momma."

"Don't worry, baby. When I get up to heaven I'm gonna watch over you. And you're gonna make me so proud. The angels are gonna see me peeping down off of my big old white cloud, and they're gonna ask me, 'Whatchoo smiling about, sister?' and I'm gonna point and say, 'You see that one right there? That's my boy.'"

It was a long ride back to Atlanta. Florida tried to have a conversation with Marcus, but it never really lasted very long, and they always returned to the subject of "those white devils and what they did to your mother". The hate and grief that Marcus had been holding in acting like a "little man" finally came to the surface as Marcus talked about what happened. Fat tears rolled down his cheeks. Soon it was as if he couldn't stop crying, and Florida began to worry about him.

"You're really going to like Atlanta," she said, forcing a smile. "You're going to make a lot of new friends."

She couldn't think of anything else to say. After he cried himself out, he fell asleep.

Life in Atlanta was different. At school, instead of being welcomed by the other boys, he was challenged to fight. After refusing to fight two white boys, they ambushed him and beat him bloody anyway. When Marcus got home that afternoon Aunt Florida was horrified to see his swollen eye and the cut across his chin. She wanted to call the principal and make Marcus report the names of the boys who had beat him up. But Marcus said he wouldn't tell. He said that telling on those boys would be the best way to make sure that he got another beating.

Boys who fought earned a reputation for being tough and not taking anything off of anyone. And boys with a good "rep" were respected at school. Marcus quickly learned that the same was true of the community. The men who were accorded the most respect were "crazy niggers" who were liable to kill you for crossing them.

Marcus knew that he had to even the score in a very public way. In the lunchroom the next day he could sense the pointing and the whispering that was going on behind his back as he sat at the end of a table of black boys all by himself.

He didn't have to look long to find the white boys who had beat him up. Trey and Larry sat in the middle of another table, surrounded by other whites. The other boys saw Marcus watching them and threw food at him when the teachers had their backs turned. He ate quickly and everyone watched as he returned his tray. Trey and Larry watched him with derisive smiles on their faces as he walked towards them. Marcus never looked away from Trey's face.

"You wanna throw down right here?" Trey taunted.

"Why not?" Marcus turned to Larry, "You want in on this, too?"

"I ain't got no problem kicking your behind again," Larry said loud enough to be heard by the whole table of boys.

"Well, here I am," Marcus said.

Larry stood up out of his chair, and as he did Marcus pulled a switchblade knife out of his pocket.

"You come at me and see how far you get," Marcus challenged.

Marcus jabbed the knife at Larry's face, and Larry scrambled screaming over the top of the lunch table sending silverware and plates and trays clattering to the floor.

As the teachers marched him out of the lunchroom in front of all of the students Marcus heard someone say, "That New York nigger's crazy!" and then he knew that his life had changed for the better.

The police charged Marcus with one count of assault with a deadly weapon. He was arraigned in juvenile court. Aunt Florida was ashamed to be in juvenile court and scared that Marcus would be taken from her and sent to juvenile hall. The judge went leniently on him because it was a first offense. Marcus received probation from the court, but the school suspended him for a month. Nevertheless, he had a reputation, and he got respect.

Other young men gravitated towards Marcus, and soon he had his own crowd of young rowdies. He told them stories, mostly made-up, of drug deals and gang fights he had been in back in Harlem.

They played on the community basketball courts after school where Marcus easily outclassed everyone his age. Word got around that he could play, and soon he was filling in when the men took over the courts in the early evening.

As he became more and more popular, he began staying out later and later and testing the patience of Aunt Florida. Marcus wore his house key around his neck, and he was supposed to go directly home at five o'clock and wait for Florida to return, but a "man" like Marcus wouldn't be ruled like that and he gained respect and admiration from his friends for the way he stood up to Florida.

Florida complained that Marcus had "gone wild", and she tried to rein him with little success. She stopped short of beating him for two reasons: she felt strange about beating her sister's child, and she didn't know if he would let her beat him.

When a man she met at work at the hospital started showing interest in Florida, Marcus had all but won his freedom. Florida started staying out on weekends and sometimes she didn't come home until the early morning. The later Marcus stayed out the more he got drawn into the "night life".

It wasn't long before Marcus was running with a crowd of older boys who dealt drugs and ran hustles. Nate and Jenks and Ham and Kenny played basketball with Marcus in the evenings, and all had good reps. They were impressed with Marcus and took it upon themselves to educate him about life on the street. Marcus began dodging school to hang out with his new friends, who seemed to know more about real life than all of his teachers put together.

Notes came in the mail to Aunt Florida that Marcus hadn't been in school for days. Sometimes he didn't even come home at night because he didn't want to catch any grief. Florida tried to get her new boyfriend to discipline Marcus, but he was as scared of Marcus as she was. At fifteen, Marcus was growing quickly and developing the body of a true athlete.

As Marcus matured, the young women began to notice him. He was boyishly handsome and had a good rep and hung with an older crowd known to be a little dangerous. The young women liked him, and he liked them. Ham and Jenks pulled him aside and told Marcus how to handle all of the attention he was getting from the women. They warned him not to fall in love. They told him that getting women was a game.

"You got to get love without giving any love," Jenks told him. "Because if you fall hard, she won. And you just got whipped."

Marcus got around, and he developed a strong rap. All of the young women wanted their chance with him, because every one of them thought that she was going to be the one to tame him. But Marcus was careful not to stay too long with any one woman. The young women who had been with him gave him a nickname: "Doctor Coffee" because they said, "He grinds so fine!"

But there was one girl Marcus couldn't charm: Daria. Pretty, sharply dressed, and full of attitude, she wouldn't give Marcus any attention. She thought he was "nothing but a thug" because she knew his reputation and had heard about all of his fights.

Having a reputation meant backing it up. Marcus was a target for anybody who wanted to get a reputation in the neighborhood. After seeing him come home with blood on his shirt for the third time in two weeks, Florida finally appealed to the principal of the school for help. She said she was afraid that if he didn't get Marcus back into school the boy would be as good as dead.

Five

After graduation in 1958, I went to work in South Carolina National Bank's trust department, and a year later I accepted a job with the International Paper company. By that time Katie was in her junior year at the University of South Carolina, where she was studying for a career in medical technology. While she was home for Christmas, she came to see me. She said she still loved me and had never loved anyone else.

I said, "Show me you love me. Marry me."

Although Katie was a Christian, and she knew I did not believe in God, she accepted my proposal on two conditions: I was to take her to church, and I was never to drink. I promised. We agreed that our families shouldn't know about the marriage until she finished school, and a month later we eloped.

Katie returned to her studies, and for nineteen consecutive weekends I drove 135 miles to Columbia to spend the night with my wife in a motel. The routine was interrupted when I began six months of National Guard training at Fort Jackson, South Carolina.

Again athletics smoothed the way for me. Assigned to Special Services, I was chosen for the football and basketball teams, helping both teams win the Fort Jackson championship. As a reward, the players received weekend passes. Instead of going to see Katie, I spent the time drinking.

In the spring of 1961, Katie was graduated from the University of

South Carolina. We made our marriage public and started house-keeping in Greensboro, North Carolina, where Katie entered a hospital program to study medical technology. At her encouragement, I gave college a try. Guilford College accepted me (I was on academic probation because of my poor high school grades, and I was forced to go to night school for one semester before they would accept me), and I chose economics as a major. Between classes I did housework and hated every minute of it.

To enliven things, I joined a basketball team in an industrial league. Katie detested sports and refused to go to my games. I was a standout in the league, scoring 51 points in one game, but when the college showed an interest in offering me an athletic scholarship, Katie insisted that I turn it down.

Marriage hadn't been too bad when Katie and I lived apart. Now that we were together, I found myself growing tired of her. I wanted to be free to sow some wild oats. Instead of talking with her about my feelings, I began staying out late with my buddies from school and running around on Katie. I started drinking more and more, and I stopped going to church.

Katie asked the pastor to see me, and he quizzed me about my drinking. He even opened the refrigerator looking for beer. I resented that and jumped on Katie about it. Realizing our marriage was in serious trouble, Katie did everything she could to save it. She even violated her own convictions and agreed to drink and go to parties with me.

Katie finished her training and took a position at the hospital. I still had no goals for the future, so I dropped out of college during my senior year and found a job with a clothing company. When Katie learned about it, we separated. Yet, Katie really cared about me and asked for a reconciliation. She tried her best to make our marriage work, but I was unwilling to be as committed to her as she was to me.

One day as Katie arrived home from work I announced, "I've packed my car. I'm leaving. I don't love you anymore."

For a moment she just stood there, as though she were stunned. When I turned toward the door, she grabbed all of my sports trophies off the mantle over the fireplace and smashed them on the floor, one by one. I was infuriated.

"Now I hate you!" I shouted, storming out the door.

Katie filed for a legal separation when I did not return, and then she moved to California. I didn't see her again for more than a year. During that time my dad died of cancer, and with him died my last hope of having his approval. It seemed everyone had abandoned me. One night when I was drinking, I called Katie and asked her to take me back.

"Harold," she said, "if I knew you meant business and could change, I'd come back. But you'll never change." We didn't talk again until July of 1967, when she called to say she was coming to finalize our divorce. I let her use my car while she was in town.

After the divorce was settled, she came by my apartment and asked me to drive her to the airport. There was a bikini-clad girl of nineteen with me, but when I compared her to Katie, I realized once again that Katie was the most beautiful woman I'd ever seen. She smiled at me and said, "Well, you're a free man now. Are you happy?"

"Yes, I am," I lied.

On the way to the airport, Katie told me she would always love me and that she regretted our marriage had failed. She repeated her view of me: "If I thought you could change and be the man I once thought you were I'd re-marry you. But you have very serious problems. You'll never change, Harold. I'm sorry. You need help."

I watched her walk up the ramp. Both of us were crying. She turned to me and waved, then stepped into the plane and out of my life forever.

And from that point on my life went downhill - and fast.

Six

O ne afternoon Marcus came off the court after a game and saw an older black man watching him intently. The older man waved him over and away from his crowd of friends. He was the coach of the high school basketball team, Coach Butts. He said he'd heard around the school that Marcus was a player, and he'd wanted to come out and see for himself.

"You know, our high school has a great basketball tradition," the big man rumbled in a gravelly voice, "but we've never won a state championship. You could help us do that. You could make your mark on the hard court the same way you've made your mark on this basketball court here."

Marcus shook his head, "I don't think so."

"Then you'll never know how good you can be at this game," the coach said.

"I'm already good enough."

"Good enough ain't good enough. I think you can be great."

Marcus smiled.

"But you'll never know how good you are just playing out here, young man. You can already beat the pants off everyone. You won't know what kinda player you are until you go up against the best, and the only place to do that is in the state championship."

"I ain't going back to school."

"Well, you can't play on my team unless you go to school."

"Then I won't be playing."

"I want to see you make something of yourself. I care about you. You may not believe that, but I've seen too many young men like you standing out on street corners until all hours of the night. You know what happens to those young men? Somebody finds them face down on that corner the next morning. And the next Friday there's another young man standing on that same corner like nothing happened. I don't want that to happen to you. I been watching you, and you've got all the potential in the world, son."

Butts could tell by the young man's expression that he'd got him thinking.

"The boys who die out there do it because they think it's the only thing they can do," he continued, his tone urgent. "They don't have the talent you have. You have another way out. You don't have to do what they do. You don't have to end up in a pool of blood on a street corner. You can make something of yourself, but first you've got to really develop the talent you've got. I want to help you do that. I know what you can do. But I don't think you know what you can do. All I'm offering you is a chance. No free ride. I'm gonna ride you hard. It'll be my way or the highway. I'm gonna find out what you're made of."

Marcus was touched by the man's interest in him. Deep down, he desperately wanted a father, and he thought that maybe he'd found one in the coach. But in order to play he needed to return to school.

By bringing his grades up and starring on the basketball team Marcus suddenly and unexpectedly became much more attractive to Daria. She went to every basketball game, and every time Marcus made a basket he would turn to her and wink as he ran back downcourt.

Soon they were eating lunch together. Marcus' life had made a turn for the better. He had a father figure in his coach and someone to love that loved him back in Daria.

The team didn't win the state championship that year, but in his junior year Marcus established himself as the leader of the basketball team and in his senior year they won the championship.

Many of the same boys who played on the basketball team also

played on the baseball team. Marcus had never had a chance to play
organized baseball, but he'd played stickball on the streets of Harlem.
He went out and watched his friends play after school. But most of
the time he was hoping for a glimpse of Deborah, the coach's daughter. She was his age and blonde with green eyes. A cheerleader and
the homecoming queen, she wasn't overly friendly.

One afternoon his friends goaded Marcus into the batting cage
before practice. After striking out four times, he got his first solid hit.
And then another. The ball was jumping off his bat when the baseball coach, Mr. Larsen, arrived.

Larsen encouraged him to take a few more swings, and then he put
Marcus on the team as a project. But Marcus quickly excelled and was
soon the starting center fielder. By the end of his second season on
the baseball team, Marcus, then a junior, had attracted the notice of
professional baseball scouts. They seemed to think that he had
tremendous potential, and Marcus' coach loved to tell and re-tell the
story of how he had discovered Marcus hitting balls in the batting
cage.

"He's been leading the team in hitting since the middle of that first
season," Larsen repeated to one scout after another. "He's a very special player. The best talent I've ever seen, fellas."

While Marcus listened to his coach and the scouts sing his praises,
he watched Deborah. He had started to like her, and he'd let her
catch him staring, hold her gaze for a moment, wink, and then look
away.

Walking home from practice one day, Marcus noticed a small powder blue roadster slow beside him. He turned to see Deborah staring
at him. She reached over and opened the passenger door.

"We need to talk," she said seriously. "Get in."

"About what?"

"The way you've been staring at me."

He smiled, but she didn't smile back.

"If my father catches you looking at me like that do you know what
he'll do to you?"

Marcus got in, and they rode in silence until she stopped the car
on a quiet tree-lined street. Marcus looked and felt like he was sitting

in a dentist's chair. She smiled at his nervousness.

"If you're going to watch me," she began coyly, "you have to be more discrete."

She enjoyed his confusion, and a sly smile curled her lips.

"W-what?" he stammered.

"I've been watching you, but you didn't know it did you?"

Marcus shook his head.

"And ever since you started watching me I've been wondering whether you're ever going to do anything besides watch me."

Inch by inch, he slowly leaned forward until he could feel her breath on his face, his eyes never leaving hers. Then they kissed. He wrapped his arms around her and pressed her to his chest.

"I can feel your heart beating," she whispered, her breath hot in his ear. "Am I the first white girl you've kissed?"

"No," he lied.

"Well, you're the first black boy I've kissed," she whispered. "Only, you can't tell anyone. My dad would kill us."

She continued to pick him up in her car after baseball practice, dropping him off a block from his house. Sometimes they met on weekends, mostly afternoons, when they'd drive far away and return before dinner. Marcus made sure that no one knew, especially not Daria.

Seven

"**D**rive! Drive! We shot a man!" shouted my friends as they scrambled down the street toward my car.

I gunned the engine and, without waiting for an explanation, spun the car around and headed in the very direction from which Frank and Al had come.

"You fool! You're going to get us caught!" Al yelled.

The two men slumped in the back seat as several police cars and an ambulance sped into the supermarket parking lot, their lights flashing and their sirens blaring.

I made a right turn on Ponce de Leon Avenue - the only route I knew out of Atlanta - and took the interstate north. For some time all I could hear was the rapid breathing of my friends in the back seat, and my head pounded with questions.

A shooting! How could this have happened? When Frank and Al finally started to relax, they told me the story. They had walked into the supermarket, pulled guns, and ordered the manager to open the safe. As one of them grabbed a handful of money from the cash register, a bystander reached in his belt and produced a snub-nosed .38 pistol. There was a scuffle, and the would-be hero was shot.

"Fun is one thing," I thought, "but being involved in a supermarket robbery - suppose that man dies! Should I go to the police?"

"Wonder what that fool was doing with a gun?" Frank asked.

Al laughed, "Wouldn't it be something if he was waiting to rob the place?"

Soon they were both laughing, and Al must have noticed that I wasn't because he hit me on the shoulder. "What's the matter with you?" he wanted to know.

"Did you kill him?" I asked, afraid to hear the answer.

"Nah!" Frank answered, sniffing. "He took it in his side, but he was standing when we ran out. He'll live."

I breathed a sigh of relief. At least the wound wasn't fatal, and I was glad that no one had seemed to notice us when we drove by the supermarket. Although I felt remorse for the wounded man, the farther we got from Atlanta, the more reassured I became. He would recover, I reasoned, and we had escaped. Everything would work out all right.

Frank and Al seemed to think the incident was closed, and they didn't take my concern for the man seriously. We stopped for food and beer, and then we continued the 350 miles to our homes in Greensboro, North Carolina. The six-hour drive gave me plenty of time to review the events of the past four months.

I had met Frank and Al at a topless nightclub in Greensboro shortly after separating from my wife. The idea of spending the rest of my days with one woman had lost its appeal, and I made no secret of my drinking and girl chasing. After the divorce, I began spending a lot of time at the nightclub, the first topless club in the state of North Carolina. It was a fast life, and I was running - but I didn't know where.

I had a respectable job with an insurance company, a new Cadillac, and the freedom I thought I wanted. I had never been in trouble with the police before, and I'd never known an ex-convict prior to this. But that soon changed. The nightclub attracted the shadiest of characters - hardened alcoholics, drug addicts, drug pushers, ex-cons, and prostitutes. This life was new to me, and I found myself falling deeper and deeper into the mire.

While I put up a good front for my friends, inside I was miserable and confused. My drinking increased until my days and nights were consumed with alcohol and women. I discovered amphetamines, and pills called "black beauties" soon became part of my life.

Finally, I quit my job. A little money trickled in from insurance poli-cies that I had sold, but it was not enough to support my lavish lifestyle. I worked a few hours at the nightclub and lived on credit cards, running up debts totaling several thousand dollars.

Shortly thereafter, my girlfriend introduced me to two of her friends who it turns out were nothing but hoodlums. Frank and Al were sharp dressers, fast talkers, and big spenders. They were also hand-some and popular with women. The three of us hit it off immediate-ly. All we did was sleep during the day and party all night.

Tiring of the Greensboro party scene, my two friends and I sought women and excitement in other cities, from Myrtle Beach to New York. Frank always had pocketfuls of money, and sometimes he picked up the tab for the entire week. The night life in Atlanta lured us like moths to a flame, so we went there to party.

On September 18, 1968, we checked into a room at the Heart of Atlanta motel and then hit one nightclub after another while high on alcohol and pills. After a week of this, we'd spent our cash, leaving only credit cards to cover our expenses. I was ready to return to North Carolina anyway. So, on the 25th we checked out of the motel. Before leaving town, my friends insisted on visiting some girls we had met earlier in the week.

I drove to the address they had given us - North Highland Avenue. We knocked on the door, but no one answered. As we waited for the girls to come home from work, Frank and Al started down the street saying they were going to get some beer and that they'd be right back.

Soon the girls arrived, and I went inside the apartment with them to get a drink. Minutes later I returned to the car as Frank and Al came racing down the street, breathless and obviously shaken, shouting that they'd just shot a man.

But now we were approaching Greensboro, and neither Frank nor Al seemed shaken anymore. As they dozed in the back seat, my con-fidence gave way to doubts. I fell deeper and deeper into despair.

"You've reached the bottom of the barrel now," I told myself. "Dad always said you'd never amount to anything. Maybe he was right. But maybe he wasn't right. And if that's true I'll have to break away from

Frank and Al if I'm ever going to do something with my life."

My decision was made. I would leave Greensboro. I dropped them off at Frank's apartment, making no mention of my plans to leave town. Then I gathered my things and caught the next flight to Houston, Texas, where a friend had offered to share his apartment.

I was there only a few weeks when my friend suddenly accepted a new job in Atlanta. With no other connections in Houston, I decided to move with him. I heard nothing more about the shooting and put the incident out of my mind.

Although I was removed from my former friends, I did not break from the women-and-booze lifestyle.

In Atlanta I hit the party scene heavier than ever. The months passed, and I almost totally forgot the robbery until an old girlfriend called from North Carolina.

"You made the front page today," she said.

"What do you mean?"

"Your picture is on the front page of the newspaper. You're wanted for armed robbery and murder."

"Murder!" I gasped. My stomach tightened as the reality hit home. Frank and Al had killed the man in the supermarket.

"The F.B.I. has been questioning me, Harold," she said. "They say the man you shot only lived a few minutes."

"I didn't shoot anybody," I protested.

"Well, your two friends are locked up, and the F.B.I. is looking for you."

When the conversation ended, I sat thinking about the night of the robbery. I knew I was guilty of some despicable things, but I wasn't a robber or a murderer. I hadn't run from the authorities, and I wasn't hiding. I waited in Atlanta for several days, expecting officers to come for me. When they didn't, I decided to return to North Carolina to see an attorney friend. We had played the party scene together, and I thought I could trust him to find out what was going on.

The attorney had already heard of the charges against me, and he wanted to know about my involvement in the crime. He said he believed my story, but he advised me to wait for a while before going to the police. First he would check around the courthouse to see what the two captured suspects were saying. Then I'd go to the police and tell everything. For testifying against them, I'd probably be freed, he said. After all, I had been implicated simply because I knew them; I hadn't killed anybody. There was no problem, he assured me.

When I called the attorney a few days later he seemed baffled. Everyone was hush-hush about the case, he said, but he had learned that Frank and Al were not in the local jail. He needed more time, and it seemed important to find out what was going on before turning myself in to the police. I'd risk arrest if I stayed in Greensboro or if I returned to Atlanta, so my only alternative was to run.

I sold my car for traveling money and rode to Myrtle Beach with a friend. After several days of partying there we went to Charleston, Savannah, Columbia, and finally to Greenville, South Carolina, where my friend left me saying he would return in a few days. On his way back to North Carolina, he was stopped for speeding and driving under the influence. To avoid losing his license he made a bargain. In return for having the traffic charge dropped he would help solve a murder. He told the officer where to find me. I was staying at a motel with a girl I'd met in Columbia, but we had separate rooms so I would be free to see other women.

On September 18th - almost one year after the shooting in Atlanta - I returned to the motel about 9 a.m. after spending all night with a new girlfriend. When she dropped me off, I bought a Pepsi and a newspaper on the way to my room. Sitting by the window to read, I closed the draperies about 10 a.m., latched the door, and settled into bed.

Thirty minutes later, a knock awakened me. Groggy with sleep, I opened the door but found no one there. Thinking it must have been the maid, I dozed off again.

Bam! Bam! Bam!

The maid again! I was really agitated over being bothered a second time. As I unfastened the night latch, the door was kicked open, and a dozen officers burst into the room, thrusting pistols against my head.

"If you move, you're dead!" they shouted, throwing me onto the bed and handcuffing my hands behind my back.

"Where's the gun?" they demanded, emptying dresser drawers and wastebaskets. I had never owned a gun in my life. The scene taking place before me could have been from a gangster movie - and I was playing a part.

"Read him his rights and take him downtown and book him," snapped the officer in charge.

"Are you going to carry me out naked?" I objected as they grabbed my arms and started to push me out the door.

"Put some clothes on," he said.

"How do you expect me to dress? Do you think I can stretch like Gumby?" I quipped.

They loosened one hand so I could get into my clothes.

"How about my money?" I asked.

"Count his money. He thinks he's smart," the F.B.I. agent grumbled.

"Listen, you've got me. All I want is my money and what belongs to me," I said.

They never knew about the girl in the other room.

During the drive to the county jail, they bombarded me with questions: "When did you get into town? What have you been doing?" On and on they pressed, insisting I give them the information they wanted. Knowing I had the right to have an attorney present during questioning, I answered nothing.

When we arrived at the jail, the officers become furious when I objected to being fingerprinted. Threatened with a beating, I finally agreed. Arraignment was before a federal magistrate who set bond at $10,000 for interstate flight to avoid prosecution. Then, I learned that I was charged with armed robbery in Greensboro. That really threw me.

How could I be wanted for an Atlanta murder that I did not commit but charged with a Greensboro robbery which I knew nothing about? I figured the officers didn't know about the murder. By raising a $10,000 bond, I could be free.

I used the one phone call that I was allowed to contact an attorney recognized as one of the best in the state of South Carolina. His secretary said that it would cost $200 just to talk with him. I had $500 in cash. The attorney, however, was out of town, and it would be several days before he could see me.

About two hours later an F.B.I. agent came to my holding cell and wiped out all hope for an early release.

"Harold Donald Morris, I have something to read to you," he said. He read six indictments for armed robbery and one for murder and robbery. Plus a federal conspiracy charge.

"There is no bond," he announced.

The other men in the cell were relieved. Because I was stylishly dressed in a double-breasted sports jacket, they had thought I was an informant planted by the F.B.I. But when those charges were read, they decided I was a desperado much more dangerous than any of them.

Seven armed robberies, murder one, a federal conspiracy charge, no bond - how could this have happened to me? I had seen myself as a country boy who had made it to the big time. I had adopted a playboy lifestyle because it promised me the freedom to do whatever I pleased. This must be a hideous nightmare, I told myself. When I wake up, everything will be okay. But the jail bars told me otherwise.

Eight

By the time his senior year rolled around, Marcus seemed destined to play baseball in the major leagues. College and pro scouts flocked to his baseball games. A scout from a major league team promised Marcus that he would draft him in the first round.

Deborah got a bottle of champagne to celebrate. While they were driving out of town that Saturday a motorcycle cop pulled Deborah over for speeding. She showed the officer the registration for the car, which was in her father's name. The patrolman eyed Marcus suspiciously and asked for his name.

They drove on and parked in a secluded spot. The officer followed them at a distance.

That evening, Mr. Larsen received a phone call even before his daughter got home. Irate, Larsen demanded that Marcus be arrested for rape. That very night the police rousted Marcus out of bed and marched him down the front steps of Aunt Florida's house in handcuffs.

Marcus used his one call to phone Coach Butts. He said that he'd been charged with rape and that he'd been seeing Deborah for almost a year and that they were in love. The next morning Butts called a black attorney friend who was a civil rights activist.

The lawyer found the case against Marcus preposterous. He said the charges were "ridiculous, baseless, malicious, and based solely on race". He supplied the district attorney with the names of white boys Deborah had been with.

"You didn't arrest any of those white boys did you?" the lawyer asked the district attorney point blank.

The district attorney had a hard time explaining to Mr. Larsen that he could not proceed with the case. He said he would have to expose Deborah's whole past and her role as a willing participant. Finally Larsen acquiesced, but he promised he'd have Marcus expelled.

The principal refused. The best he could do, he said, would be to see that Marcus didn't return to school by graduating him early.

"If I catch you near my daughter again, I'll kill you," Larsen hissed at Marcus over the phone. "And I'm going to make sure you never play baseball again. You ruined my daughter's reputation, and now I'm sure going to ruin you. You're through, boy!"

Larsen burned up the phone lines to the collegiate and professional recruiters that had expressed an interest in Marcus. He would say whatever he had to to make sure that their interest in Marcus was gone before he hung up.

Aunt Florida cussed Marcus for being "white women crazy".

"You need to stick with your own kind," she said. "All these whites are devils. All they did was use you. You should be thanking the Lord that you ain't swinging from some old tree!"

When Daria learned how Marcus had been cheating on her, she said he had humiliated her and refused to talk to him. Strangely, she never seemed more beautiful to him than she did when she told him that and she never wanted to see him again as long as she lived.

He didn't sleep or eat for two days after that. He'd just seen all of his hopes for his future blown away, and he didn't know who to turn to or what to do next.

The diploma Coach Butts delivered to the house was just a piece of paper to Marcus. He was convinced his life was over. Coach Butts saw that Marcus was despairing and tried to talk some sense to him. He tried to tell Marcus that he hadn't lost everything, but Marcus knew that his dreams of being rich and famous were gone.

"You could still go to college and get an education," Butts said. "Ain't a college in the country that don't want you. Pick your head up, young man, the game ain't over yet. I never saw you give up on that basketball court. Don't let anybody tell you you ain't a winner."

"I can't win in the white man's world," Marcus said. "And I don't want to talk about it anymore."

Marcus knew he was going back to the streets, and he was going to be a dealer. Many of the people he'd hung out with in the street before had gone to jail or were now strung out. Nate and Jenks both had bad habits. They had turned into real junkies - the kind who would steal from their parents to get money for a fix. They remembered Doc, but they weren't good for any more basketball games. Kenny was doing a short stretch for dealing pot. Ham had been arrested along with an accomplice for the armed robbery of a liquor store.

While trying to track down his old friends, Doc met a big, square-shouldered, serious-faced drug dealer named Tito Evans who said he'd heard about what happened. He told Doc that ten years ago he was the three sport star at the local high school.

"Football, basketball, baseball, baby. I did it all," Tito said. "Everybody knew my name. I was the man. Just like you. But you got to know that that ain't gonna last, bruh. You can't be eighteen and a jock your whole life. But that's okay."

Doc shook his head sadly.

"Man, it's good that this happened to you now."

"Are you crazy?" Doc gaped.

"You didn't really think that you was gonna be playing pro ball and running with all the women, did you?"

Doc lowered his eyes.

"Come on!" Tito laughed. "I'm your friend. I'm trying to educate you to some of the realities, and that is the same junk that ol' house niggers like coach feed niggers to keep them in line! Man, he gave me the same old speech he gave you. Ain't one word of truth in it."

Tito saw that Doc was getting angry.

"I'm sure he believes it," Tito quickly pointed out. "I'm not saying ol' Coach Butts is trying to trick you. He believes it, but that's how these house niggers is, bruh. Let me ask you this: how many players has he put in the pros? Can you name one? I can't. So, I'm just trying to educate you to the realities, like I said."

Tito felt sorry for Doc and gave him a connection and some advice about dealing.

"You can't let anybody take your stuff off you," Tito warned. "You can't let 'em get away with it because if you do they'll all try it and then you're done as a dealer. If you ain't got a gun, get one. You got to live by the code, bruh."

The connection turned out to be a very good one, and soon Doc was dealing. He immediately invested the money he made back into more product. He smiled to think that Coach Butts' prediction had already come true: he was a success.

Aunt Florida noticed Doc's new wardrobe and told him straight out that she didn't want him carrying any drugs in her house. Doc ignored her. When he was out of the house Florida searched his room, but all she found was a suitcase full of neatly stacked piles of bills secured with rubber bands. Then, she noticed a new car parked in front of her house.

Doc was having the time of his life and for the first time Tito's words made sense to him. He was already forgetting the life he'd left behind. The life he was living seemed to be the life he'd been destined for all along. He was feeling like a man and acting like a man and making enough money for three men.

"My operation's getting so big I'll probably get busted one of these days," he told Tito, "but right now I'm living for today."

"Hey, you know the only thing a real nigger's scared of is living too long," Tito smiled.

And with the money came the women. Doc no longer trusted women, but he still enjoyed their company, and a parade of young women marched into and out of Florida's front door at all hours. This was the last straw for her.

"You got a different girl in here every week!" Florida laid into him. "Dealing drugs, catting around, drinking up all the liquor in the world, killing people, what kind of life is that to live? It's gonna catch up with you one day, and I don't want to be there when it does!"

"I ain't killed anybody," Doc said.

"I want you out of my house!"

Tito arranged for Doc to have a penthouse in an apartment building where all of the young thieves and dealers and hustlers lived. Doc felt that these were his people and that he'd finally found his place in the world. Doc was among the "in crowd" and something was happening almost every night. At one of the parties he was invited to he saw Daria. After he had done a line of cocaine Doc hit on her. She smiled to see him, and he handed her the rolled up bill. After she had done a line, he and Daria got along so well it seemed like the old days. In a moment, their past was forgotten and a wonderful future lay ahead.

After their first night together, Doc saw Daria regularly, but not exclusively. Kenny got out on parole, and Doc hired him as protection. Everyone on the street knew that Doc was the man and always had a large roll of bills in his pocket. Life in the fast lane came to a grinding halt when Daria told him that she was pregnant.

"I thought you were on the pill!" Doc shouted, rising from his seat and walking to the other side of his apartment.

"I must have forgotten to take one," she said meekly.

"How do you even know you're pregnant?" Doc pressed. "Are you sure?"

"I'm sure."

"Have you been to a doctor?"

"I'm having your baby."

Doc stared into her face and knew that she had gotten pregnant on purpose. She was single-handedly trying to wreck his life, he thought. The next thing he knew he was slamming the door in her face and locking it.

Four days later, he took her in. He still cared for her, and he cared for the baby she was carrying. He didn't want that baby to be without a father.

"I'll do what I can," Doc said, trying to be reasonable about it. But the next month he couldn't stand to be with her. He stayed out late and came home early in the morning drunk or high. He cheated on Daria every chance he got. She tried to complain, but every time she did Doc went back out the front door. Sometimes he didn't come home for days. She learned that if she wanted him home at all she should keep quiet.

Doc knew that he'd probably go to jail sooner or later, and he dabbled in the drugs he sold to push the thought that he might get caught out of his mind. He used either weed or cocaine every day. At home, drugs were the only thing that kept Doc and Daria from fighting constantly.

When Doc was leaving his apartment one Friday night a junkie put a gun in his face and pushed him back through his door. Daria screamed when she saw Doc standing in the middle of the living room with his hands in the air. The junkie turned the gun on her and told her to be quiet.

"Just gimme all you got, or I'll kill you both."

Doc could see that the junkie needed a fix, and he knew how desperate junkies could get when they were strung out.

"Hey, man, just calm down. I don't have a gun. You can have anything you want."

The man was sweating, and the gun shook in his hand.

Doc reached slowly into his jacket and brought out a bag of pot and a bag of coke and tossed them on the floor.

"And the cash, nigger!" the junkie screamed.

Doc nodded nervously and then produced a roll of bills and threw it on the floor with the drugs. The junkie picked it up without another word and scampered out the door. Doc pretended nothing important had happened, but he knew in the back of his mind that he'd probably have to kill the junkie to protect his own reputation.

Nine

For three days I sat in a filthy cell trying to sort out the puzzle of my existence. I had failed in many areas of my life - school, work, marriage. Even athletics had proven to be an illusion. And now my choice of friends had plunged me into a nightmare.

I was still wearing the clothes I'd scrambled into when I was taken into custody. On the third day after my arrest, a policeman took me into a room where two F.B.I. agents delivered my toiletries from the motel. A radio and some other personal items were missing, but I didn't mention it to the two men. Instead, I signed a form releasing them of responsibility for my possessions.

"You're not what we expected," one said. "You're a pretty decent guy - not the kind who would do the things you're accused of doing. In fact, during the six months that we were searching for you, we interviewed many of your friends. Only one said anything bad about you. One of your former coaches said you were a little bit hot-head-ed. But he said he liked you and couldn't believe you'd be guilty of such a crime."

"What happens next?" I asked.

"You were arrested for interstate flight to avoid prosecution. You'll be turned over to the authorities in North Carolina first and Georgia later. You're really in trouble. The case is out of our hands, and we won't be back."

"We do have one question," the other agent added. "Looking over your personal things we found a woman's wig, panty hose, panties, shoes, and make-up. I don't understand. What were you doing with a woman's clothes?"

They still didn't know about the girl at the motel! By that time I had lost everything except my sense of humor.

"Don't you know?" I said with an affected lisp but a straight face, "I'm a drag queen. You mean, you don't dress drag on Saturday night? I thought everyone cross-dressed on Saturday night."

"Get him out of here," the first agent snapped to the guard. "He's a sorry fag!"

"Sir, please watch your language," I said, seriously, "I got my girl-friend's picture in my pocket, and he's cute."

"Get him out of here!" the agent shouted.

I laughed all the way back to my cell, but then I stopped. I had no idea what was in store for me.

My attorney was still away when Greensboro detectives came to interrogate me. They began with a friendly approach, trying to win me over while building a case against me. When I refused to talk with them or to sign extradition papers, their approach changed to cursing and threatening.

Finally, I talked with my attorney, and I was greatly encouraged that he believed my story. We discussed the possibility of fighting extradition, but he felt it would be a waste of time and money because I was bound to lose. He advised me to return to North Carolina and offered to recommend an attorney there.

Shackled like an animal, I was taken to Greensboro, where Frank and Al had implicated me in every crime they had committed. Knowing I was innocent, I felt optimistic about being freed. My new attorney was very impressive.

"If you're telling the truth, you don't have a thing to worry about," he said. He left to investigate further and returned three hours later. "They don't have a thing on you, but they want to work a deal," he said.

In exchange for information about the men I had known at the nightclub, all charges in North Carolina (which I had not committed) would be dropped. The term for this is *nol pros.* I told everything I knew (which was nothing), and plans for an arraignment in North Carolina were dropped.

My attorney paid me a final visit and offered to stay on the case, working out of his Charlotte office. He would bring in another noted attorney, and the two of them would work through a lawyer in Atlanta.

"For $7,000 you'll never get a day," he promised. "I have investigated the case, and it's very weak. They only have the testimony of Frank and Al. That's the whole case against you."

I was out of money, in debt, and feeling cocky.

"If I can get the money and put it in escrow, will you accept that?" I asked, knowing he would be paid only if he won the case. He agreed to the arrangement.

"I've got news for you," I grinned. "I don't have any money."

"You have a family," he suggested. My grin faded.

"You leave my family out of this! I'm willing to take my chances."

Facing the charges in Atlanta didn't really worry me. After all, I wasn't guilty. I'd be honest with the authorities, and they would understand that I wasn't a murderer. At the very worst, I'd be placed on probation. I didn't realize the authorities had spent a year building their case, and Frank and Al had worked a deal to get a lighter sentence in return for testifying against me. The trap was laid, and I stepped into it.

After six months in county jails, I was shackled to another prisoner for the trip to Georgia in the custody of two detectives who had been told I was extremely dangerous. They stopped at the county jail in Charlotte, North Carolina, so we could take a bathroom break - with our hands cuffed to our waists and our feet shackled to each other. It was only one of a multitude of humiliations to come.

After a night in Atlanta-Fulton County jail, I was taken in handcuffs to appear before the distinct attorney. Because I was not represented by counsel, this was an illegal procedure. Unfortunately, I did not understand that then.

The district attorney pulled my file and said, "See this? We know all about you. I got your partners. They'll say you threatened to kill them if they didn't rob the store and murder everyone inside."

That was not what I had expected to hear. I'd been led to believe that he was going to offer a deal. I'd tell everything, and he'd give me a break. I was shocked.

"I understand you have told some people in North Carolina about your innocence," the district attorney continued. "I don't believe it. You are a mastermind criminal, and if this case goes to trial I'll go for the death penalty and I'll get it."

"The *death penalty?*"

"That's right," he said. "But I don't want to see this case go to trial, you see, I was a minister before I was a prosecutor. And I understand how a young man like you can get on the wrong path in life. You're not what I expected at all. You're not an animal. You're clean-cut, a college man. I'll tell you what, Morris, I'll make you a deal: twenty years for both counts - armed robbery and murder - if you'll plead guilty. There will be no trial. You'll just go on down to the prison and start doing your time. What do you say to that?"

By now I realized I was in trouble, but clearly this man was my enemy. I was sarcastic.

"That's awfully nice of you. I appreciate that. Tell you what, mister district attorney, I'll take ten years and you take ten. Let's go on down there and do it together."

"I've put five men on death row, and you are going to be number six, you miserable smart mouth," he snarled. "Your life is coming to an end! Get him out of here!"

I was taken back to my cell, and for two weeks I didn't hear from anyone. Finally, on a Friday afternoon, I was told, "Your attorney wants to see you." How could that be? I had no money to hire an attorney.

A cage of metal bars separated me from the man who identified himself as the head of the public defender's office.

"I've studied your file," he said. "They have an open-and-shut case against you. Two men are going to testify that you're a mastermind criminal, that you threatened their lives and forced them to go into a store with instructions to kill every person in there. They can send you to the electric chair. I have connections with the district attorney, and I can get you twenty years if you'll plead guilty."

"I can see that you know nothing about me," I said in disgust. "You believe I'm guilty."

"I know you're guilty," he said.

"Let me tell you something," I yelled, trying to reach through the bars to choke him. "You're not my attorney, and I will not plead guilty! Tell the district attorney that my original offer stands: I'll do ten if he'll do ten, and I'm ready to go anytime he's ready."

"You're going to die, you sorry piece of white trash," he promised. "You're a murderer, and you're going to die! I'm dropping off the case, but let me tell you something - you'll regret the day you were born."

A week later I was told to be ready at five o'clock in the morning to go to trial. I was charged with a capital offense, and I didn't even have an attorney!

After a sleepless night I was taken to a holding cell at Superior Court for hours of waiting. About 10 a.m. a guard marched me into the courtroom. I recognized the prosecutor and the public defender who had cursed me at the jail when he dropped from the case.

The first case to be announced was "Donald Harold Morris." Even my name was backwards! "My God!" I thought, "What am I going to do? They're going to railroad me! I'm going to die!"

The public defender walked over to me and whispered, "I can get you twenty years. Will you plead guilty?"

"I'm ready for trial, but I'll be tried for your murder. I'm going to break your neck!" I threatened.

"Your Honor, may we approach the bench?" he said.

He and the prosecutor conferred briefly with the judge. The prosecutor announced that because key witnesses from South Carolina had not arrived the case would be delayed.

Later that day I lay in my cell thinking, "I've made enemies . . . I can't win . . . they're going to kill me!"

The jailer interrupted my thoughts, "I have been authorized to offer you twenty years," he said. "Will you take it?"

"Authorized by whom?" I asked.

"The chief judge," he replied.

"Tell the chief judge that I'll do ten if he'll do ten, and let's get started on it today. Tell him we're wasting time!"

"You're going to die," he declared. "They're going to fry you!"

Ten

By the next afternoon it seemed like everybody knew. Doc went to talk things over with Tito.

Tito saw a bit of indecision in Doc's expression and pressed him, "Look, man, if you want to keep on dealing drugs this cat's got to pay. Your rep is at stake. If you don't back it up now, you're through. You might as well leave town."

"You're right," Doc nodded. "I know you're right."

"It's a shame, man," Tito said. "But it's the price of doing business."

Kenny offered to find the junkie for Doc, but Doc told him to sit tight. Doc knew that he had to do it himself, and he put the word out on the street. After three days of searching, Doc got a tip.

The junkie was holed up in the basement of an abandoned house. The man lay on the floor in a nod, a blissed out expression on his thin dirty face. Doc slowly pulled the revolver from behind his back. He pointed it and looked at the man over the front sight of the weapon. One shot in the face would do it. He cocked the hammer back. He just had to pull the trigger. A moment passed, and when it did Doc knew that he would not be able to kill the man.

The next day he told Kenny that he was through dealing, "It ain't worth it - not when I got to kill a man over $200."

"Man, what are we gonna do for money?" Kenny asked.

"Where do they keep the money?"

"Where?"

"In a bank! And it is time we made a withdrawal!"

After two weeks of scouting out banks and locations Doc decided that hitting a bank was too risky: there were too many customers to keep track of and too much security. Then he hit upon a better idea: finance companies. He figured three armed men could do a finance company in no time at all with little risk and a big reward. He recruited an older man known as Fish who had just been paroled from prison after serving eleven years for armed robbery. Fish had experience and know how, and was a stand-up guy. Doc learned so much talking to him he began to think it would be foolish to try to rob without Fish.

After seven successful jobs, the finance companies in the area significantly increased their security. Based on their stakeouts, Doc and Fish decided that there was just as much risk robbing finance companies as there was robbing banks. And there was more money at the banks.

The bank guard sat on the floor looking up into the twin barrels of a sawed-off shotgun. Kenny, dressed head to toe in black, watched the bank guard and watched the front door. Kenny had taken the bank guard's revolver, but he had missed the .32 the bank guard kept in his ankle holster.

The bank customers lay quietly on the floor with their hands behind their heads. Two men, also dressed in black, held revolvers in the faces of two young female bank tellers. The young women smiled nervously as they heaved two gray sacks across the counter. Moments later, the two men raced past Kenny and out the doors with the bulging sacks slung over their shoulders. As Kenny lowered the shotgun and turned to leave, the guard grabbed at the .32 in his ankle holster.

Doc leaped into the back seat of the getaway car, and Fish raced the engine as the first shots rang out. Jerking off his mask, Doc spun around and saw Kenny fall heavily to the pavement five feet outside the bank. The bank guard stood in the doorway, and fire bloomed from the muzzle of his pistol. Doc pulled the back door shut and reached for his .45 automatic. But before he could fire he heard Fish emptying his gun. For seconds the air pulsed with reverberations of shots fired and whined with crisscrossing bullets shattering the bank's tinted glass doors, plunking ominously into the getaway car, bullets ricocheting off the bank's granite facade and the pavement and then, suddenly, silence. A red mist floated down onto Doc's face.

"Fish? You okay?" Doc asked wiping his face with the back of his sleeve.

Blood. Doc sat up cautiously and peered out the window. The bank guard lay on his back atop a pile of broken glass, his body propping the bank door open. In the front seat, Fish was slumped over staring blankly at the ceiling, a bullet hole in his right cheek, his head resting on the bags of money.

Kenny made a wet, gurgling sound in the back of his throat as Doc picked him up by the shoulders and dragged him into the back of the getaway car.

"We'll, get you fixed up, bruh," Doc said breathlessly as he heard sirens approaching.

Shoving Fish's body across the front seat, Doc squeezed behind the wheel and dropped the car into gear. The tires spun, and the car lurched forward. He couldn't tell which direction the sirens were coming from. In his panic it sounded like the sirens were swarming him from all directions.

Doc turned left and hurtled down a narrow side street. As he raced blindly out into an intersection the ink bombs secreted into the gray sacks of money exploded, one after another, on the seat immediately to his right. Startled, Doc reflexively jerked the wheel sharply to the left raising the car up onto two tires in a harrowing sideways slide through the intersection, the car skidding across the street and smashing into several parked cars.

As Doc clambered out of the car with a gray sack in each hand he saw three police cars pull into position behind him, boxing him in and blocking his avenues of escape. Four officers jumped out with their weapons drawn.

Doc dropped the sacks and raised his hands.

Doc picked up the phone, but his eyes never left Daria's face.

"I'm so sorry. Please forgive me," he pleaded, his eyes searching hers.

She nodded her forgiveness, unable to speak. He could see that she was upset, and he wanted desperately to pick her up in his arms and hug her and comfort her, but the glass between them made that impossible.

"Will you forgive me?" he asked, longing to hear her voice. "I never meant to put you through this."

"Are you okay?" Daria asked after she had composed herself. "Are they treating you all right?"

Her voice sounded high, strained, coming through the phone.

"I'm fine. Don't worry about me. How are you?"

"Well, I've explained it to him," she said in a matter-of-fact tone, nodding towards his son, who stood beside her staring sullenly through the glass. "He understands that you won't be coming back for a while. One of the boys in his kindergarten class has a father who-"

"At most, I'll get a dime," Doc assured her. "I ain't killed anybody."

He could see that she wanted to believe him.

"I'll be out in a few years," Doc continued confidently, trying to convince himself as much as Daria. "That's it . . . so don't go nowhere."

Doc forced a smile, but Daria could not return it.

"I know this looks bad," Doc continued into the silence, "but we're gonna be all right."

She nodded slightly.

"Matter of fact," Doc whispered, glancing over his shoulder at the guard, who couldn't help but hear, "there's a suitcase in the attic behind the chimney. It should hold you until I get out of here."

Doc enjoyed the look of sheer surprise on Daria's face.

"Ima take care of you," he promised. "I'm always gonna take care of you and little Doc. You ain't got nothing to worry about. All you got to do is wait on me."

She nodded and mouthed the word "okay".

"Baby, don't give up on me," Doc whispered urgently. "You got to be strong. I'm gonna need you behind me at the trial. You and little

Doc. I ain't got nobody else. Florida won't have nothing to do with me. You're all I've got, baby."

She smiled and wiped her nose and passed the phone to the boy. His eyes were sad and his mouth was turned down at the corners. Doc knew that his son understood exactly what was happening.

"Is that your Christmas suit you wearing, little fella?" Doc asked playfully.

"Mommy said I had to put on my good clothes before we could come see you."

"She did?" Doc asked. "Well, you looking like a little man in them bad threads. Do you think you can be the man of the house for a while?"

The boy nodded.

"You know I love you, son," Doc said.

"I love you, too, Daddy."

"Could you do a favor for me, little man?"

"Uh huh."

"Could you give Daddy a smile?"

The boy stretched his mouth into an imitation of a smile, and Doc's heart sank.

PART II
1969-1970

Eleven

The days dragged by. On a Friday afternoon about a month later, I was told that my new attorney wanted to see me. Again, I was puzzled. In the visiting room stood a well-dressed successful-looking man who said he had been appointed by the judge to represent me. After asking several questions about the crime, he said that a trial was set for Monday - ten days away.

"I've studied your case," he said, "and I've received a Bill of Particulars. I know what we're facing. Two criminals are going to testify against you - a man who has never been in trouble. We'll discredit their testimony. They've been given a sweet deal, and we will prove this to the jury. They don't have a case."

What a relief to hear a man say that he believed in me! He thought I was innocent and that we could win the case!

On Monday morning, June 15, 1970, at 9 a.m. in Superior Court, downtown Atlanta, I went on trial for my life. I had already spent nine months of my life behind bars.

At three o'clock every morning during the trial I was taken from my cell to the courthouse to wait until the proceedings began at 9 a.m. The prosecutor had done his homework, and he ate my attorney alive. I learned that mine was a civil lawyer who had never tried a criminal case, and we made some grave errors. I intended to tell the truth and wanted to be sworn in, but my attorney objected to my taking the witness stand.

"This prosecutor is sharp, he'll make a fool out of you," he warned.

I had told him I had no family, and we did not subpoena any character witnesses. How could we? I met the attorney on Friday, and we went to trial ten days later. He insisted that I didn't need character witnesses anyway. Furthermore, he said that in the state of Georgia, I could take the stand without being sworn in and say anything I wanted to say without being cross-examined. That was the greatest news I'd ever heard.

"You're the only witness we need to win this. Just let them present their case, and we'll attack that. They don't have a case." He was confident.

But the trial was a farce. The police officers and detectives who had investigated the shooting, the ambulance driver, and the people who were at the scene all testified to establish that a murder had been committed but none could link me to the scene of the crime.

Not until the trial did I learn all the facts about the robbery. There had been twelve people in the store. The man who had been killed was the husband of one of the cashiers. A total of $590 was stolen during the robbery.

Early in the trial, Frank and Al sent me a message by way of another inmate. They said they had made a deal, and they advised me to plead guilty for a twenty year sentence so I would avoid the death penalty. Their concern for my future was not so evident when they took the witness stand to testify against me.

They were brought in separately, and neither looked at me except when the prosecutor asked him to point out the alleged criminal mastermind. Listening to their false testimony, I wanted to kill them. It's a good thing I didn't have a gun!

Essentially, they testified that I had planned each of a series of robberies and had threatened their lives if they didn't help me carry out my plans. Sometime before the supermarket robbery, they testified, I had gone to the store to determine the best way to carry out the theft. Frank and Al said I had ordered them to kill everyone in the store.

The manager of the store and the cashier whose husband was killed were each called to the stand. They gave details of the murder, and the widow wept as she spoke. When asked if they had ever seen me before, both said they had not.

When the prosecutor finished presenting evidence, I took the witness stand. On the advice of my lawyer, I made an unsworn statement, which would prevent the prosecuting attorney from cross-examining me. I told of my college days and stressed that I had never been in trouble. After testifying for over an hour, I stepped down with a feeling of confidence that I had done a very good job portraying the kind of person I was. At the same time I felt optimistic because none of the eyewitnesses had ever seen me before. My nightmare was about to end, and I was relieved.

Then it was time for the prosecutor to begin his closing arguments. "Ladies and gentlemen of the jury," he began, "weren't you impressed with this man? He's a college man - well-dressed, with a stirring vocabulary. Did you notice how he handled himself? He's not a normal criminal; he's a mastermind!"

After reviewing all that the men said about my supposed involvement in the Atlanta robbery and shooting, he said I had killed other people as well. His statement should not have been allowed, because I had never been indicted for any other crimes.

Walking over to the jury, the district attorney held up a Bible, "This case is really very simple. Two young men put their hands on this Bible, admitted their guilt, and swore Harold Morris masterminded their crimes. Now, the defense says that those two young men are lying. But let me ask you something. Did Harold Morris put his hand on this Bible and deny his guilt? No. He did not. Now, of course, no man is required to testify in his own defense, but if you were in his place and you were innocent, what would you do?"

The district attorney placed both his hands on the front of the jury box and looked each juror in the eyes. "Any man who will not put his hand on the Bible is a lying cheat, a snake in the grass. Morris is a murderer! And if you don't convict him, I'll take my wife and kids and leave this town! I won't walk the streets with him!"

He rested his case.

The jury retired about 9 o'clock that night, and at 11 p.m. they returned, unable to reach a verdict. They asked the judge if I could receive a lesser sentence than death, but he refused. Later, the jury retired for the night, and I went back to jail. At 3 a.m. I was awakened and taken to the courthouse to await the verdict.

At 11 a.m. on June 18th, I entered the courtroom in handcuffs. When the jurors had filed in, the judge asked for the verdict. The foreman handed it to the clerk, who gave it to the prosecutor. A grin spread over his face as he looked at me.

"Guilty as charged!" he declared.

The judge received the written verdict and noted that the jury had recommended mercy, meaning that I would automatically receive a life sentence instead of the death penalty.

The judge said, "Donald Harold Morris . . ."

Again, my first and middle names were reversed. Grasping at a straw, my attorney had filed a motion that I was illegally indicted because of the confusion over my name. The motion was denied.

Forever the words of the judge would ring in my memory, "Young man, for the crime of armed robbery, I sentence you to hard labor at the state penitentiary for the rest of your natural life. And for the crime of murder, I sentence you to hard labor at the state penitentiary for the rest of your natural life. Take him away."

"Your Honor, I can't do it!" I cried. "There's no way that I can serve two life sentences!"

"Young man," he said, "you go to the prison and do your best. I'll do the rest."

"Wait a minute. May I say something?" I asked.

"What is it?"

"Your Honor, two days ago when I was taken from this courtroom in handcuffs and shackles three of the jurors saw me. I request a mistrial." (The shackles indicated that I was already incarcerated and that I was considered dangerous, which would lead the jurors to an assumption of guilt.)

Angrily, he overruled the request.

Seeing that my chances were running out, I quickly added, "I would like to poll the jurors. I want each of them to look me in the eye and tell me they want me to spend the rest of my life in prison. I want them to say they did not see me in handcuffs."

"That is your right," the judge agreed. "Poll the jurors."

Each juror said that I was guilty, but not one of them looked me in the eye. Although three admitted to seeing me in shackles and handcuffs, the judge held to his decision to overrule the request for mistrial. Reaching into my pocket, I pulled out an appeal that I had prepared during the night.

"Your Honor, I respectfully appeal my case and ask that I be allowed to remain in the Fulton County jail until all of my rights have been fully exhausted."

I knew that if I could stay there without getting a number on my back, my chances of appeal were much greater.

"You have thirty days to appeal your case," the judge said.

Throughout the proceedings my attorney had appeared more nervous than I. Beads of perspiration stood on his forehead. Hearing the verdict, he cried. He said he was sorry and promised to appeal the case. I told him that I no longer trusted him. I was still upset over the unsworn statement I had given. He should never have encouraged it.

The prosecutor smiled as I walked by in shackles. I stopped in front of him.

"So you're a Christian - a preacher," I said. "I hope to God I never get religion!"

As I walked to my cell, I passed the cell in which Frank and Al were being held. How I wanted to kill them!

"They say that I'll die here. Don't believe it! I will live to kill you both! And if I can't get you, I'll kill your wives, your mothers, your kids! You will die! You will die! You give me a reason to live!" I spit as far as I could to reinforce my promise.

I didn't sleep that night, knowing that down the hall were the men who had destroyed my life.

Twelve

Doc went on trial for murder, armed robbery, and conspiracy in June of 1970, in Atlanta, Georgia. The bank guard, Fish, and Kenny had all been killed. Only Doc was left to take the blame.

"This is a man who has deliberately placed himself outside the law and outside society," the district attorney railed. "He has put himself there! He's nothing but a thug, a hard core criminal. He's a menace to society, and today we have a chance to send a message. Enough is enough! Please don't let your conscience bother you. He deserves the electric chair, and that's where he belongs. So today, I'm asking you to render a death verdict. This animal came from nothing, and he will always be nothing."

Enraged, Doc bounded over the defense table, and before anyone could react he attacked the district attorney, slamming him to the courtroom floor.

"Don't you ever talk about my mama!" Doc screamed maniacally.

Three officers of the court tackled Doc to the floor and held him there while a fourth handcuffed him.

On the day the verdict was delivered, Doc sat behind the defense table in handcuffs and leg shackles with an officer of the court over each shoulder. The jury could not agree on a death sentence.

"For the crime of armed robbery, Marcus Eugene Odomes, I sentence you to hard labor at the state penitentiary for the rest of your natural life," the elderly judge said with a withering stare. "And for the crime of murder, I sentence you to hard labor at the state penitentiary for the rest of your natural life. These sentences are to run concurrently. God have mercy on you, because I will not."

He knew his life was over. Doc immediately turned around and looked into the faces of his heart-broken wife and child. He fought back tears. He wanted to stay strong. He wanted his wife and child to remember him taking his punishment like a man.

As he was led out of the courtroom he wanted to hug them good-bye. Doc asked that his hands be uncuffed so that he could hug his son, but the officers refused. Doc swore that he just wanted to hug his son, but the officers would not uncuff his hands from behind his back.

Doc bent down and little Doc hugged his father around the neck. Straightening up, he looked at Daria with glistening eyes. Doc saw in her face that she was trying to be strong for him.

"I'll wait for you," she said.

Doc choked up when he heard this. But now was not the time for half-truths, and he knew it.

"Please take care of my little man," Doc whispered in a barely audible voice. "And take care of yourself. You know I love you both more than anything in the world."

Duck-walking down the hallway in leg irons, Doc scowled at a white convict as the man emerged in handcuffs and leg irons from a nearby courtroom. The white convict returned his hard stare.

"What are you looking at, spook?" the white convict snapped.

Still trying to get control of himself, Doc did not respond.

"Are you gonna let that cracker talk to you like that, boy?" one of the bailiffs taunted.

Doc remained stony-faced, and the bailiffs laughed. But as soon as they took off Doc's handcuffs he turned and grabbed at them through the bars of his cell, calling them every filthy name he could think of.

"How could this have happened?" Doc thought as he sat in his cell, the faces of his wife and son still floating before his eyes. "Oh, God, my precious wife and baby, all alone."

His chest tightened with anguish. He had never known the depth of his devotion to them until the moment that he was taken from them. He felt like he had abandoned them. Even though she had promised to wait for him, he knew that there was no way she could wait through a life sentence. He didn't know if he could survive a life sentence.

Just the thought of her with another man was enough to send Doc to his bunk in tears. He wanted to protect her. He wanted to tell her that all men were dogs. They couldn't be trusted. They would only want to use her, just as his father had used his mother.

His poor mother! She would be looking down on him right now and see him jammed up in a little cell with nothing but a cot, a sink, and a toilet and barely enough room to turn around. After everything she had done for him - after all that she had sacrificed so that he would have a chance to be a man - he had failed her. He wept bitter tears when he realized that everything that his mother had tried to do for him had been in vain. She had worked so hard, and despite her best efforts her son had turned out to be nothing more than a common criminal - even worse - a convicted murderer.

When Doc thought of his poor mother he suddenly envisioned what life would be like for Daria and his son. He knew from his own life the kind of hardships a single black mother had to endure, and his heart ached for them. He shuddered to think that now Daria would have to go through the kinds of humiliations his mother had endured.

And his son. He'd have to grow up without his father, just as Doc had.

"I'm no better than my own sorry father," Doc thought. "Oh, God, I'd give anything for just one more chance! I want to go back and do it all over! I could be playing major league baseball! I could have married Daria right out of high school, and then I never would have gone back to the street or met Tito! I had it all. I could have done anything, and what did I do? I chose the street! Why didn't I listen to my dear mother, Aunt Florida, Coach Butts, my teachers? It's all my fault. I put myself here."

He paced the cell tirelessly that night piecing together the events of his life, trying to understand how it had all gone so wrong. As night turned into day, Doc's sorrow turned into anger.

"I'd have been better off born dead in the back seat of that police car!" Doc concluded.

When breakfast was served on a plate under the door the next morning by an inmate, Doc kicked it back out into the hallway. The old white guard standing beside the food cart smiled as if he'd seen the same thing happen a hundred times before.

"You'll be licking it off the floor one day, boy!" the old guard said. "You'll learn to love it. Where you're going, you'll be eating hog's head stew for the rest of your sorry life. I spent twenty years down there - I seen 'em make it."

"You got the life sentence, you old fat cracker!" Doc spat. "You ain't nothing! You got to bring my meals to me! You're too stupid to do anything else! Your wife hates you! Your kids hate you! And you'll be walking around in a jail until the day you die! At least I might get out! I might make parole!"

The old guard laughed sarcastically, "Boy, they're gonna bury you on Pissant Hill!"

As he sat on his bunk with his face in his hands reflecting on his life, Doc began to hate himself for the life he'd lived. He thought that Daria and his son would be angry with him, too.

"I know they hate me for not being there," he reasoned. "And they should hate me. I'll never be with them again. I can never be a father to my son or a husband to my wife. I'll never be free again. If whitey wouldn't let me out of the ghetto, he sure ain't gonna let me out of prison."

He wanted to go to sleep, and he didn't want to wake up. Thoughts of suicide alternated with dreams of escape. But neither seemed real to him. All of his hopes for freedom gave way to a paralyzing despair.

As he cried himself to sleep, he told himself that this must be a dream - a nightmare - that when he awoke everything would be all right. And then one morning the old guard came to his cell and told him to get ready to take a ride.

"Ride? Where?" Doc asked.

A grim smile came to the old guard's face as he said, "On the blue goose, to the classification center in Jackson, and then to the white elephant, boy, for the rest of your life. You will die there."

"The white elephant?"

"Georgia State Penitentiary," the old guard said. "The vacation's over. It's time to start earning your keep. We're gonna make a man out of you or else kill you. Get a move on!"

Thirteen

T he night of my conviction was one of the loneliest of my life. There had been hope until I was sentenced, but as I lay in my cell, the finality of the verdict began to soak in. Over and over I heard the words of the jury: "Guilty as charged! Guilty as charged! Guilty!"

I am guilty, I reasoned, but not as charged. I am guilty of associating with scum, guilty of living a low life, guilty of some irresponsible choices - but not guilty of robbery and murder!

In my mind I retried the case, remembering every word spoken on the witness stand, every facial expression, every emotional response. I had been so confident I would win. My family would never even have to know about the trial, and none of my friends back home in North Carolina would hear about it, either.

But it hadn't worked that way. I'd played a deadly game, and I had lost. Since that time I've watched the faces of many people who received the death penalty or multiple life sentences. Some tried to fight the district attorney. Some cried. Some fell to their knees. Some fainted. Some laughed at the judge. Some tried to commit suicide.

Although I made attempts to change the outcome of the trial by requesting the jury to be polled and asking for a mistrial, I hadn't raised my voice. Except for my comments to the prosecutor as I walked out of the courtroom, I had controlled my temper. I took the verdict calmly, even though I was not prepared for it. I had even read my appeal calmly.

As the hours ticked by and the shock began to wear off, I began to realize, little by little, what the guilty verdict and the double life sentence meant. I was so young, my whole life was ahead of me. But my life was virtually over. To spend the rest of my life in prison was little more than a living death.

"How could I have wasted my life like that?" I thought. "I could have used my opportunities to become whatever I wanted."

Around three o'clock in the morning, the full impact hit me, and there was no stopping the tears. The only thing I could hear was the sound of my own sobbing. Darkness engulfed my soul as I remembered my mother.

"She doesn't even know where I am," I thought. "I'll never survive the violence of prison life: I'll die! But I don't want to die. More than ever before in my life, I want to live!"

Throughout the long night I wept. "Why has this happened to me?" I kept asking myself. "Why am I here?" I tried to remember the name of the man who was killed in the robbery. I reminded myself to look in the newspaper to find out who he was. Finally, exhausted, I fell into a fitful sleep.

The next morning a guard showed me a copy of the Atlanta Constitution. My conviction was big news, and when the guard handed me the paper, I snapped, "You should have been there and seen it firsthand!"

As I read the account, I was astonished at the distortions. The story described a heinous murderer - a villain I could not even recognize.

"That's not me!" I thought. "They're talking about somebody else! If only they knew me, knew who I really am . . . They're going to find out how wrong they are!"

I never saw my attorney again after the trial. He sent a letter stating that he had appealed my case directly to the Georgia Supreme Court.

The days dragged by as I awaited the outcome of my appeal in a musty eight-by-ten foot cell in the Fulton County jail. With the conviction of a felony came the loss of my United States citizenship. Stripped of my rights, I became a ward of the state.

Once a week I was allowed out of the cell for a shower. My meals were served on a tray the guard pushed under the door. There was a tiny window in the cell, but it was too high for me to see outside. For month after month after month I never saw the sky, the sun, the moon, the stars. It was my first encounter with solitary confinement, and each day I drifted further from my sense of humanity.

The longer I remained in the cell, the more enraged and distorted my thoughts became. Everyone was my enemy, and I began to hate my own mother. "She knows where I am!" I thought. "She's left me here alone. Like everyone else, she has turned against me."

My hatred and rage evolved into a seething thirst for revenge. I wanted to hurt people - to kill the prosecutor and those who testified against me. Then one day a new prisoner who was being released came to the jail, and he gave me some information that intensified my determination to get even with Frank and Al.

The new inmate knew both of them. He had done time with them and knew what prison they were in, and he told me what had happened. The two had been sentenced to twenty years for their part in the robbery, but because of their cooperation their sentences were commuted to time served. Shortly after my trial, they walked out of jail and into freedom.

"They bragged about how they set you up," the new prisoner told me. "It's a shame they got away with it."

I offered him all the money in my account if he would kill them for me. He promised to do it and took my money, but I never heard from him again. Still, it gave me satisfaction for a short while to think that something might have happened to my two enemies.

Day after day I paced the floor of my cell waiting for some word about my appeal. My hatred for Frank and Al and for the prosecutor energized me, and I began to wonder - am I even human? It was a question I repeated many times in the days and weeks that followed. My behavior certainly belied my humanity: I screamed at the guards, waving my arms at them, and I even threw filthy commode water into one's face.

That behavior landed me in a "strip cell," also known as a "slicker". Authorities claim that this tiny cell with metal walls and a concrete floor is designed to keep a prisoner from hurting himself.

Although its construction appears to support this idea, clearly, its purpose is total humiliation. It is an effective way to break the spirit of a
man.

Usually, the inmate's clothing is taken away if he is considered suicidal, because he can use the clothes to hang himself. But I was being
punished, so I was allowed a shirt and a pair of pants and I was also
permitted to have a bed. There was no running water, so I had to ask
the guard for water when I was thirsty. I was literally reduced to beg-
ging for this necessity of life.

While I was in the slicker an inmate in the next cell stopped up his
toilet, flooding his cell and mine with human waste. As we waded
through the filth that eventually became a foot deep, the guards
turned water hoses on us, laughing all the while. I'll never forget their
mockery of us. I threatened to kill one of them, but he continued to
laugh.

I had other opportunities to witness the devastating psychological
effect that slickers had on inmates. On one occasion in a cell adjoin-
ing mine a man began hallucinating. Convinced that someone was
trying to kill him, he beat his brains out on the bars. Another prisoner unscrewed a long bolt that was used to flush the toilet and swallowed it. Another swallowed bedsprings, and others ingested knives.

When I was released from the slicker and returned to my cell,
depression subdued me. I lay on my rack lost in loneliness and
despair. Occasionally, I thought about asking for help, but I had too
much pride. Besides, there was no one to ask. "No one cares, anyway," I told myself. For my entire life I had felt that there was not one
person on whom I could depend, and so I never cried for help.

I didn't call on God to help me, either. My thoughts traveled a different course. "There is no God," I decided. "If He were real, He
would never allow this to happen."

For months I wavered between wanting to die and wanting to live.
At some point during those endless days I finally made up my mind
to live. Then, finally, the Georgia Supreme Court made its decision
about my appeal.

"Hey, big boy, read this!" a guard said, slapping me on the
shoulder as he handed me a newspaper clipping. I glanced at the

headline:

"Georgia Supreme Court Denies Harold Donald Morris a New Trial."

My eyes blurred as I read the words. I could scarcely take it in. But the guard did not allow me time to consider the news.

"Now you really belong to us!" he beamed. "Today you start digging ditches!"

He gloated about what the other prisoners would do to me at Georgia State Penitentiary, and I shuddered at his repulsive prophecy: "You're gonna be raped, Morris, 'cause you ain't tough."

Shortly after that I received a letter from my lawyer saying that he had bypassed all of the usual channels and appealed directly to the United States Supreme Court. He had done all he could do, he said, and he wished me luck.

"Get your stuff," a guard said. "You're being transferred."

My "stuff" consisted of the clothes I was wearing. When I was arrested, everything I owned disappeared, and to this day I don't know what happened to my personal effects. Facing two life sentences, I didn't worry about leaving things behind.

It was a forty mile trip to the classification center in Jackson, Georgia, where inmates underwent psychological and physical testing before being taken to the penitentiary.

A male social worker with long hair and a master's degree in sociology started to explain how to survive in prison. Of course, he had never spent a day behind bars.

"Have you ever been there?" I asked.

"No," he said.

"Well, I don't want to talk to you."

As I started to leave the room, he asked about my family.

"I have no family. I'm an orphan," I lied.

"You're a first offender," he noted. "I've looked at your record. There's nothing against you. You're not like the rest. Most inmates fit a pattern. You're different. You're intelligent. I'm going to try to help you. I can recommend placement if you tell me where you want to go. What's your first choice?"

"Georgia State Penitentiary," I replied.

"That's the worst prison in the country!" he said. "No one wants to go there. You're crazy!"

He didn't realize that I was playing games. A man with two life sentences doesn't tell the system where he wants to go! I knew no prisoners other than the two men who had testified against me, and they had been freed. The social worker assumed that I had friends at Georgia State Penitentiary, so he recommended another facility. I didn't care. I was just trying to blow his mind.

When aptitude tests were given, I played games again, deliberately giving incorrect answers. Why should I try for high scores? I was going to die in prison.

After my tests were finished two months later, I was taken to the prison bus, along with other inmates. A large square-jawed officer swaggered around the parking lot with a shotgun as inmates were shackled in pairs and led onto a big blue prison bus called the blue goose. No one bothered to explain what was happening.

The officer with the shotgun suddenly spoke up, "You're all going to the white elephant! Georgia State Penitentiary! And you're gonna work like you've never worked in your sorry lives! You're going to be out in those fields digging ditches and picking peas all day long! And when you get back to the old elephant somebody is gonna make you his galboy! Yeah! They're gonna rape you boys! They're gonna turn you inside out! And if you don't like it, they're gonna kill you!"

The transportation officers were about to shackle me to a black. The same black I had seen coming out of the courtroom. Blacks outnumbered whites about two to one. I switched places with a man behind me so I could be shackled to a white convict.

The gray winter morning reflected the gloom in my soul. During the ride, I had plenty of time to think about the events that had led to my incarceration. As we were driven to the penitentiary I stared out the window at the rolling countryside, the only sound in my ears was the humming of the bus engine.

"What are you in for?" I heard someone say. I turned and saw the convict I was shackled to, a small man with short greasy hair and a sparse mustache, staring at me.

"Are you gonna do part of my time, you little runt?" I asked.

"No, I got enough myself."

"Then shut up."

I looked away and noticed that some of the others on the bus were listening.

"All right," I said, "I'll tell you. You look like a decent guy. I got two life sentences for stealing a fishpond."

"How'd you steal a fishpond?" he asked with a puzzled look.

"That's why I got two life sentences," I answered, trying not to smile. "One for stealing it and one for not telling the judge how I did it."

The square-jawed officer with the shotgun at the front of the bus began laughing, and some other men joined in but most were not in the mood to laugh.

"You about got a smart mouth, ain't you?" the small man wanted to know.

The black convict I had almost been shackled to, the same one I had seen in the courthouse hallway, turned around in his seat and stared at me. I held his gaze long enough for him to know that I wasn't afraid of him, then I looked away.

"Hey, honky," the black convict said to me, "there are three things I live for: driving a white Cadillac, killing a white man, and taking his white woman away from him. And since they ain't no white Cadillacs or white women where we going, you gonna be my galboy."

At this, the other black convicts on the bus burst into laughter.

"Hey, black boy," I said, "you are living proof that Indians mated with buffalo."

Laughter erupted from the white convicts as the black convict pointed at me and promised to kill me.

"You belong to me," he said. "You mine, honky. I'm gonna kill you when we get to the prison."

PART III
1970-1973

Fourteen

T he inmates rode in silence through acres of dark, thick, impenetrable swamp, which opened onto a long, lush sweep of green and, in the distance, the imposing façade of Georgia State Penitentiary, a massive five story structure enclosed by walls and fences all topped by razor wire. Doc saw that all of the buildings were painted white. The main building resembled a huge motel standing four stories high.

The prison reservation encompassed 10,000 acres of farmland growing cabbage, broccoli, squash, cucumbers, peas, corn and wheat. Doc's eyes were drawn to a gentle knoll in the shadow of the prison walls. There he saw rows and rows of small white crosses and a hand-painted sign that read, "PISSANT HILL".

Chains rattled as the prisoners disembarked the bus and assembled in two lines. "Welcome to Georgia State Penitentiary," the sign at the entrance made an ironic attempt at a warm greeting.

Above the front gate, a tower guard shouldered his high-powered rifle and pointed it at the new prisoners. A few cringed, and the tower guard smiled from behind his mirrored sunglasses.

"I'm Captain Tucker, the captain of the guard," boomed a stocky, barrel-chested man with piercing eyes. In his right hand he held a four-foot staff of polished hickory with a large key protruding from the lower end.

Behind him, a fat, hypertensive man in a standard gray suit scowled at the inmates. Pale and flabby, he seemed to belong behind a desk.

"This here is the white elephant," Captain Tucker continued at the top of his voice, "turn around and take your last look at freedom, ladies, because inside you are property of the Georgia State Penitentiary and Warden Edwin Kelso!"

"This is my prison," Kelso began in a flat monotone that Doc strained to hear after Captain Tucker's shouting. "You play by the rules and we'll feed you, clothe you, and give you a place to sleep. But if you think you're a hard case, I'm here to tell you that inside these walls I've got the hardest, meanest and most violent men anywhere in the world, and not one of 'em wants to cross me."

The corners of the fat man's mouth curled up into a self-satisfied smile as he slowly looked over the faces of his new convicts.

"If you don't like it here you can try to escape, but you gotta get through twenty miles of God-awful swamp and if the water moccasins don't get you, the gators will," the warden sneered as his gaze rested on Doc. "That's if you can swim. Niggers, don't even think about it. Y'all swim like rocks!"

The warden turned his back on them and walked back through the prison gate.

"What are you smiling at, big boy?" Captain Tucker barked.

Leaning forward, Doc saw that Captain Tucker was in the face of the white convict he'd threatened on the bus.

"How much time you got?"

"Two life sentences," the white convict said calmly.

"Double elbows? You can forget about it! They're gonna carry you outta here in a pine box!" Captain Tucker guffawed.

He stepped back and pointed with his staff to the gentle knoll where Doc had seen all of the crosses.

"Over there is Pissant Hill!" Captain Tucker rumbled. "That's where the state sticks your dead body when nobody else claims it! You do what I tell you when I tell you or you will be under the next cross! Now move!"

As he hobbled duck-fashion in his shackles through the prison gate, Doc gazed in the direction of Pissant Hill, dread in his heart. He had heard frightening stories about Georgia State Penitentiary, where thousands of inmates who had committed every crime conceivable to man were thrown together.

As the last of the new inmates shuffled through the colossal gate it clanged closed, and the sound reverberated in Doc's ears. He knew at that moment that it wasn't all a dream as he had hoped; it was a nightmare, and it was just beginning.

In the final stripping of his dignity, Doc's head was shaved and his body sprayed for lice, a routine procedure for all inmates arriving at the prison. Standing naked, Doc watched as a high-pressure hose scoured the body of the inmate in front of him. At Captain Tucker's command, the man was hit in the chest and then in the back with delousing powder that clung to his naked, wet body.

"Next!"

Doc stepped into the place the man had just vacated.

"By the way, when you get to your cell it don't matter if you stand or squat over the commode 'cause them there crabs can jump ten feet!" Captain Tucker barked.

Captain Tucker smiled when he saw Doc staring at his unusual staff.

"This here is the elephant key, boy, and it's the only way out of the white elephant," the big man grinned. "Spray 'im down!"

As Doc shook the water out of his eyes he heard Captain Tucker say, "See, what you do, boy, is you use this key to unlock his trunk!"

His booming laugh echoed in the shower.

"Delouse 'im!"

Doc was issued a pair of coveralls and a new identity - number 62346. He was also given three pairs of white socks made at the prison, three sets of underwear stamped with the numbers of three inmates who had worn them previously, a pair of boots and three sets of clothes with white and blue stripes down the side. "State Prison" was stamped in black letters on the pants and the back of the shirt along with Doc's prison number.

To add to his humiliation, the inmate who issued the clothing gave Doc size forty underpants (he was a thirty-four) and an extra-extra large T-shirt. Everybody laughed at the "greenhorn". Doc was fresh meat.

New arrivals were detained for six weeks to three months in quarantine in M-building to determine if they could live in the general inmate population. There were three tiers of twenty cells each, with one man to a cell. The place was also called the catch-out building, where inmates were taken for protection if their lives had been threatened within the prison. Doc was allowed out of the cell once a week for a shower, and he received his meals on a tray that was slipped under the door.

After eight weeks, Doc left M-building and was assigned to a dormitory in A-building. When the guard slammed the door behind him, Doc scanned the faces in the dormitory. All of them were black. One hundred and sixty men milled around. Some watched TV, some played cards, and others talked amongst themselves. Some looked at Doc and looked away while others seemed to be studying him. There were no friendly faces.

The house man told the new inmates to follow him to their bunks. Doc walked with his shoulders back and his head high, not looking to make eye contact, but not avoiding it either.

When he got settled he stretched out on his bunk with his hands behind his head, trying to seem casual, but his heart was pounding so hard he could feel it in his ears. He lay there for a long time, not knowing what to do next until he heard someone sit on a bunk three feet away.

"Hey, man, what'd you get jammed up for?" a man asked.

"Armed robbery and murder," Doc said without turning to look at his questioner.

"Come on!" the man said. "You don't look like no cold-blooded killer to me!"

Doc looked at the man, but he didn't say anything. He was tall and thin, like Doc, but he had a big afro and a big smile.

"How much time you get for all that?" the man pressed.

"Look, man, I don't want to talk about it," Doc said, turning his attention back to the underside of the bunk above him.

"I catch your drift," the man nodded. "This is my bunk here. And if you want anything, anything at all - weed, horse, pills - I'm your man. I'm the Sears and Roebuck of junk, you know?"

"I used to deal," Doc said, thinking back to a much happier time.

"Yeah? Whereabouts?"

"Southside, man, where else?"

Doc learned that the man's name was Charlie, but everybody in the dorm called him, Feelgood. He was in for possession and distribution. Feelgood was ten years older than Doc, and they traded stories about dealing on the Southside but the only person that they had in common was Tito.

"Is he still running the junkies?" Feelgood asked in surprise.

"Far as I know," Doc said.

"That cat has got to be bad to stay on top for that long," Feelgood rhapsodized. "I was there when he started, and he made his from the curb. That cat has no fear."

"He told me that the only thing a real nigger was scared of was living too long."

Feelgood nodded and laughed, and the two men became fast friends.

"Where do you get the junk you sell in here?" Doc asked in a low voice.

"You ain't got to whisper," Feelgood said. "Everybody knows. The screws bring it in."

"The guards?"

"Yeah! They bring it in, find a guy like me with a long stretch to do, a decent guy they think they can trust, you know, and we deal. Make some big money, too! A little ol' joint, you know, 'bout like a matchstick, goes for two dollars 'merican, and a 'black beauty' or any drug you can shoot up goes for twelve or better. I can get you any kind of drug you want. No problem."

"And nobody says nothing?"

"Oh, sometimes the guards get caught. And then they have to resign, but the penitentiary writes 'em a letter of recommendation for their next job."

"Come on . . ."

"Nah, man," Feelgood said, "the only witnesses is inmates!"

Feelgood smiled, and Doc shook his head.

Fifteen

When I left M-building I was assigned to dormitory G-3 where 115 of the most hard-hearted, petty, and quick-tempered men in the state of Georgia shared two commodes and one shower. The toughest inmates, the "tush hogs", sat at two metal tables at the front of the dormitory playing cards and arguing over the sound of a small flickering black and white television high on the wall.

The cots were stacked in triple decks, and the responsibility for assigning bunks fell to the house man, an inmate who was known as Latcheye after a prison stabbing had left one of his eyes drooping half-closed.

"If you've got any money, I'll give you a bottom bunk. Top bunk's free," he said after leading me to a deck of cots.

I couldn't believe it - a man with two life sentences, doomed to die in prison, paying for a bunk to sleep in!

"You're crazy!" I said. "I'm not paying you anything! I've got two life sentences! I think I've earned a bunk!"

"You can pay Latcheye now or pay Latcheye later," he said with satisfaction, "but I think you'll find that heat rises."

"You take a check?" I quipped.

A man I came to know as Double Ug (because he was the ugliest man in the prison) laughed as he strode out the door, "Does he take a check! That's funny!"

"You better wait 'til the ink dries on your behind, sweet meat,"

Latcheye sneered. "You got a lot to learn in the old elephant."

It had been so long since I'd shaved or showered that I couldn't stand my own stinking odor. I asked Latcheye to let me borrow a towel and a razor.

"I'm not giving you anything," he barked.

Nearby, an old man was busy lacing leather wallets. He looked up and spoke.

"Young man, you can borrow my towel and razor."

"I appreciate that," I said, surprised by his kindness. "I'll gladly repay you."

"Hey, you don't associate with people like that," Latcheye interrupted. "That man is a baby raper. He's the scum of the earth."

"I don't think I know you," I said to Latcheye.

"No, but I know you," he replied. "I've already pulled your file. You're somebody. You're a murderer."

I was dumbfounded! Accepted because I had supposedly killed someone! The prison seemed to have a kind of social hierarchy, with murderers receiving more "respect" than many other criminals. Thrust together in that filthy prison were killers, robbers, rapists, and homosexuals - 3,200 of the worst of Georgia's 16,000 prisoners. One man had killed his entire family. Another had buried a girl alive. One inmate was accused of raping 150 women. Lowest in this pathological caste system were the "baby rapers" - the child molesters. I soon realized that a strong person puts no trust in baby rapers, bank robbers, and murderers.

Although I'd been convicted of murder, I knew my conviction was not enough to protect me from danger and assault. Inmates jostled for power, and survival became a daily challenge. There wasn't a doubt in my mind that I'd be killed. I wasn't tough enough or smart enough to survive. Desperate and miserable, I stayed to myself, speaking as little as possible, hoping that everyone would think I was tough while inside I was frightened to death. It was the loneliest kind of life.

Sitting on a bench in a prison hallway with all of the other new inmates, I heard Captain Tucker call my new number. I walked past him and into a room where a short man with a receding hairline was seated behind a desk. A guard stood on one side of the desk and a man I would come to know as Dr. Ortiz stood on the other side. The door closed behind me.

"I'm Deputy Warden Grimes," the seated man said as he closed my file. "Huh. Very interesting. So you can type? What kind of work did you do on the outside?"

"I was an airplane pilot," I said.

I kept a straight face, but the guard and Dr. Ortiz smiled.

"Let me tell you something, smart boy!" Grimes said as he looked into my face for the first time. "I'll have you digging ditches and picking peas faster than a rattler can strike. You mess with me, and you'll die in solitary, you understand me, joker?!"

He exchanged a glance with Dr. Ortiz and asked, "You sure you want this one?"

Dr. Ortiz did not change expression.

"Normally, you have to work six months on the outside before you can get an inside job," Grimes explained. "But Dr. Ortiz here needs someone who can type to work on the hospital floor. Lucky for you, you can type."

"Well, I'll think about it and let you know," I said.

"Let me know?!" Grimes said, rising from his chair. "You'll type or you'll go straight to the hole!"

As Dr. Ortiz and I exited the office he pulled me aside.

"That went pretty smooth, didn't it?" I smiled.

"Your smart mouth is going to get you into a lot of trouble in here," Ortiz warned, his expression serious. "You just made an enemy of the wrong man."

As I learned my way around, I discovered there was a convict code, an unwritten set of rules governing behavior behind bars. An inmate who violated the code could expect harassment from inmates as well as guards.

The prison was dominated by a handful of inmates who had built a reputation for toughness. They controlled everything in the prison, including the television, which blared constantly. It was close to my bunk, but I didn't dare adjust it. Only the tough guys known as the "tush hogs" were allowed to do that. On Saturdays, about fifty smoking and tobacco-chewing inmates huddled around my bunk to watch cartoons. That nearly drove me out of my mind.

It had been a long time since I watched a ball game, and I was desperate to see one. As I headed to lunch one Saturday, I gathered my courage and said, "Fellas, the Celtics play the Lakers in basketball at one o'clock today, and I'd like to watch the game. You know, we're all in here together. I want you to know I'd really like to see that game."

"We don't watch sports in here," Latcheye said gruffly, adding, "I don't know who you think you are, but you ain't watching nothing on that television."

I wished I'd never mentioned it. But now that the issue was raised, it had to be settled.

"Let me tell you something," I said. "This is as much my home as it is yours. I haven't touched that television, but I'm telling you that at one o'clock I will watch that basketball game."

I turned and walked out. Shakey, a narrow-shouldered man, a stuttering chain-smoker, caught up to me outside the dormitory.

"C-can't f-figure out wh-whether you're the b-b-bravest or the s-s-st-upidest m-m-man I've ever s-s-seen," he said. "R-railroad and Latcheye are m-mean c-cons. They'll c-cut your head off for s-saying things like th-that!"

I didn't answer.

"D-do you have a knife?" he asked.

"Man, I don't have anything!" I said, feeling the grip of fear.

"You c-can't b-back down n-now. If you d-do, you're f-f-f-finished. You'll b-be a n-nobody. They'll r-rape you and s-s-steal everything you own. U-understand?"

I nodded.

"There's a m-magazine under m-my b-bunk with a s-s-sh-shank in it," he said.

A shank is a homemade knife long enough to almost pierce through a man.

"G-go over to my b-bunk and g-get it. If th-there's tr-trouble, you'll have a w-weapon. You t-tell where you g-got it, I-I'll k-kill you myself."

When I returned to the dormitory, I did exactly as he said. If his warning hadn't frightened me, the touch of that razor-sharp blade certainly did. What if I had to use it? Never before had I faced anything like this. I'd started something, and I had to go through with it. I leaned against the wall, afraid to turn my back to anyone. Time crawled.

At one o'clock an old western movie was playing. With the magazine in one hand, I walked over to the set and turned the channel to the ball game.

"You touch that television again, and I'll kill you!" warned Latcheye as he switched back to the movie.

"Fellas," I tried again, "can't we work this out? I live here too, and I've never asked to watch anything. I should be allowed to watch one program. I don't want any trouble, but I'm going to watch that basketball game. When it's over you can watch anything you choose for the rest of the day. That's the way it should be. I hope we can get along."

"You touch that television and you're going straight to Pissant Hill!"

The voice came from a bunk where Railroad lay with his young galboy lover. Every inmate at Georgia State Penitentiary knew who Railroad was because he controlled the prison rackets: gambling, drugs, galboys, and even some guards. An ex-professional boxer with tattoos down each arm and a scar across his cheek that resembled a railroad track, he was the most feared man in the prison and his word was law in G-3. The other inmates wanted him to take up the fight.

"My fight is not with you," I said, "but I've watched you turn the channel. It's only fair I have the same privilege. I don't want any trouble, but I'm ready to go to Pissant Hill, if that's what it takes."

I waited through an interminable silence, my body tense and drenched with sweat.

Finally, he spoke, "You're the only man in this place who has any guts. I like you. What you're saying makes sense. As far as I'm concerned, you can watch anything you want."

Then, he turned his attention to the boy lying with him in the bunk.

"I'd like for you guys to watch the ball game with me," I said, changing channels again.

Still grasping the magazine with the shank carefully concealed, I sat on a stool without turning my back. The inmates began walking away, disgruntled and mumbling. Only one stayed to watch the game with me.

A strange thing happened that day. Through a challenge made in ignorance and innocence, I gained respect. Knowing nothing about me, the other inmates gathered the impression that I was dangerous. If I had backed down, they would have persecuted me. It was a terrifying introduction to the law of the jungle - win, or you're through.

The only time I found that I could really relax was at yard call when I could play basketball. One day as I played I saw a young boy standing at the prison fence dribbling a basketball. When he saw me looking at him he waved. After a moment's hesitation I waved back. I didn't know what to make of the boy, but after the game was over I walked over to the fence, which was actually two fences, ten feet apart, topped by razor wire. A shotgun guard walked a turn between the fences. I was wondering how the boy could get to stand between the fences when he smiled.

"Haven't seen you before," he said.

"Convict 62345."

"So what? You don't scare me."

"Come over on this side of the fence and say that," I joked.

Turning to the nearest tower he shouted, "Guard! Open this gate!"

The guard smiled at him from behind his mirrored sunglasses.

"My dad's an officer in the state patrol," he explained, "and my mom's a nurse in the prison hospital. I live in that house right there."

He pointed to a small white house just across the road on state property.

"Hospital floor? That's where I work," I said.

"So where'd you learn to play like that, convict?"

"High school. I was all-state."

"You? If you can be all-state I'm gonna be the best basketball player in the world," he said, smiling. "So what happened to you? Looks like you got drafted by the wrong team."

"I never was too smart," I replied. "I didn't go to school but two days. One to sign up and the other to tell them I wasn't coming back."

He laughed and smiled at me. He was the first person who'd smiled at me in a long time. Then the horn sounded, ending yard call.

"I'm Jimmy Hale," he said.

"I'm Harold. I'll catch you later, Jimmy. I gotta go. Yard call's up."

Sixteen

P rison existence proved daily that when men are treated like animals, they will do whatever is necessary to survive. Consequently, violence became a way of life. Doc never got used to it. Although he'd been a physical person and athletic, he realized that brute strength was no match for psychopathic killers, and he was scared. It was a rare thing for anyone to be prosecuted for murdering an inmate, and the penalty was usually an additional sentence to run concurrently with the existing one. That hardly served as a deterrent to murder. Much of the violence in prison was drug related.

One night Doc was awakened from a deep sleep by the sound of a nearby struggle. Through bleary eyes, he saw Feelgood wrestling on his bunk with three men. Doc was still groggy when one of the men raised a shank over his head and jammed it between Feelgood's ribs. Doc heard a muffled scream. Then the man stabbed Feelgood again and again as Doc watched. Somewhere in the back of his mind Doc knew that by the time the knife had plunged into Feelgood's chest a fourth time there was nothing he could do to help his friend, and he didn't have a weapon. He closed his eyes and kept them closed until he was sure that the attackers had left.

They were junkies who had owed Feelgood money, so he'd stopped dealing to them. He'd bitched about them to Doc more than once. Feelgood felt these men were his friends and that they had taken advantage of him. It was doubtful whether they'd ever pay, and

Feelgood spread the word. Soon, nobody would deal to the men, and when they couldn't score any drugs their habits came down hard on them so they decided to take it out on Feelgood and steal his drugs.

Doc wondered how long he had to lie there. He peered out of half-opened eyes and saw that everyone around him was still sleeping - or pretending to be. Doc knew the convict code, knew that no one would say anything to the guards. If a convict did, he had to be moved out of the dormitory or he'd be killed.

Pretending to rouse from his sleep, he stood and stared down into the face of his friend. Feelgood's eyes had been gouged out. His chest was a bloody mess. Doc hurried to the bathroom where he hunkered down over a toilet and vomited. He was sick to the very depths of his soul, sick with the knowledge that his friend had been killed while he watched, three feet away, helpless to do anything. He told himself it was over before it started; it was probably over after the first time the knife pierced Feelgood's chest. But he still felt horrible, and he knew that the only thing that could make him feel better would be to see the men who had done it punished.

At the morning count Feelgood's body was discovered by the guards. Captain Tucker arrived soon afterwards. He looked at the body and then at Doc.

"What happened here?" he asked Doc.

As Doc stared at Captain Tucker he felt the eyes of the entire dormitory on him.

"Answer me, boy! What happened here?"

Captain Tucker swung his staff and clipped Doc on the left knee, dropping him to the floor.

"I didn't see anything!" Doc protested.

"You were sleeping three feet away from this boy and you didn't see anything? Well, I know somebody saw something!"

Helmeted riot guards roved up and down rows of naked inmates standing at attention in front of their bunks. Captain Tucker opened the door to the interrogation room and sent another naked inmate back to his bunk.

"Odomes!"

Doc walked naked across the cold floor and into the interrogation room where he stood before Deputy Warden Grimes.

"Sound off," Grimes snapped.

"Odomes, 62346."

"He's a new monkey, sir," Captain Tucker offered. "He was sleeping three feet away when the crime occurred."

"Tell me everything you saw," Grimes demanded.

"I didn't see nothing," Doc responded bluntly.

Grimes tried to stare Doc down, but Doc would not look away.

"I know you saw what happened."

Doc shook his head, "I wasn't in my bunk."

"Oh, no? Where were you?"

"On the toilet."

"On the toilet," Grimes repeated looking at Captain Tucker and shaking his head. "Explain this to me, Odomes. I've already interviewed half of this dormitory and seventeen of you were on the toilet when this happened. There's only two toilets in here, and one of 'em is broken! So just where were you? Top or bottom?"

"About halfway, sir."

Captain Tucker smiled, but a stern look from Grimes quickly wiped it off of his face.

"You think you're smart, huh?" Grimes glowered. "You're already playing the game, nigger? One day I'll be in here asking some new monkey how your dumb behind happened to get carved up! Get him out of here!"

Doc learned never to interfere when hostilities between inmates flared into violence. In such a situation friendship counted for nothing. He knew he could not count on anyone. And no one could count on him. If his life was on the line, any inmate who chose to fight for Doc would end up fighting for his own life, too. It was every man for himself, and in the end Doc was alone.

After Doc refused to talk, Muscle Jaw, the man who ran the dormitory, approached him. Tall, muscular and bald, he had a jaw as big as a horseshoe and a violent demeanor.

"You did the right thing in there, not talking to those turnkeys," Muscle Jaw rumbled. "I like a man that ain't too talkative."

Doc nodded.

"I know you and him was friends. But that's how it goes."

Again, Doc nodded.

"You're gonna do all right in here," Muscle Jaw predicted. "I like the way you handle yourself. You need anything, you come to me. Okay?"

"Okay."

"You ain't thinking 'bout getting back is you?"

"Nah," Doc lied.

"That's right, you leave all that up to the Jaw. This is my house, and long as you understand that we gonna get along just fine."

Doc fantasized about getting back at the three men who he'd seen butcher his friend, but in the end reality barged into his fantasy and three beat one every time. He did not sleep well and constantly worried that the men would come back for him in the middle of the night.

The only time Doc had any peace was when he was playing basketball during yard call. The prison yard was a microcosm of prison life. Both were segregated. The dormitories for the white prisoners were on the east side of the prison and the black dormitories were on the west side. At yard call whites stayed on the east side of the yard and blacks kept to the west. Even the basketball court was divided: whites playing on the east basket, blacks playing on the west basket.

Although blacks and whites never played together, they did slyly watch each other play. As Doc picked up a ball that had rolled off the court he turned to watch the action at the east end. The inmate he'd squared off against in the bus was the obvious standout. The man caught a pass on the left wing, drove right, made an Earl-the-Pearl spin dribble and zipped a no look pass to a teammate under the basket. He turned and caught Doc watching him.

"You keep watching me and you might learn something, black boy!"

"Bring it on down here, and I'll learn you some respect!" Doc shouted.

The man just shook his head and turned his back to Doc.

"You think you could take him?" Doc heard Muscle Jaw grunt.

Turning to see Muscle Jaw striding towards him, Doc said, "No problem."

"Hey, Road!" Muscle Jaw called out. "Bring your Super Honky down here so my boy Doc can teach him a lesson!"

Doc saw the white inmate, an enormous man with short-cropped, fiery red hair and tattoos snaking down each massive arm.

"You gotta make it worth something!" Railroad said.

"You're covered, man!" Muscle Jaw shot back. "You're on!"

Convicts, black and white, surrounded the west end of the court until the crowd was four men deep. Afraid that a riot might break out at any minute, yard guards fought through the mob to get onto the court and watched the two players closely.

The game seesawed back and forth. Fighting for a loose ball under the basket, the two men butted heads violently and instantly began throwing punches.

The basketball game quickly turned into a street brawl as they both fell to the court. The crowd cheered wildly. The guards descended on the two men and tried to pull them apart. Tower guards, fearing for the safety of the guards on the court, fired warning shots over the heads of the inmates. The crack of high-powered rifles quickly restored order. The inmates who had not scrambled back to their dorms for safety were sent back inside for the rest of yard call.

The fight had gotten Doc's blood up, and that evening in the dormitory he found Muscle Jaw playing chess on his bunk with another inmate. Doc told Muscle Jaw that he wanted a weapon. Muscle Jaw shook his head silently.

"What difference does another life sentence make?" Doc argued. "Man, if I do live long enough to get out, I'll be nothing but an old broke-down nigger."

"You see what I'm doing, here?" Muscle Jaw asked angrily as he turned from the board.

"Yeah."

"What am I doing?"

"Playing chess."

"Chess! You never make a move without thinking about what's gonna happen next! Now, you're lucky you didn't go to the hole or start a riot today," Muscle Jaw lectured Doc sternly. "You kill him, and you will start a riot. Proper timing is everything."

"Who cares if I cause a riot? I don't care if the whole place burns down! I'm gonna die here anyway!"

"That's just the ol' elephant coming down on you," Muscle Jaw said calmly. "You got to get past that."

"Get past that? To what? To sit around this stinking place staring at the walls waiting for a visit and ain't anybody coming? Man, my life is over!"

"You'll adjust after you become institutionalized," Muscle Jaw said, turning his attention back to the chessboard. "We all do. You got plenty of time to deal with that honky. He ain't going nowhere."

Seventeen

I was working at my job on the prison hospital floor one day when Doctor Ortiz said, "Harold, tell that inmate I want to see him."

I got up from my typing and walked over to a tall white inmate with his back to the door. I tapped him on the shoulder.

"Hey, man, Doc Ortiz wants to see ya."

The man spun around, and I discovered that his eyebrows were plucked and his ears pierced.

"How dare you address me as such," he chided in an unnaturally high voice, placing his hands on his hips. "My name is Diane, and you will address me as such or never speak to me again, you brute!"

The inmates on the bench in the hallway doubled over with laughter. Diane sashayed past me into the room, and I saw that even Doc Ortiz was laughing. I wheeled on Diane, furious, clenching my fists.

"Hey, fag!" I growled. "How'd you like a roll in the hay?"

By being derogatory, I thought I could prompt a fight. I was ready to knock his teeth out for humiliating me.

"A roll in the hay?" he sang out. "Honey, together we'll light the hay on fire!"

Laughter cascaded into the room from the hallway. Even I had to laugh.

I said, "Doc Ortiz, you gotta help me, I think I'm in love."

I was to learn that homosexuality was a way of life at Georgia State Penitentiary. Although inmates were sentenced to the hole for being involved in homosexuality, the practice was widespread. When the dormitory door would open and a young fellow would step inside, you would see the old cons smile. Then one would say, "Hey, fellas, it's happy hour!"

As I lay on my bunk the next evening I saw Latcheye approaching me. Slowly reaching under my pillow, I gripped the handle of the shank Shakey had given me.

"Get your stuff," he said gruffly. "You're moving."

"Moving? Where?"

"Railroad wants you to have the bunk next to him."

This was an offer I couldn't turn down. I quickly collected all of my things and moved. My new bunk was on the bottom, next to Railroad. As I got settled in, the guard came to the door and shouted, "Mail call!"

Practically all of the other inmates stampeded to the front of the room to receive letters and packages, leaving me alone with Railroad, Latcheye, and Ringo. Ringo was one of Railroad's flunkies and without a doubt one of the toughest men in the prison.

"How come you never go to mail call?" Railroad asked me.

"Nobody knows I'm here," I said.

"Why not?" he wondered.

"I don't want 'em to know."

Railroad smiled, "I like a man who can hold his tongue. You know that scrawny little runt calls himself Shakey?"

"Yeah."

"Friend of yours?"

"Yeah," I replied cautiously.

"He's the reason Cow Daddy's in the hole."

"Shakey? He'd never rat."

"He's a rat," Railroad stated flatly. "You make sure he goes with you to the theater Saturday morning."

"The theater?"

"It's nice 'n dark in there. Latcheye's gonna put him on Pissant Hill."

"Lemme stab the snitch, Road," Ringo pleaded. "I wanna do him."

"Nah, Latch can do him."

I didn't think that Shakey would rat anybody out, but I could see that Railroad wasn't going to change his mind. If I tried to protest, Railroad might decide that I was a rat, too. It was a simple choice: I was either with Railroad or against him.

At yard call, I passed a basketball between my hands as I walked around the perimeter of the fence. I wanted to be alone to think.

"Hey, 62345! Why aren't you playing?"

It was Jimmy. He was wearing a T-shirt that read, "I'm a winner! God don't sponsor no losers!"

"Trying to think," I said.

"Don't hurt yourself!" he quipped.

I smiled.

"Yeah," I said, "if I was smart I wouldn't be in here in the first place."

"What'd you do, anyway?"

"I got convicted of armed robbery and murder and was given two life sentences. I got mixed up with drinking and drugging and the wrong people and I was at the wrong place at the wrong time," I said as earnestly as I could. "But I didn't kill anybody."

"I believe you," Jimmy said without hesitation.

Tears sprang into my eyes. It had been so long since anyone told me that. I would have hugged him if I could. Choked up, I wanted to say "thank you", but I was afraid that my voice would betray my emotions.

"So, are you gonna teach me some basketball or what?"

"Jimmy, I'm gonna make you the best basketball player in the world," I said after a long moment. "First drill: pass me that ratty old ball over the fence."

He looked at me like he wondered whether I was serious or not, but then he heaved the ball over the razor-topped chain link fence. I tossed him the prison ball that I had, which was almost new. He smiled ear-to-ear.

"You right-handed?" I asked.

"Yeah."

"Dribble around that guard tower and back to me with your left."

He dribbled off with his left, lost the ball, and had to chase it down.

"That's all right!" I shouted. "Stick with your left! We're gonna turn that weakness into a strength! When we get through there's gonna be no stopping you!"

As he dribbled off I had to admire the courage of that young boy. He'd watched me play basketball through a prison fence and wanted to learn from me. He didn't treat me like a dangerous animal that needed to be caged up. He talked to me like he talked to any other decent human being.

He repeatedly lost his dribble as he rounded the guard tower, but he didn't give up.

When he got back to the fence he looked me in the eye and said, "That's wasn't very good, but I'll do better, you watch."

He was determined. I really admired that little boy. And I was determined to learn from him.

I found Shakey, and I told him that I was giving him back the shank he had loaned me.

"You c-can ha-have it," he said.

"You're gonna need it," I whispered.

He looked at me strangely.

"Don't go to the theater on Saturday."

"W-why not?"

"They're going to kill you."

"That's f-funny," he smiled nervously. "No-nobody wants to k-k-k-kill m-me."

"Stay out of that theater and watch your back, that's all I'm saying."

"Why would a-anyone w-want to k-kill m-me? You're c-crazy."

"You ratted on Cow Daddy?" I whispered.

"N-no!"

"Railroad thinks you did."

His face drained of the little color it had.

"I d-d-didn't!" he protested. "You-you g-g-gotta t-t-t-talk to him!"

"I'm talking to you," I said. "Catch out if you have to. There's nothing else I can do for you."

Shakey didn't return to the dorm after yard call, but Railroad and Latcheye did.

"You're dead, Morris!" Railroad roared, pointing a finger at me.

"Nobody talks to this snitch, or they'll have to answer to me for it! Freeze him out!"

It wasn't hard for Railroad and Latcheye to figure out what had happened. I lay awake that night sweating in my bed wondering if I would live to see the morning. I kept a tight grip on the shank Shakey had given me. He was probably sleeping like a baby in M-building in a cell of his own, but my six weeks in M-building had been enough for me. I'd have rather died in population than be moved to a solitary cell for the remainder of my two life sentences.

I couldn't carry the shank with me under my clothes, and I couldn't conceal it in the shower. Clearly I would need to find a way to defend myself if somebody came after me in there. In the corner of the bathroom I noticed a bucket with a mop-wringer - a metal bar used to squeeze the mop. It measured nearly three feet long and was attached to the bottom of the bucket with a nut and bolt. During the night, while everybody was asleep, I removed the nut and bolt and refastened the bar with a small piece of wire. The mop wringer still worked, but by yanking away the wire I'd have a deadly weapon within seconds.

The next morning I caught Double Ug looking at me as he smoked his first cigarette of the day. He stopped by my bunk and stared at the floor as he spoke.

"I can't believe you did it," he said sadly. "Can't believe it. I can't talk to you anymore."

"I saved an innocent man's life," I protested, "doesn't than mean anything?"

He dropped the cigarette on the floor by my bunk and stubbed it out with the toe of his boot before walking off. I had no friends left, and the dormitory was now a sea of hostile faces. I was constantly on my guard because I had no way of knowing which one of my fellow inmates might try to kill me. Railroad could come after me himself, or he could put a contract out. As I tried to stay alert, the days and nights ran together. My peace of mind was gone. But after three weeks nothing had happened. I began to relax a little. I let my guard down. And that's exactly what they were waiting for.

I was in the bathroom trying to shave in a fogged up mirror when

I thought I saw someone move in behind me. I turned just in time to
see Latcheye swinging a board at me. The board glanced off the side
of my head, opening a gash in my scalp. I dropped to one knee and
blood poured into my eyes. As Latcheye reared back to finish me off
I drove my fist into his groin, and he fell in a heap in front of me.
And then I saw Railroad standing behind him. He advanced on me
with a shank in his right hand.

Remembering the mop wringer, I scuttled sideways along the wall,
all the while wiping blood out of my eyes. I yanked the mop wringer
loose and brandished it.

"C'mon!" I shouted. "Let's get this over with!"

The riot alarm sounded, and Railroad smiled grimly. Behind him,
inmates jammed the entrance to the shower to see what would happen next. I held the pipe in front of me in both hands. As he lunged
at my neck with the shank I ducked and slammed the pipe into his
left knee, sending him howling to the tile floor. I raised the pipe over
my head and brought it down hard, only to have the blow deflected
by Latcheye's board. Before I could get my balance Latcheye
whacked me in the ribs and swung for my head. I got my pipe up in
time, but he hit me on the left hand, snapping my little finger.

I inched along the wall in a defensive crouch as Latcheye cut the
air with his board again and Railroad struggled to his feet. Suddenly,
riot guards clad in helmets and armed with shields and clubs burst
through the mob jamming the doorway and rushed Railroad,
Latcheye and me - pinning us to the wall.

Captain Tucker strode into the bathroom and picked the shank up
off the floor at Railroad's feet.

"What's this Railroad?" he asked sarcastically, running the shank
over the hair on the back of his hand. "That's a bad blade! This thing
could shave a floating dog turd!"

After I had gone to the hospital to be sewn up, I was marched into
kangaroo court. I was a terrible sight as I stood before the board of
three prison officials, presided over by Deputy Warden Grimes. My
head had been shaved and thirty-nine stitches laced my scalp together.

"Well, whaddya know?" Grimes began. "After three years our ol' airplane pilot is still messing up. I knew I'd be seeing you again, boy.

You are charged with inciting a riot in a dormitory. How do you plead?"

"Nolo contendere."

I knew my plea didn't matter. But Grimes leaned back in his chair to confer with the other two officials anyway. When he leaned forward again he was smiling.

"We find you guilty," he said. "Fourteen days in the hole. Get him out of here."

I smiled bitterly and shook my head. As the guards appeared on either side of me to escort me out, I just couldn't let it go.

"Oh, by the way," I said, "I saw your wife a few minutes ago with a mattress on her back headed towards cell block six."

He leapt up out of his chair and said in a voice trembling with rage, "Forget the hole! Put him in the slicker! Then throw this piece of trash on death row! And you're gonna stay there as long as you're in this prison!"

Panic set in as I realized what I'd done.

"But I got two life sentences!" I said. "That means forever!"

The hatred of many years rose in his voice as he said with a satisfied laugh, "Nothing lasts forever!"

Captain Tucker and another guard, Dobbs, took me, stripped to my shorts, down a long hallway stopping before a large iron door. Dobbs opened a waist high hatch. Inside, the slicker resembled a shower stall: no cot, no toilet, just a hole in the middle of the floor. I struggled as best I could, but Captain Tucker beat me down onto my knees with the staff, kicked me like a dog through the hatch, and slammed it closed.

Cold meals came once a day on a plastic tray. The roaches that I shared my cell with swarmed my tray for whatever I didn't eat. Whenever the guard opened the slide on the door a shaft of light would cut the darkness and spill onto the floor and the roaches would scramble into the dark corners. One day I asked the guard to see the doctor.

"What for?" he asked, his eyes narrowing.

I leaned my head into the light and showed him that the stitches were growing into my head and needed to be removed before they became infected.

"Man!" he said. "That looks awful!"

"Go get the doctor," I pleaded.

"Don't you tell me what to do, boy!" he snapped. "You just look on the bright side - if gangrene sets in they'll have to cut your sorry head off and then you'll be out of your misery!"

He closed the slide, and I was once again immersed in darkness. The doctor never came.

Eighteen

After three years of infrequent visits, Daria sent Doc a letter saying that she and Marcus were moving away and most likely wouldn't be back. The money had run out and it was time, she said, to move on. Doc was crushed. He cried almost every day in the shower so that no one would see him.

At the same time Daria was leaving him, Doc was given an inside job in the hospital floor's dispensary doling out medication to inmates. Pill call was at 6 p.m. every day. Doc stood behind a half door which opened into a small square room lined with rows and rows of shelves filled with hospital supplies and medications - cold pills, aspirin, salve, and cough syrup. The job was simple enough, and it was much better than working out in the fields under the broiling Georgia sun or in the steaming penitentiary kitchen. But the job had its drawbacks; inmates whose medication ran out constantly tried to bully more medication out of the dispensary attendant.

At the front of a long line of prisoners stood an agitated Kung Fu. A small wiry man with black beady eyes and a face like a hatchet, he spent his yard call not playing basketball or lifting weights but practicing the martial arts by himself.

"Just gimme another bottle of that cough syrup, boy!" Kung Fu shouted.

Doc looked down at his chart.

"No, you had your 'lowance this week," Doc said calmly.

"You're new here, so I'll spell it out for you: gimme the cough syrup or I'll knock your nappy head in, nigger."

A hush fell over the crowd of inmates as Doc and Kung Fu stared one another down. Finally, Kung Fu let out a banshee scream and leaped into the air, gyrating wildly, landing in a fighting stance before the half door.

"Kung fu! Hah!"

Doc slammed a claw hammer into the side of Kung Fu's head spinning him around and sending him slumping to the floor.

"Claw hamma! Hah!"

The rest of the inmates in the hallway were hysterical. Some even slumped to the floor, holding their sides as Doc opened the half door and dragged the twitching and unconscious body of Kung Fu out of the way. He returned back behind the door and closed it, returning the hammer to its place under the counter of the half door.

"Next!" Doc shouted over the laughter.

"I think I'll skip pill call today!" Double Ug said smiling. "Suddenly I'm feeling a lot better!"

"It ain't funny!" blustered Ringo as he stormed to the front of the line. "I'm gonna bust your head open, nigger!"

Hall guards quickly restrained Ringo before he could get to Doc.

"I'll get you on the yard, boy!" Ringo threatened as the guards moved him away from Doc and down the hallway.

Threats had been flying back and forth between Ringo and Doc for three days when the house man sang out, "Get ready to love your honky brothers! The warden says we gonna be integrated!"

The house man finished tacking up a memo on the bulletin board as confusion reigned in the dorm. Everyone talked, yelled, threatened, and questioned at the same time. Many men crowded around the board to read the memo for themselves. Muscle Jaw shouldered through the crowd and scanned the memo before tearing it down and ripping it up.

"You brothers with me or against me?"

Many in the dormitory shouted their approval, but there were also many anxious inmates, including Doc.

"Doc, you with me?" Muscle Jaw asked him loudly.

"Yeah!" Doc piped. "I ain't got my limit yet!"

"We're going to battle!" Muscle Jaw shouted as he stalked back and forth in front of the dormitory, his eyes feverish and sweat streaming off of his bald head. "If you ain't with me you're against me and if you're against me catch out now! I don't want to see you in here tomorrow if you ain't ready to fight!"

Kneeling before Doc's bunk, Muscle Jaw placed a shank on Doc's chest. Doc raised his head off the pillow but did not pick up the shank.

"You ever killed a man?" Muscle Jaw asked.

Doc didn't answer.

"Now's the time to get that honky! When everything goes down tomorrow, you can do him!"

The next day yard call had all of the tension of a combat zone. Blacks and whites eyed each other, sensing what was coming. A group of whites led by Ringo and a group of blacks led by Muscle Jaw milled near the center of the yard.

"We gonna roll the head of the first honky that comes to the west side," Muscle Jaw taunted.

"What if it's me, black boy?" Ringo shot back, stepping towards Muscle Jaw. "You gonna roll my head?"

Eyeball to eyeball, Muscle Jaw smiled at Ringo before turning his back and looking at his group of toughs.

"You hear what he called me?" Muscle Jaw asked.

Then, without warning, Muscle Jaw wheeled on Ringo, jamming a shank deep into his neck. Dark blood spewed onto the ground, turning black in the dirt.

This was the spark that set off the powder keg. The prison yard exploded into violence as the white toughs yelled and pulled their weapons, quickly converging on the blacks. Other inmates ran to the fight with shanks or razors or baseball bats. Doc pulled his shank, suddenly ready to fight for his life as the pandemonium spread over the whole yard.

A group of blacks chased down a lone white and beat him to the ground with boards from broken benches. In another part of the yard, a group of whites with shanks and razors surrounded two unarmed blacks and stabbed them to death.

Many, black and white, rushed to the safety of the dorms hoping to escape. Yard guards fled to safety inside the prison as alarms sounded and tower guards fired warning shots.

"Get down! On the ground!" shouted the megaphoned voice of a guard. "Now!"

More shots rang out as the tower guards tried to restore order. Many of the inmates hit the dirt, but many continued fighting until tear gas canisters hit the ground and the yard was suffused with choking yellow gas. Tears streamed from Doc's eyes. He dropped his shank, and he knelt over wiping at his eyes frantically, unable to see anyone or anything clearly. Moments later, the fighting had stopped, and the bodies lay strewn around the yard moaning, writhing, bleeding, crying, or dead.

Nineteen

After fourteen days in the slicker I was sent to death row. There is no hope among condemned men. On death row the desperate wait to die. Some forty men were there when I arrived.

I looked around at my new accommodations: another eight-by-ten foot cell with a bunk, a small sink offering only cold water, and a commode permanently cemented to the wall to resist the strength of the insane, who would attempt to rip the fixtures from their mountings. There wasn't enough room to exercise, and it appeared the cell hadn't been swept in six months. The door was padlocked. I would be allowed to leave the cell only once a week to shower. I had one shirt and a pair of pants; underwear, socks, and belts were not allowed to reduce the possibility of death by hanging.

Meals - usually cold - came on a tray pushed under the door three times a day. A television mounted on the wall outside the cell was controlled by the guards. It did not help to pass the hours, because I found it difficult to try to watch television through two sets of bars. There was constant noise and pressures I can't begin to describe.

"Hey, next door," someone called through the metal partition that separated our cells.

"Yeah?"

"If I get out of this cell, I'm going to kill you!"

A man I'd never even seen wanted to kill me! The first day on death row, I knew I was through.

Later I learned that my violent neighbor had been convicted of murder. After being sentenced to prison, he had killed a guard and an inmate. He swore he'd kill again, and I was to be his next victim. Thank God, we were never out of our cells at the same time.

The man in the cell to my right had murdered thirteen people. Alone in my filthy cell, sandwiched between two killers, I entered the darkest days of my life.

Lying in bed, I looked at the metal wall and noticed a word that had been crudely scratched there. "Help." Month after month I stared at it. I could almost see the man who had written the message. In my imagination, I watched his face as he heard someone call, "All right, number seven, you're next. Time to go to the electric chair." Hopeless, he scratched on the wall a last plea for help and walked out the door to his death. The reality of it almost drove me crazy.

What does it take to be broken? I'd survived prison violence with numerous wounds, culminating in thirty-nine stitches in the head. I'd survived prison punishment and the continued taunting of the guards. I'd survived the loneliness - four years without receiving a letter or a visitor because I was too ashamed to let my family know where I was. But the absolute hopelessness is what finally broke me.

Convinced that I would never get out of prison or off death row, I decided to take my life. Having worked on the hospital floor, I was familiar with the solution used to test for diabetes. I was told if taken internally, it would be fatal.

Not long after my fateful decision the door of the cell opened, and there stood Dr. Ortiz. He grimaced at the sight of me.

"The warden is really ticked," he said as he plucked the stitches out with a pair of tweezers. "The whole prison's on lockdown. Railroad and Latcheye are on lock-up in M-building. It'll be years before they get out."

"I need a favor," I said.

"Sure. Anything, Harold."

"I want you to send a letter to my mother."

"Your mother?"

"Are you ready?"

He stopped pulling stitches and picked up an empty pill envelope and a pen. I struggled to find the right words to convey my sorrow and despair.

"I love you, and I'm sorry I've disgraced you," I said, trying to keep a rein on my emotions. "You have been a great mother. Don't think you have failed me. I have failed you. You're the best thing that ever happened to me. I don't want to die, but I can't live under these conditions any longer. Please forgive me. I'm sorry."

"No!" Dr. Ortiz shouted in disbelief.

Then I asked him to bring me some of the solution used to test for diabetes.

"I'll go to the warden," he pleaded. "Okay? I'll get you out of here. Please give me one day."

I shook my head. It was hopeless, I told him. I didn't want to die. But I had evaluated my life, and I saw no reason to continue.

"I'll do all that I can to get you out of here. But I won't help you kill yourself!"

A man condemned to death row - and unable to die! I cried all night.

About three in the morning I sat in absolute silence. I was completely broken. For as long as I could remember, I had steadfastly refused to believe in God. At the same time, I shook my fist in the air and dared Him to exist.

Once, on the prison baseball field, I had screamed to the thundering skies that rained out our game, "I don't believe in you, God! If You are real, strike me dead!"

There was no God. If He were real, how could He have allowed the things that had happened in my life?

Now I sat on death row, without hope, unable to live and unable to die. For the first time in my life, I knelt and prayed.

"God, if you are real, take my life or free me! I can't stand this place anymore."

Later that day, the cell door opened.

"62345! Ho!"

I recognized the voice of Captain Tucker. He took me out of the cell and gave me a chance to shower and shave without explaining why I had been released. The next thing I knew I was given clean clothes, and I was walking into the warden's office. He looked up at me from reading some papers with no real expression on his face.

"He's all yours warden," Captain Tucker said before slamming the door shut.

I jumped. I still wasn't used to loud noises.

"I had a visit from three federal officers," the warden began in a serious tone. "They say we are the only prison in the country that ain't been integrated. They give me a month to do something about that, or they say they'll take over. Well, I ain't gonna allow that. So, I'm gonna cut you a break. Ortiz came in here the other day and told me about you, and it gimme an idea. I got plans for you, Morris. I'm moving you over to W-8. You're going from the outhouse to the penthouse in one day! How 'bout that?"

I choked up as I looked at the ceiling and whispered, "Thank you, God."

"Well, it ain't all good news," the warden was quick to caution. "You gotcha a new cell mate. A black."

"You can't put me in a cell with a stinking nigger!" I croaked.

"You wanna go back where you came from?" he asked in a deadly serious tone, his demeanor changing instantly. "You will get along with that boy or, by God, you will be sorry I ever took you off death row! I'm gonna make an example out of you one way or another! Do you understand me?"

I was marched over to W-8 by Captain Tucker, Dobbs, and another guard. The W-8 building was also known as the "trusty" building - the 450 or so inmates who lived in the facility at the edge of the prison property were considered trustworthy and therefore were given special privileges. The cell doors were locked only at night, giving them much more freedom than other inmates. On weekends they were allowed in the prison yard anytime before 6 p.m., though they were still counted every two hours. It was the best place an inmate could hope to be within the prison, but it felt like the longest walk of my entire life.

"You a nigger lover, boy?" Captain Tucker taunted me.

I didn't say a thing. Then I felt his staff running up between my legs from behind, and I jumped forward as the guards laughed.

"He's gonna be tonight!" Dobbs hooted.

Captain Tucker grinned in my face and said, "Now don't you two fall in love!"

Stopping outside an eight-by-ten cell, I looked through the bars and saw the black that I'd threatened on the bus and fought on the basketball court lying on a bunk inside. I could feel the stares of the guards. They were really enjoying my misery.

"No way!" I shouted.

As I began to struggle, I was hit from behind and I fell forward, dropping my box of personal possessions. Still reeling from the blow, I felt myself being picked up and tossed like a sack of potatoes into the cell. My box of things was kicked in behind me. The door slammed shut with a resounding clang!

I struggled to my feet and glared through the bars at the smiling faces of the guards.

They walked off, and I turned to find myself in a cramped cell with barely enough room to walk between the bunks to a sink and a toilet in the back. The nigger had a few books and a Bible on a small shelf.

I looked up at the ceiling of the cell and wondered aloud, "God, what did I ever do to you?"

After a moment I turned and said to the man on the other bunk, "Here's how it's gonna be, black boy. Nobody else comes in this cell. Nobody sits on my bed. Nobody messes with my stuff. If anything's gone, I'm holding you responsible."

I leaned back against the bars and crossed my arms over my chest. He just lay there like he didn't even hear me.

"You take a bath?" I prodded.

"If you're asking for a date, I ain't interested," he said, turning to look at me.

I closed my eyes and tried to forget him altogether.

PART IV
1973-1976

Twenty

That evening Dobbs appeared at the bars.

"We got a friendly bet going," he said grinning from ear to ear, "on which one of you is gonna kill the other first."

I lay on my bunk facing the wall. I didn't say anything.

"Either of you want in on it?" he prodded gleefully.

I rolled over and asked, "Officer Dobbs, did your wife tell you?"

"Tell me what?"

"That I was with her last night. I finally worked my way to the front of the line."

His face reddened, and he blustered, "If that nigger don't kill you I will, you sorry convict!"

After he stormed off, I burst out laughing, and I saw a hint of a smile on the nigger's face as he rolled over to face the wall.

The next morning my cell mate peered into the sheet of metal over the sink that passed for a mirror as he picked out his afro and sang "My Girl". I'd been waiting for the sink for so long that the toothpaste had hardened on my toothbrush. Barely holding my anger in check, I watched as he patted his hair down like he expected someone was going to paint his picture that morning.

"I'm gonna 'My Girl' you if you don't hurry up!" I said.

Finally, he turned from the mirror, and I stood to go to the sink. But then he turned back to the mirror and started picking his hair out all over again.

After more than a minute of standing there with my toothbrush, I sat back down on my bunk, disgusted. As soon as I did, he turned from the mirror again and lay down on his bunk.

The basin of the sink was full of springy little tufts of black hair.

"What is this junk?" I asked through clenched teeth.

He pretended not to hear me.

"Hey!" I shouted, kicking his bunk. "What is this mess in the sink?"

"You touch my bed again, and I'll stick your sorry head in that toilet!"

Scooping up a big handful of the hair from the sink basin, I sprinkled it onto his bunk. He was on his feet in an instant, and he sprang at me, knocking me back onto my bed and jamming his forearm across my throat.

I slammed a fist into the side of his head and then shoved him onto the floor. Coughing and gasping for air, I struggled to my feet only to have him pull my legs out from under me. As he crawled on top of me I caught him square across the bridge of the nose with an elbow. A spurt of blood suddenly coated his lips and chin and the front of my prison shirt. I rolled over and tried to scramble out from under him when he drove a fist into my kidney.

We scrapped on the floor between the cots until the guards got the cell open and pulled us apart. To my surprise, we were marched directly into the warden's office. When he saw us he shook his head in disgust.

"We're gonna integrate this prison, and if you think crippling each other is gonna get you out of it you're dead wrong!" he said angrily. "I got plans for you two. You will get you some teams, and you will get out there on that yard with everybody watching and you will play me a game of basketball. I mean to show this prison that whites and blacks can get along."

Out of the corner of my eye I could see that my black cell mate was shaking his head.

"You got something to say?" the warden barked.

"Ain't nobody gonna go out there, warden," he said.

I knew he was right. There was no way we could recruit enough players from the inmate population to field two teams. Any inmate who played would be hounded and harassed mercilessly by the other inmates.

"How'd you two like to go into the hole together?" the warden bullied. "You ain't got no other choice! You're gonna go out there!"

I looked down at the floor. I wasn't going to give the warden any reason to throw me back into the hole with that black.

"This game is just what we need to cool things off, so I'm willing to throw some breaks your way," the warden continued in a softer tone. "You and your players can have any kind of food you want out there - as many candy bars and Co-colas as you can put away. You can even have steaks!"

Neither of us said a word.

"And if you two pull this off you should have a special reward, don't you think?" the warden bribed. "How 'bout I let you both run the athletic department for me? How 'bout that? You pull this off, and we'll talk about it."

A long silence ensued before the warden ordered, "You go get them teams. Tucker, get them out of here!"

I knew I had my work cut out for me, trying to get four more men to agree to break ranks with their fellow inmates and play basketball with niggers. As I went around from cell to cell I got spit on, grabbed at, and cussed out by nearly everyone I talked to. Finally, I decided if I couldn't bribe them or appeal to their good nature I'd do just the opposite.

"I need you to help me beat 'em," I told Stick, a lanky inmate with a sparse beard and cheeks pitted with acne scars. "Let's show them niggers we're better than them!"

"Get outta my face, nigger lover!" he scowled, turning his back to me.

"I don't love 'em! I want to beat 'em, and I need you, Stick!"

He lay down on his bunk and tried to tune me out. At last, my frustration boiled to the surface.

"If you don't like playing 'em, we can always put a shank in 'em and go to solitary!" I shouted.

He rolled over and looked at me for a long moment.

"We could beat some coons out there in front of God and everybody, couldn't we?" he smiled.

Double Ug was also a hard sell.

"Do you know what you're asking me to do?" he hissed through the bars of the dormitory cell. "Nobody'd talk to me. They'd put the freeze on me. They'd -"

"Stick's playing," I interjected.

"Stick is?" he said, a surprised look stamped on his face.

As we were let back into our cell that night my black cell mate said, "I got mine."

His tone implied that he didn't think that I'd be able to get enough players.

"I got four," I shot back.

Walking out to the court with the rest of my team, the white prisoners still locked in their cells cursed us every way they could think of. The niggers that walked onto the court heard it from the black dorms. As we shot around before the game it got so that you couldn't hear the individual voices any more. It was like standing in the middle of a storm of words that battered us from every direction.

The warden pulled Doc and me off the court and stood between us as a photographer posed us for a picture. The photographer eventually had the warden put an arm around each of us. The whole time the warden was talking to three federal officials standing a few feet away.

"Blacks and whites have never played an organized game like this in all the years I've been at this prison," he beamed. "Gentlemen, this here is a historic day!"

"Smile," the photographer warned.

The flashbulb popped, and I tried to pull away from the warden but he wouldn't let me.

"Take another one!" he said enthusiastically. "This here is a red letter day! I want you to send the best one to the paper!"

"Are all of those armed guards necessary?" one of the feds said, pointing to the small army of riot guards that surrounded the court.

"Ready?" the warden said to the photographer, ignoring the question. "Say his-to-reee!"

There were about four times as many guards as there were basketball players, and they wore helmets and wielded batons and shields. This show of force was supposed to keep us from fighting - the idea being that if you started a fight on the court you'd take more punishment from the guards and their batons than you could ever dish out on whoever you took a swing at.

The barrage of insults from the other inmates continued even as we lined up for the tip-off. They hurled every insult they could think of at us.

"Galboy!"

"House nigger!"

"Dogboy!"

"Uncle Tom!"

The game was about like I expected it to be. The play was rough, and a couple of times I thought a fight was going to break out. I was being guarded by my black cell mate, and Stick set a high pick that knocked him onto his butt. I drilled an open jumper. As I ran back up court grinning, the warden shook his head and frowned at me.

It was a close game, and as the lead went back and forth the insults from the other inmates turned to cheers. As long as we were going to play the game, each side wanted its team to win. I was so into the game, I didn't notice that the warden had opened some of the dorms until the inmates rushed towards the court screaming and yelling. The game stopped. No one knew what would happen next. The riot guards turned their backs to us to face the oncoming horde. There were about two hundred inmates, black and white, stampeding towards them, and the forty or so riot guards tensed up and stood shoulder-to-shoulder as they nervously handled their batons.

But the inmates just surrounded the court and cheered; whether it was for the game or just because they were happy to be out of their cells, I don't know.

Warden Kelso waved his hands over his head and declared a break time for everybody. The prison cooks threw steaks onto the outdoor grills, and the smell of the sizzling meat filled the yard.

"Let me at them steaks!" shouted Jelly Roll, a 300 pound black inmate whose stomach sagged heavily over his belt, "I'm so hungry I could eat the rear end off a walking giraffe!"

The inmates still on lockdown pressed their faces to the bars to inhale the sweet smoke. We piled our plates high with tossed salad, baked potatoes, and steaks.

As we sat down to eat I heard one of the feds ask the warden sarcastically, "How many steaks do you think you'll need to integrate this place, Kelso?"

The warden fumbled for a moment over the idea that he was simply buying our cooperation. But then a sly smile appeared on his face.

"I'd be gratified if the only ones that died during the integration of this prison were cows," the warden intoned. "Wouldn't you?"

I had to laugh over that. By the time we'd finished stuffing ourselves there was no way we could finish playing the game. It was all I could do to drag myself back to my cell. It had been a great day in prison until that moment. To make things worse I could feel him eyeing me from across the cell. He was ruining what peace of mind I had, and I turned my head and sneered at him.

"You don't like me, do you?" he asked.

"No," I said, "I hate your guts."

"Why?"

"Fifty reasons," I blurted out, trying to shut him up.

"Name one."

I would have bet I could have thought of fifty, but at that moment my mind went blank.

"C-cause you're black," I finally said.

"That's right," he said. "You hate me because of the color of my skin. I don't hate you because you're white. I hate you because you'd be sorry in any color."

I opened my mouth to fire back, but I was dumbfounded. I had no reply. And I didn't say another word to him that night. I still didn't have a comeback the next morning when the warden surprised us in our cell.

Twenty-one

"I'm gonna cut you out of your afternoon duties, and instead I'm gonna let you two coach me a basketball team," Warden Kelso said as he casually looked around our cell.

As the three of us stood awkwardly in the small space, the warden picked up my cell mate's Bible. The warden shared a private smile with Captain Tucker before putting it back down again and dusting his hands.

"I want whites *and* blacks on this team," the warden stated. "We'll get you some uniforms. Outfit you. Set up a locker room. You'll get to take a ride once a week to league games, but, by God, if you go, you will bring back that trophy, or I'll have both of you out in the fields picking peas! Do you understand?"

He looked me right in the eye. I nodded. My cell mate nodded, too.

"I'm gonna let you two name that team and pick the players, but if anybody tries to run, I'm holding *both* of you accountable. Understand?"

And so we were set to our task of putting together a team that could win but couldn't escape. Many of the players I wanted to recruit were just the kind who would use an opportunity to play basketball outside the prison as a chance to escape. We went around from dorm to dorm with sign-up sheets trying to see who'd be willing to play on an integrated team.

It was no little thing to ask a man. Yes, he got out of his afternoon duties, but the resentment he would incur from the other inmates could quite possibly get him killed. By the time we looked over the sign-up sheets the pickings were pretty slim. We spread the sheets on the floor between our two bunks and peered down at the names scrawled in barely legible handwriting, trying to piece together a team.

"What about your boy Psycho?" my cell mate said to me. "He's good."

I looked up and down my lists of names.

"Didn't sign up," I said, unable to find his name anywhere.

"I guess he don't want to play neither."

"He's got a bad attitude, and he's dangerous, anyway," I said. "And, he might try to escape."

I shuffled the papers on the floor looking for another white guy for the team. We already had five black players we'd agreed on but no whites.

"So, you gonna be the only one on the team?"

"The only what?" I said, distracted.

"The only smart-mouthed punk."

I looked up. He wasn't smiling. I honestly didn't know whether he was joking with me or not.

"Not by a long shot," I said, "as long as you're on the team."

The team was finally composed of six blacks (Doc, Jelly Roll, Weasel, Tree Top, Big Money, and Lug Wrench) and four whites (Stick, Big Six, Double Ug and myself). Doc and I led practices in the afternoons out on the yard. The first thing we did was get the players into shape. We ran in the dirt path around the perimeter of the prison fence until we turned it into a shallow ditch. Most of the players who were tall like Weasel, Tree Top and Stick came through the physical conditioning okay, as did the smaller guards like Big Money, Big Six, and Double Ug. But Jelly Roll and Lug Wrench almost quit on us. Together they had to weigh over 600 pounds, but Lug Wrench was big whereas Jelly Roll was just plain fat. Jelly Roll couldn't run fast, and he wasn't quick. He didn't dribble well, and he was a poor defender. But he could shoot the basketball. Twenty, twenty-five, or thirty feet - it didn't matter where he shot from; it always seemed to go in.

After we got the team in shape, we concentrated on the fundamentals: dribbling, passing, and defense. When Jimmy got home from
school in the afternoons he'd come to the fence with his basketball
and do the same drills the rest of the players did. When we took a
break from practice, I'd go over to the fence and Jimmy and I would
concentrate on improving his left-handed dribbling. During the drills
I made Jimmy look me in the eye - that way he had to keep his head
up and he couldn't watch the ball. One afternoon I saw that something was wrong.

"What's the matter, little buddy?" I asked.

"Can I ask you a question?"

"Sure . . ."

He stopped dribbling and sat down on the ground.

"You were one of the cool guys in school, right?" he asked, his eyes
searching my face.

"You could say that . . ."

"Well, I got invited to this party, and all the pretty girls are gonna
be there . . ."

"And you got your eye on one of them?"

"Yeah, but they'll all be smoking and drinking," he said as he
rocked back and forth, "and if I don't they'll all think I'm a wuss."

"Do you know about Sheephead Kelly?"

"Sheephead Kelly? No, who is he?"

I pointed over to Pissant Hill.

"He's buried over there on Pissant Hill," I began. "He first came
here when he was 16 years old. He had a one-year sentence for stealing a Pepsi-cola and a pack of crackers. His first day in prison he was
raped."

I paused for effect. I definitely had his attention.

"He got into so many fights that every facial bone had been broken. He looked like a sheep. He became so violent that he killed several inmates and a guard. One night in a fight he took a meat cleaver,
chopped a guy up, and flushed him down the toilet. He got everything down but his skull."

Jimmy's eyes were as big as dinner plates.

"They put him on death row, and he stayed there for eight-and-a-half years before the governor commuted his sentence to life. He died of cancer after spending thirty-four years of his life in prison. Unwanted. Unloved. See, the little things can grow into big ones."

He nodded silently.

"I can't make your decision for you," I told him, "but you're smart. And you gotta make your own choice. But listen to your parents, teachers, and those of us that care. We don't always have the answers, but we care."

And I did care about that boy. Because of my loneliness in prison, I knew how important it was to have others who cared for you. I had been in prison for four years, and not one person from the outside had visited me. I had not sent or received a letter and there had been no phone calls. Then one morning a guard came to the cell.

"You have a visitor," he announced.

"I'm not going," I said, thinking it was just a counselor with news that my job had been changed.

"If you don't go I'll put you in the hole," the guard threatened.

I wasn't stupid. I went to see the visitor.

When I walked into the prison lobby, there stood my brother Carl. No woman could ever look more beautiful than he did to me that day. We hugged each other and instantly re-experienced the love that we had for each other.

"How could you do it?" he asked. "How could you not let us know? We love you!"

I went into tears as Carl told me that my mother loved me, and then he explained how he had found me. A neighbor in Georgetown, South Carolina, was looking through some old magazines at the beauty parlor when she came across a five-year-old copy of *True Detective*. There was my picture along with an account of the crime I had supposedly committed.

"We found him!" she cried as she carried the news to Carl. He then tracked me to Georgia State Penitentiary.

"Carl," I said finally, "Carl, I didn't kill that man."

"I know, Harold," he said.

I can't describe what it meant to learn that my family loved me and wanted to stand with me. I was no longer alone! Knowing that gave me hope. Carl spent the day with me, and when he left sadness engulfed me. But I carried on with the prison routine and tried not to let anyone see my pain.

One day after the Bandits' afternoon practice, Doc and I put the basketballs away in the athletic shed as usual. During practice someone had delivered a large box to the shed. Doc and I looked at one another.

"Open it," I said.

Doc pulled off the top of the box and inside were royal blue basketball uniforms with white piping around the edges and "GSP BANDITS" written in white letters across the chest. They were beautiful. I could hardly believe they were ours. It was at that point that it sunk in that I was really going to get on a bus and go outside the prison for the first time in four years. It seemed like it was too good to be true, but there were the uniforms - proof that it wasn't all just a dream.

When we got back to the cell Doc picked up a letter off the floor of the cell. He handed it to me. The handwriting was very familiar. I lay down on my bunk and turned the letter over and over in my hands before I opened it. A flood of emotions swept over me as I read my mother's spidery handwriting. I had to stop reading several times as I blinked back tears.

I could feel Doc's eyes on me. It felt like he was invading my privacy. I put the letter down and stared back at him.

"Some uniforms, huh?" he smiled.

"What?"

"Uniforms. For the team."

"Yeah, you did a good job of picking the color," I said, turning my attention back to the letter in my hand.

He laughed, "Bandits! That's pretty good. I wish I'd thought that up."

I tried to concentrate on the letter. But he wouldn't leave me alone.

"That's the first letter you ever got," he said. "Who's it from?"

I was starting to get angry. I folded the letter over and put it down.

"My mother," I stated flatly.

"I can't talk to you?"

"You can talk to me," I said, my voice edgy with impatience. "Now what do you want to know?"

"What's she say?"

I hesitated.

"What do you care?"

"Is she dying?"

"No, she's not dying. She just wants to come see me," I said. "But I ain't letting her."

"Why not?"

I got up off my bunk and walked over to the window at the back of the cell. From there I could see the road leading away from the prison.

"I ain't allowing my mother to be strip-searched for drugs like a criminal when the only thing she's guilty of is loving me and bringing my sorry behind into the world."

"You can't turn your mama away!" he said, shocked.

"I don't want her to see me walk out there with ink on my behind! She doesn't deserve that!"

"She's never seen you in prison?" he asked, incredulous.

"I never told anyone I was here. I haven't had a letter in four years."

"Man, I don't understand that. My mama died when I was fourteen, and I miss her every day."

"What was wrong with her?"

"She was poor. She wouldn't be dead if we'd had money."

I stared out the window and imagined what it would feel like to see my mother driving towards the prison. My heart rose into my throat.

"You're a proud man, and I am too," he said. "But if my mama were alive, I sure wouldn't let pride keep me away from her."

"She knows I love her," I said softly.

"She don't care about the ink on your behind!" he shouted, startling me. "A mother's love is special. Mothers are the backbone of any family - not fathers. After my father left, my mama worked three jobs. She worked for whites who talked down to her and treated her like nothing her entire life. They gave her food to eat off their plates, like she was a dog!"

I turned around and looked him in the eye for the first time.

"If they did that to my mother I'd want to kill them!" I ranted.

He looked at me sadly and said, "Believe me, man, when you come to prison everyone who loves you comes with you."

I was already in the visitation room when I saw two female guards escort my dear gray-haired mother into the room and then directly into a side room used for strip searches. I felt sick inside, but what could I do? I sat there with my face in my hands so that no one could see my sorrow. I listened for the side door to open. When it did, I quickly stood. Through teary eyes, I looked on my mother's face for the first time in more than five years. I saw the sorrow in her eyes but no shame. She seemed smaller and more fragile than ever, and as I hugged her to me the tears streamed down my face.

"Mama, please forgive me," I pleaded. "I'm so sorry to put you through this."

"I was so worried," she said, looking up at me. "I was afraid that you were dead. Why didn't you tell us? It hurts me that you went through all this by yourself."

"I didn't want to hurt you . . ." I sobbed. "That's why I didn't call. The whole time I thought that things would work out."

We sat at a table, and I told her in detail what had happened to me.

"That sorry lawyer I had, he was about useless," I complained bitterly. "If I'd had any money I wouldn't be here now."

"We'll get you a new lawyer," she promised.

"It's too late," I said, shaking my head. "They're not giving me another trial. The only chance I've got is parole, and that's years away."

"I promise you I'm going to do everything I can to get you out of here," she said as she squeezed my hand. "Carl's already talking to attorneys about helping you."

I smiled thinly and nodded, but I knew that she wouldn't be able to change things. When time was up we hugged once more, and I told her again that I loved her.

She smiled bravely, "I love you too, no matter what happens."

It was at that moment that I realized a man is not really a man until he's in touch with the woman in him, and that's why mothers are so special.

As I turned to leave the room, another inmate caught me by the shoulder and stopped me.

"I'da thought you'da killed that nigger by now, man. I bet on you. You cost me two packs of smokes!"

I gave him a hard look and shrugged his hand off my shoulder.

"Whassa matter with you? You a nigger lover now?" he scowled.

"You want me to break your neck?" I said, squaring my shoulders. "He's more of a man than you'll ever be!"

As I walked back to the cell I couldn't believe what I'd done. I had squared off with another white man over a black.

Twenty-two

As the bus taking us into the free world pulled through the prison gates all of the players on the team, black and white, began to smile.

"I see you dumb idiots smiling," Captain Tucker growled. "You just enjoy the ride, because every door and every exit at that there gym will have a shotgun guard by it. You can sit on that bench or you can go to the john, but you stick your head out a door and it will get blown off."

The prison bus drove down Main Street in Metter, Georgia, and the stores were lit up in the early evening as shoppers walked from store to store carrying brown paper sacks. I marveled at the colors of Main Street - bright reds and greens and yellows. Inside prison everything is painted either drab yellow, drab green, or gray. I had nearly forgotten that there was a world of color outside the prison walls.

The bus finally stopped by the side of a small gymnasium. When we got off the bus in our new royal blue warm-ups we looked like a real basketball team - except for the shotgun guards. It was the first time in four years that I wasn't wearing a prison uniform.

As I sat stretching out on the floor near center court, I felt like everyone in the stands was staring at me. The capacity for the gym was probably 1,500, but on that night not more than 100 people turned out to see us play. Suddenly someone tapped me on the right shoulder. I turned, but no one was there. Then I heard his laugh.

"Hey, buddy," a familiar voice said from over my left shoulder.

Jimmy stood behind me with a smile that stretched from ear-to-ear. We hugged for a long time without saying anything. Then he pointed to where his mother was sitting in the stands, and I waved to Mrs. Hale.

As soon as we started our warm-up drills I could see the surprise in the faces of our opponents. Nearly every player on our team could dunk, and we put on a pre-game exhibition that made the people in the stands gape. Afterwards, a young boy walked over to where Jimmy and I were standing and pointed to the letters on my jersey.

"What's GSP stand for?" he asked.

"Georgia State Patrol," I said with a straight face.

"Mister, you've got the best team I've ever seen," he said earnestly. "I'd give anything to play for you someday."

"No problem," I said as I knelt and put my arm around him.

"Really?"

"Just go down the street and knock off that 7-11 on the corner," I said seriously. "We'll pick you up on the way by."

The young boy was confused and looked to Jimmy for a clue, but Jimmy just laughed.

"Son," I said, "GSP stands for Georgia State Penitentiary. Every man on this team has got at least one life sentence. Don't admire us, son. You don't want this kind of life. You're gonna think about that and stay out of trouble, right?"

He nodded.

"Why don't you sit on the bench with us?" I proposed. "You two can be our ball boys."

As Jimmy and the young boy raced over towards our bench, I saw that Doc had been listening to what I'd said. He nodded at me like he approved. I just shrugged.

As we stood at center court for the tip, I went around the circle shaking hands with the players of the opposing team, who were all white. But when Tree Top tried to shake hands with the white team captain the man refused.

"I'll shake hands with Casper, but not with any of you bluegums," he declared.

Tree Top was about to square off with the man when Doc stepped in.

"Don't mess with me, honky!" Tree Top shouted.

Doc pushed Tree Top back from the circle and said calmly and quietly, "Shut your mouth. They got a lock on us, okay? They make the rules. We gotta beat them on the court. I'm gonna pin my man. You just tip it towards their basket."

When the referee tossed the ball up for the tip-off, Tree Top easily outjumped the other team's center and batted the ball down the court. Doc streaked down the floor and put the ball in the basket before the other team even knew what had happened.

Because our team was so deep and had so many outstanding players we substituted freely and quickly wore the other team down. Our aggressive defensive pressure kept our opponents from getting into their offensive sets and forced them to take a lot of outside shots, which set up fast breaks for us. Grabbing a rebound, I'd look for Doc to break and then hurl a baseball pass downcourt. It worked in the game just like it had worked in practice: Doc caught the pass, dribbled, jumped, spun all the way around in mid-air and dunked the ball. The opposing players were stunned, and the crowd was stunned. I was only amazed. I'd seen him do it before.

Throughout the first half of the game the partisan crowd cheered for the home team even as we outclassed them in every aspect of the game. At halftime, the Bandits led 41-26.

From where I sat at the end of our bench, I could see the opposing players slumped over on their bench, bickering and sniping and pointing fingers at one another.

In the second half our opponents didn't fare any better. Tired and outmanned, their defense broke down and they began fighting amongst themselves. After Doc drove by his man for an easy basket the white team captain snarled, "Are you gonna guard that nigger or just wave at him as he goes by, Mort? Foul him if you have to!"

"Foul him!" Mort snapped back. "He'd probably kill me as soon as look at me!"

"I'm guarding him from now on," the white team captain said.

The next time we brought the ball up, I got the ball to Doc, because I knew that the white team captain could not guard him. Alone on the wing, Doc faked a drive to the basket, sending the white team captain scrambling backwards while Doc calmly hit a jump shot. Doc stared long and hard at his hapless defender, but he didn't say a word.

The white team captain was incensed - I could see the color move from his neck up into his face. He probably never expected to lose so badly to a group of convicts while his friends and neighbors watched from the stands.

The next time we had the ball, I got it to Doc again. Doc again faked a drive to the basket and squared up for a jumper. As the white team captain jumped towards Doc to block his shot, Doc pulled the ball down and dribbled in for a dunk. As he came down, the white team captain rushed over and pushed him from behind, knocking Doc to the floor. He then stood over Doc as Doc slowly rolled over.

The next thing I knew I had shoved him away from Doc, and if the referee hadn't clamped his arms around me I would have done worse.

"You got something to say, Casper?" the white team captain jeered.

"I'll stomp your guts out!" I shouted back.

Doc went to the bench, and I joined him there, thinking it better not to start anything that would get us knocked out of the league after our first game. As we sat there watching our team thoroughly demoralize the home team, Jimmy brought Doc a bag of ice for his back.

"I'm Jimmy Hale," he said.

Taking the bag of ice from him, Doc offered his hand, "Doc."

"I know," Jimmy said. "Harold told me you're the greatest athlete he's ever played with."

I straightened up. Neither of us said anything.

"He's never told you that, has he?" Jimmy asked Doc.

"C'mon, Bandits!" I yelled, pretending to watch the game.

"Well, I expect he would if he could," Jimmy said loudly.

After the game was over, Jimmy walked with the team to the bus. I think that everyone on the team took a lot of satisfaction from beating the other team so badly. Even as we filed onto the bus that would take us back to prison we were still smiling.

"When I play high school ball, I'm gonna wear number 30, just like you," Jimmy told me.

"You are?" I said.

"Yeah, but I'm gonna be a heck of a whole lot better than you are, monkey."

Doc, who was right in front of me, turned and laughed.

During the ride back to the prison the euphoria of the win wore off and my mood soured.

"Where do they get off treating us like that?" I wondered.

Doc looked at me for a long moment before saying, "What are you griping about? I been listening to that junk my whole life, and you couldn't take it for one night. You oughta try it for a lifetime."

I suddenly realized that not too long ago I had treated blacks with the same disdain that the opposing players had treated us. I knew he was right. I was sure of it, and I was sorry. But I couldn't bring myself to say it out loud.

The next morning in our cell I stared down into the sink at the clumps of wiry black hair, and instead of getting mad I gathered the hair up into a ball and held it up to Doc.

"Man, we don't need a Brillo pad," I said jokingly, "we can use this stuff here!"

I pretended to scrub the sink with the handful of hair and said, "I'll make this sink sparkle! Hey, I got another idea! You ever heard of astroturf?"

"Yeah," Doc said.

"Why don't you and me start an afro-turf company when we get out? There's no way you could fall down if you were running on this! And if you did, you couldn't get up!"

He stared at me like I had lost my mind.

"You take care of the afro, and I'll handle the business end!" I shouted, a loopy grin on my face. "We'll make millions!"

Then he laughed, "You are one crazy white man, Harold."

As soon as he said it, I realized that it was the first time he'd called me by my name. I felt like I should do the same.

"Say, why they call you Doc, anyway?" I asked.

"It's short for Doctor Coffee," he said.

"Doctor Coffee?" I repeated.

"Yeah, the girls used to call me Doctor Coffee, because I grind so fine!"

I busted out laughing, and Doc laughed with me and we gave each other a high five.

As the basketball season went on we collected more wins and got more attention from the local newspaper. After a while we even won over the crowds that came to see us play.

By the time we played in the championship game we had more fans than the local team did. After we won the game handily, the fans mobbed the floor, hugging us and slapping us on the back. Photographers snapped pictures of Warden Kelso holding the league championship trophy with me standing on his right and Doc to his left. That picture made it onto the front page of the paper.

The basketball Bandits were such a success that the warden gave us permission to create a softball team. We didn't have any problems recruiting players for the softball Bandits. Everybody wanted to play. I was surprised that so many whites would volunteer to play with blacks, but at the same time I felt a little pride. It seemed that Doc and I had started something. If blacks and whites weren't willing to love one another, many of them were willing to tolerate one another for the first time.

The warden got his picture in the paper again, this time holding the league championship trophy for softball. And he got his picture in the paper again when the headline read, "STATE PEN INTEGRATED".

Not long after the prison was integrated I got a phone call from my mother. She informed me that Carl had gotten two lawyers to take up my case at no charge. Even though I knew it was probably hopeless, I still felt cheered by the fact that I finally had someone fighting for me.

Twenty-three

In 1973, normal prison routine was interrupted when actor Burt Reynolds and producer Al Ruddy paid a visit to Georgia State Penitentiary to determine whether the site would be suitable for filming a motion picture. They began work on September 15th for "The Longest Yard" starring Reynolds. Doc and I were among several inmates who were given small roles in the football and swamp scenes. A catering service brought our meals to the filming sites.

The contract with Paramount Studios offered each inmate $5 a day and an additional $50 every time an inmate made contact in a football scene. One of the professional actors said jokingly to Burt, "Morris and Doc have bigger parts than I have!"

An inmate nicknamed Bank Robber was used as a stand-in so that the film crew could adjust the lighting before a scene was shot without troubling the actors, who always sat off in the shade sipping something cold. The film crew got a kick out of the inmates' nicknames, and enjoyed using them. One afternoon as the director was setting up a shot, he needed Bank Robber to stand-in, and he couldn't find him. Finally, he called out, "Bank Robber!" About fifty inmates called back in a chorus, "Right here!" and raised their hands. The director and the rest of the film crew broke down in laughter.

Prison officials wanted the inmates to stay away from the actors, but Burt often came to sit and talk with us as did many of the other actors. In one scene Burt and I were standing on a ditch bank in the swamp.

"What are you in for?" he asked.

"Armed robbery and murder."

"You don't look like a murderer," he said.

"What does one look like?" I asked.

"Guess you got me there," he said.

He wanted to know about my family and seemed genuinely interested in my life. We talked a great deal during the coming weeks.

One day a member of the crew wanted to charge inmates $2 each to have souvenir photographs taken with Burt. I had no money and neither did Doc or any of the other inmates. In fact, we weren't allowed to have money on our person. If caught with money, an inmate would be sentenced to fourteen days in the hole.

"Take all the pictures they want," Burt told the photographer. "I'll pay for them."

An old-timer who had been in prison for many years asked Burt, "Where do you live?"

Burt said that he had a home in Florida and one in California. The inmate then asked for his address.

"Why do you want my address?" Burt wondered.

"I've been stealing from people who ain't got nothing," the old-timer said without cracking a smile. "When I get out next week I want to steal from somebody who's got something!"

Burt said, "He means that, doesn't he?"

When the filming was completed, the movie crew gathered up their equipment and started to leave prison.

"Do you think you'll ever get out?" Burt asked me.

I said, "No."

"I wish you would. I'd get you a job in Hollywood tomorrow. Is there anything I can do for you?" he wanted to know.

"Yes, I'd like to have some pictures for my nieces and nephews," I said.

He took an hour to autograph fourteen photos, personalizing each with the name of the recipient and adding, "It was great being with your Uncle Harold."

I told him I'd like to have some good reading material. From that time on, I received a best seller every month from the Book of the Month Club, compliments of Burt Reynolds. After I finished reading the novel, I would give it to Doc. After he'd read it, we'd put it in the prison library.

The premiere of "The Longest Yard" took place in Atlanta in 1974, and they also came to the prison for a showing. After viewing the motion picture, I was told the warden wanted to see Doc and me. At 10 p.m.? Nobody ever went to his office at that hour. When we walked in, we found the room jammed with members of the news media.

"Fellas, I guess being in a movie with Burt Reynolds is the greatest thrill of your lives isn't it?" a lady reporter asked.

I said, "Ma'am, the biggest thrill of my life hasn't happened yet. When I walk out that door as a free man, that will be the biggest thrill."

I couldn't believe what I read in the paper later: "Harold Morris, a baby-faced gent five down on a double-life sentence, said that being in a movie with Burt Reynolds was the biggest thrill of his life."

Another interruption in the normal routine was when Doc and I got the choice assignment of working in a little hobby shop located at the front gate of the prison. The shop carried hand-crafted leather items made by the inmates, and Doc and I sold these items to the public. The money was credited to the inmates' accounts, providing a few dollars to buy cigarettes, candy, and soft drinks. Although there was no money in it for us, we gained a great deal of prestige because we were dealing with the outside world (though we were still in our prison clothes and there was a guard tower just a few feet away).

"Hey, convict! I want the best wallet you've got," said an old guard who was uneducated and particularly surly whenever he was out-smarted by the inmates.

I reached for a hand-tooled wallet of quality leather - the nicest one in the shop - and handed it to him.

"You must think I just drove up here yesterday," he growled. "You think you can sell me anything. I said I want the best you've got!"

It was the best, but I didn't try to convince him.

"I apologize, sir. I should have known the minute you walked up that you were different. You know your leather. I have just the wallet for you."

I picked up a wallet constructed of thin scrap leather. It had been stamped in a press without a hint of hand-tooling.

"That's more like it," he said. "How much is this one?"

At $1.25, the wallet was overpriced; by my figures the cost of materials came to a mere sixty-seven cents. But we sold them for twelve dollars a dozen.

"For you, it'll be six dollars," I said.

As he whipped out the money, I shared a look with Doc, who just shook his head.

"I'll tell you what I'm gonna do," I went on. "Since it's you, and you know your leather, I'll give you a special deal if you'll take three dozen. It's close to Christmas, and you'll be the most popular daddy in the world if you buy these for your family. Three dozen for sixty dollars."

"My goodness! I'll take 'em!" he said.

As he laid the money down, obviously delighted with his purchase, I said, "Let me show you a fine wallet."

I reached for one that had been in the shop longer than either Doc or I had worked there. The inmate who had the job before us predicted that we'd never be able even to give it away. I'd tried several times without success.

"It's too bad that you can't own one of these," I said.

The curious old guard wanted to know more about the wallet.

"It ain't for sale," Doc added slyly.

When an inmate tells a guard that he can't do something, it triggers his "I've-got-the-gun-and-I've-got-the-power" reaction.

"How come it ain't for sale?" he demanded.

"That's a collector's item," Doc said.

"There will never be another one like it," I explained. (Really, there never would be another one like it!)

"How come?" He was determined to draw the truth out of me.

"This is imitation alligator," I said.

He gave me a puzzled look and hesitated a moment before asking, "What kind of gator is that?"

I realized he didn't know what imitation alligator was.

"The alligators were brought over from Australia," I began in a serious tone. "They would breed only with south Georgia alligators. Don't ask me to explain that. I don't know why. But they wouldn't breed with another gator. Because these imitation gators are now extinct, this is it," I declared, holding up the wallet.

"I want it!" he insisted.

"Sir, you're an officer, and I can't deny you. I'll tell you what - you can have it for twenty-five dollars."

He counted out the money and picked up the one-of-a-kind wallet.

After he walked off Doc and I finally let the laughter out, and tears rolled down our cheeks at the thought of him boasting to his buddies, "There'll never be another one of these. It's imitation alligator. These gators were brought over from Australia and bred right here in south Georgia." By the time we got back into our cell our sides ached.

To me, laughter is the lotion for the sunburn of your life. A sense of humor helped us endure the worst of times. And in our cell that night we laughed until we had tears in our eyes as we shared story after story about our prison experiences.

"Once," I said to Doc, "I asked an inmate, 'How much time do you have?'

"He said, 'Twenty years.'

"'Great!' I said, 'Mail this letter on your way out!'"

Doc laughed and said what really surprised him when he got to prison was how dumb many of the inmates were and that some of the guards were even dumber!

"I thought I was dumb until I met this inmate in the dorm," Doc said. "I said, 'What are you in for?' He said, 'Rape.' I asked him how they caught him and he said, 'Well, they put me in this here police line-up, and they brought this girl in and I said, 'That's her! That's her! I picked her out!'"

"That's one of the best I ever heard," I said.

Nothing tickled us more than taking the guards for a ride. As we lay on our bunks I told Doc about one of the guards, Smith, that was giving me a hard time on the hospital floor.

"I told him, 'You better be nice to me, or I'll have you assigned to tower six.'" Tower six was the most undesirable assignment for a guard, frequently used as a disciplinary measure.

"Well, the next day, by sheer coincidence, Smith was assigned to tower six. I had nothing to do with it, of course, but he didn't know. So he sent me a note by a trusty that said, 'Please get me off tower six! I never thought I'd see the day that inmates would run the prison!'"

Doc laughed, delighted.

"I wrote back, 'I'll think about it.' The next day Smith was back on regular duty. Again, I was not involved, but I didn't tell him, because I had him right where I wanted him. Smith said, 'I really appreciate this. I'll throw a favor your way.' And I said, 'Well, you scratch my back, and I'll scratch yours. You know what I mean.' After that he'd do anything for me. When he caught me stealing a piece of chicken from the mess hall, instead of throwing me in the hole he said, 'Bring me a piece, too!'"

"I got a tower six story, too," Doc said.

"Lay it on me," I said.

"Back when I was in county jail waiting to come here I was in a two man cell. You know the kind I mean?"

"I do."

"Well, I was in there with this fella named Andy. Andy was tall and thin and double-jointed. He was so limber that I could stuff him into the small locker in our cell, making it look like he'd escaped. I'd straighten Andy's bed and then stretch out on my bunk, pretending to be asleep when the old dumb guard came by to count," Doc explained. "And that guard would stop for a moment in front of the cell and finally say, 'One.' And it wasn't too long before I'd hear the guard and the captain of the guard coming towards the cell arguing. 'You never could count!' the captain'd yell. And that guard's swearing, 'There ain't but one! I'll show you!' And then I'd get Andy out of that locker, and he'd lay down on his bunk like he'd been there the whole time. And the captain of the guard would point and scream, 'There's two, you idiot!' But the guard'd say, 'I'm telling you there was just one!' So the captain, he'd say, 'That's it! You're through!'"

Doc and I nearly died laughing at that. The guards had almost absolute power over the inmates, and the only way we could retaliate was by outsmarting them.

"When I was in the dorm, there was an inmate named Chicken Yard Shorty," I said. "Well, one day as Chicken Yard was gathering eggs a hen jumped on him and spurred, and Chicken Yard got mad and said he'd kill the bird if it spurred him again. The next day the chicken spurred him again, and Chicken Yard hit it with a stick. A guard saw him do it, grabbed Chicken Yard, and brought charges against him for assaulting a chicken. In kangaroo court the next day, they told him, 'You have been charged with assault on a chicken, how do you plead?' Chicken Yard said, 'I didn't kill the chicken.' They said, 'How do you plead?'

"He pleaded not guilty, and they told him to wait outside. When they brought him back in they said, 'You have been found guilty of assault on a chicken. We sentence you to fourteen days of solitary confinement in the hole and ninety days probation. If you ever hit a chicken again, we're going to throw the book at you.' But then Chicken Yard, he said, 'Thank God that chicken didn't die! I would have gone to the electric chair!'"

We laughed because it was ridiculous and because that was the way it was. Nearly every inmate at Georgia State Penitentiary had a story about how he'd been mistreated by a guard.

"Hey, do you know Dopey?" I asked. "The cook for the guards?"

"Yeah, man, I know Dopey from when I worked in the kitchen," Doc said. "That guy's about as squirrely as they get."

"He is," I nodded. "I heard him say one time, 'If they'd give me all the drugs I wanted for two years, I'd let them kill me. I'd sign a pact right now.' Well one Saturday he found me during visitation hours and said, 'Man, I'd give anything in this world for some drugs. You know Stick pretty well. His girlfriend is visiting. See if she has any drugs. I'll give you anything if you help me.'

"So I walked over to Stick, and I asked his girlfriend if she had any pills. All she had was birth control pills, so I got her to give me one. I handed it to Dopey, and I said, 'I made a score, but you have to take it quick! I don't want to get in trouble.' He popped it right in his mouth, and half an hour later he staggered up to me and said, 'That's the best drug I ever had in my life! It's dynamite! I'll give you a carton of cigarettes if you'll get me one more.'

"I had to stifle a laugh. I said, 'Dopey, you really are high, and I'll tell you something else - you'll never get pregnant. That was a birth control pill!' Man, he chased me through the grounds for an hour."

Doc and I told stories and laughed together like we were old friends. But even as I was gaining a new friend, I was about to lose the dearest friend I had.

Twenty-four

I saw Jimmy standing at the fence, but for the first time he didn't have a basketball. At 16, he was tall and lean and his normally smiling face was downcast.

"What's wrong, buddy?" I asked. "Where's your ball?"

"My dad bought a house in town," he said sadly. "We're moving away tomorrow, and I've come to say good-bye."

I could scarcely believe it. I fought to keep my emotions under control.

"Where to?" I said automatically.

"Reidsville - ten miles away," he moped. "But I guess I could still come on my bike from time to time."

"Well, that's good," I said managing to keep my voice from trembling. "Now you show those city slickers how bad you are. You're the best, son, don't you ever forget that."

Then he reached into his pocket and pulled out a small polished wooden cross.

"I brought you something to remember me by," he said, handing the cross through the fence. "I made it myself."

I nodded, unable to speak.

"I won't ever forget you," he promised.

As he turned to walk away, I quickly wiped the tears out of my eyes with the sleeve of my shirt.

"I'll never forget you either, Jimmy."

He turned around again and looked at me. His eyes burned bright and blue. He nodded once and jogged down the road towards his house, never looking back.

"I love you, little buddy," I whispered softly to myself before turning away.

I was still red-faced from crying when Doc returned to the cell.

"Where'd you get that?" he asked, pointing to the small cross that Jimmy had given me.

"Jimmy. He's moving. His family's moving to town."

"Can I see it?"

"He made it himself," I said, handing the cross to him.

Doc turned it over in his hands as he admired it. Then he handed it back to me and sat down heavily on his bunk, his face suddenly somber.

"I don't know what I'm gonna do," I moaned. "I looked forward to going to that fence every day. He was my whole life, and now he's gone."

"I know how you feel, man," Doc lamented. "I've got a son, and I'll probably never see him again, but I think about him all the time."

"You do?" I asked, genuinely surprised.

"After a few visits to the prison my wife decided to move away and start over and she took him with her," he explained. "He's eleven now."

I thought I understood how he felt as he stared blankly at the floor of the cell.

"Drugs and running with the wrong crowd robbed me of my son," he said softly. "He'll never know who I am."

"Man, if your son knew you, he'd be proud of you."

Doc stood and shuffled to the window at the back of the cell and wrapped his hands around the bars.

"But nobody's coming for me - not my son, not my wife. Nobody to take me home. And I just don't wanna wind up as another number on Pissant Hill."

"Man, one day you'll be free, and you'll be able to go up to your son and put your arms around him and tell him how much you love him."

As soon as I said it, I knew it was wishful thinking, and Doc knew it, too.

"You know, honky, we might have come over on different ships, but we're in the same boat now."

I had to laugh when I heard him say that, and it felt good to laugh - even if it was for just a moment.

The one meal that I actually enjoyed in prison was the Brunswick stew we were sometimes served for lunch. One day I looked up from my bowl, and I saw Doc grimacing.

"What's the matter with you?" I asked.

"Man, how can you eat that slop?"

"Eat what?" I smiled, taking another spoonful. "Man this is Brunswick stew! This is my favorite!"

"Brunswick stew, huh?" he said taking a bite out of a piece of dry bread. "More like hog's head stew."

"Man, this stuff's great. It's the only meal in this place that I actually don't mind eating, so I don't need you trying to ruin it."

"I worked in the kitchen, man," Doc said. "Where do you think they get the meat they put in there?"

"Who cares?"

He smiled, "What is this?"

He reached down into my bowl with his spoon and there was an eyeball staring up at me.

"Oh, God!" I exclaimed as I jumped back from the table and bumped into a man walking up behind me.

Doc cackled to see me so unnerved. I didn't think it was funny. For a few moments I thought I was going to throw up.

"This is from the Road and Latch," the man behind me said, handing me a note.

I opened the note and read it. I passed it across the table to Doc.

Doc read it aloud, "Hey white nigger, it is time to visit Pissant Hill. Judgement day is at hand. Time to pay for your sins."

Doc crumpled up the note and threw it at the messenger who smirked and walked off. I warned Doc not to get in the middle of it. I told him that it was old business between Railroad and Latcheye and me and that it had nothing to do with him.

I was still thinking about Railroad and Latcheye's threat that afternoon when Booger Brown was rolled into the examination room by
two inmate orderlies.

"What'd you swallow this time, Booger?" I asked with a sigh.
"Another bed spring?"

"A knife," Booger said, his expression serious.

"A knife? C'mon!" I said.

Just then Dr. Ortiz entered the examination room with an x-ray in
his hand.

"That's no lie," Ortiz said, holding up the film.

"You could get another five years, Booger," I said.

"For what?" Booger asked.

"Carrying a concealed weapon."

Everyone laughed, including Booger, but as his belly shook, his
laughter was cut off with a gasp.

Mrs. Hale stuck her head in.

"What can I do for you Mrs. Hale?" I asked, standing and going to
the door.

I tried my best to keep a straight face as she told me that Jimmy's
high school team was in the state finals and that he wanted me and
Doc to listen to the game on the radio.

"Does he get to play much?" I asked.

"He's in the starting line-up as a freshman!" she boasted. "And he
wears number thirty. He still idolizes you. He talks about you all the
time. And I did want to thank you for having such a positive effect
on him."

I was deeply touched, and I wanted to tell her how much Jimmy
meant to me and how he had sustained me by being my friend when
everybody else had turned their backs on me, but all I could get out
was, "Thank you, Mrs Hale."

I couldn't wait for the game to come on the radio. Doc and I sat
on a bench in the prison yard hunched over a small transistor radio,
trying to make out the scratchy voice of the announcer. Jimmy played
as well as I could have hoped, but his team was behind by one at the
end of the game. Doc turned the radio all the way up, not wanting
to miss a word.

"There are five seconds left and Shades' Valley is down by one with the ball out on the side," the announcer said. "Murray will inbound the ball, and you just know they're looking for number thirty, Jimmy Hale, who's under the basket. The clock will start on the inbound. The referee blows the whistle, and Hale comes off a high screen and takes the inbound pass at the top of the key. He fakes . . . dribbles left . . . and shoots from seventeen . . . it's good!!!"

Doc and I jumped around the prison yard screaming like we had won the game ourselves. We pumped our fists in the air and shouted for joy.

"What are you two morons so happy about?" Railroad growled.

Doc and I wheeled to see Railroad and Latcheye standing not ten feet away. I didn't know whether they were armed or not, but I was determined not to show any fear.

"When's this gonna end, Railroad?" I asked.

"It'll end when you're on Pissant Hill, Morris."

"Why don't you guys cool it?" Doc interceded.

"You'll get plenty of trouble with me if you're siding with Morris, nigger."

In the tense silence that followed I heard the radio announcer say, "We're here with Jimmy Hale, whose last second shot won this game. Jimmy, you had a big game with 27 points and you certainly didn't play like a freshman, but you had to be a little nervous when you took that last shot."

"No sir, I had a good teacher-"

Suddenly, Railroad grabbed the radio off the table and smashed it to the cement. I was furious and started to square off with him, but Doc grabbed me.

"It ain't worth it, Harold," he said.

Latcheye nodded towards the three yard guards who had noticed the commotion and were coming in our direction.

"Catch you later, rat," Railroad said as he and Latcheye moved off.

Lying in my bunk that night, I imagined how Jimmy would have finished his sentence. "I had a good teacher-" he'd said. I was very proud of his accomplishment, and I was proud that I'd helped him.

"I guess you can mean a lot to someone and never even know it,"

I said.

"You got that right," Doc affirmed.

"No matter what I did, my daddy was always telling me how I was no good and how I'd never amount to anything," I recalled. "If you hear that long enough from your daddy and your teachers and your coaches, too, you start to believe it."

"My father ran off, which told me the same thing," Doc said. "After that we were so poor my mother had to take three jobs."

"We were poorer than you were."

"Bull."

"Poor people called us poor!" I crowed. "Man, one Thanksgiving we were so poor my Daddy showed us a picture of a turkey, and I spent an hour trying to lick the gravy off it! Not only that, my daddy was illiterate - never went to school a day in his life. He couldn't write his own name."

"Come on . . ."

"We lived in a run down old shack," I explained. "We were so poor my daddy had me write Sears and Roebuck to ask for a roll of toilet paper. And Sears and Roebuck wrote back, 'Please look in our catalogue and send us the order number, and we'll be glad to send you the toilet paper.' Daddy had me write back, 'If I had the catalogue I wouldn't need the toilet paper!' Man, we didn't even have running water!"

"Hey!" Doc laughed, "maybe if your dad had run off and mine had stayed neither one of us would be here!"

We shared a laugh in the darkness.

"I think most of the problems in this country center around ignorance and race," I said. "My father taught me from birth that blacks weren't my equal. Children aren't born racist. They're taught."

"You're right," Doc agreed. "All my life I've been judged by the color of my skin. I guess I been in prison my whole life in one way or another - and so have you. We just didn't know it until now."

I propped myself up on my elbow and looked over at him.

"Hey, man, if everybody had to live together in a little eight-by-ten cell like you and me . . ." I said, "everybody might learn something."

He looked at me for a long moment and then nodded once, accepting what I'd said for the apology that it was.

"I was talking to this old inmate today," I continued, "and I asked him who the president of the United States is and do you know what he said? George Wallace. Not Jimmy Carter but George Wallace. And I thought, 'Is that going to be me someday?'"

"That's just the ol' elephant talking to you," Doc soothed. "We're gonna be free someday."

As the days went by I noticed that Doc was reading a lot in his Bible. One Saturday afternoon he caught me staring at him as he read.

"My wife gave me this Bible when I first got here," Doc said. "Back when I was over in M-building the roaches would eat the corners and nibble on the pages. I guess they were spiritual roaches, because they sure were digesting the word!"

"That place was filthy," I said, remembering M-building. "The roaches, ants, and flies outnumbered the inmates. One time I laid a pack of cookies on a little table in front of my bed for a snack while I was reading, and when I reached for a cookie, something crawled over my hand. It wasn't long before those cookies were covered with ants."

"I didn't mind the ants as much as the roaches," Doc said.

"When I first got here I stomped every roach I saw," I said. "But then I got to where I accepted them, and as time went by I made friends with them."

"Now how do you make friends with a roach?"

"I even named them. Homer was my favorite. I fed 'em bread crumbs, and I'd play with 'em - hold up a string for 'em to climb. I never killed another roach. When one died in my cell it was of old age."

Doc just shook his head.

"So, you know anything about the Bible?" he asked.

"A little bit."

"Okay," Doc smiled. "What kind of car did the disciples drive?"

"They walked everywhere! They didn't have no car!"

"Sure they did. They had a Honda."

"A Honda?"

Doc pointed to a passage in his Bible, "It says right here: 'And the disciples were all in one accord.'"

We laughed together.

"What have you got to laugh about?" Dobbs asked, flipping a stack of letters onto the floor of the cell.

I got off my bunk and picked up the letters. One was from my mother, and I'd started to open it when I noticed Dobbs holding one more letter through the bars.

"State board of pardons and paroles," he said.

I snatched the letter out of his hand and tore into it. The letter officially informed me of the time and date of my parole hearing. I started smiling and couldn't stop.

"Thank you, God," I whispered.

"Lemme see," Doc said reaching for the letter.

"Don't get too excited," Dobbs sneered. "You know what kinda bird can't fly don't ya? A jailbird! Your sorry behind ain't going nowhere!"

As Dobbs laughed, I handed the letter to Doc.

"Officer Dobbs, you better be nice to me," I said.

"Why do I need to be nice to you?"

"Don't you know?" I baited him.

"Know what?"

"Promise you won't tell?"

"I ain't promising you a thing," he blustered.

I stepped over to the bars and peered down the hallway in either direction.

"What is it?" he wondered.

In a low voice I whispered, "The warden is my brother."

He straightened up and thought about what I'd said for a long moment.

"How could he be your brother? His name's Kelso and your name's Morris."

Again I leaned in, "Kelso's his maiden name."

"Uh huh!" he said as he nodded slowly, piecing everything together.

I kept a straight face, but Doc had to turn away and fake a coughing fit to keep from laughing out loud. After Dobbs had left, Doc and I laughed ourselves sick. Although he hadn't received his parole letter yet, Doc congratulated me on my upcoming parole hearing. However, we both knew that our chances were extremely poor. Men with two life sentences aren't often paroled after just seven years.

"And my mother says Carl's got two lawyers coming to see me," I said, folding up her letter.

"Yeah, well they better bring a sack full of hacksaw blades with them," Doc teased.

Twenty-five

The trustee building where Doc and I were housed was mostly deserted during yard call, and the cell doors were unlocked and it was then that Railroad and Latcheye chose to make good on their threat. I was at the back of the cell at the sink, and Doc was on his bunk when they appeared in the doorway and pulled shanks out of their shirt sleeves.

"No! No!" Doc shouted as he jumped out of his bunk and stood squarely between me and my attackers.

"Get outta the way, nigger!" Railroad growled.

I reached for a broom leaning in the back corner of the cell and snapped the handle off. Doc suddenly lunged forward and grabbed Latcheye's knife hand, trying to break his grip on the weapon. As Doc and Latcheye struggled, Railroad shoved past Latcheye into the cell and stabbed Doc. Doc screamed as the shank ripped into his flesh, and I jumped up on my bunk and pummeled Railroad and Latcheye with the broom handle in a desperate attempt to beat them off Doc.

Lunging around Doc, Latcheye stuck me in the stomach with his shank. I kicked him away and slammed the broom handle into his head. I continued swinging the broom handle even as I heard the sound of feet racing down the hallway.

Railroad grabbed Latcheye by the collar of his shirt and pulled him out of the cell.

They bolted down the hallway and Doc, slipping in his own blood, fell to the floor. I dropped to my knees over him.

"Guard! Guard!" I yelled hoarsely.

I pulled up my shirt and saw a deep stab wound with blood fountaining out of it. Doc had been stabbed several times. He'd lost consciousness, and I tried to revive him, but it was no use.

Dobbs and two other guards raced up to the cell.

"What happened?" Dobbs asked frantically.

"Doc's hurt bad," I said.

"Get him to the hospital!" Dobbs ordered, and the two other guards hustled him away.

"Who did it? Who was it? The black Muslims? Or Railroad and Latcheye?"

I pressed my hand to my stomach to stop the flow of blood, but it seeped out between my fingers.

"Man you're bleeding!"

I cried, staring at the pool of blood on the floor of the cell.

"We'd better get you to the hospital."

"His blood is red," I whispered. "The same color as mine. God, please don't let him die. Please, please."

The next thing I remember was Mrs. Hale's face hovering over me.

"How are you feeling?" she asked.

She told me I was in the hospital. My side was bandaged, and tubes ran into my arm. She went and got Dr. Ortiz to have a look at me.

"You're very lucky," he told me. "That knife missed your liver by about a half-inch. Otherwise . . ."

"Where's Doc?" I asked.

Ortiz and Mrs. Hale exchanged a worried look.

"He's not dead," I said.

"No, he's not dead . . ." Ortiz hedged.

"Where is he? I want to see him."

Ortiz tried to break the news to me gently, "He's in a coma, and we don't know if he'll ever come out of it."

"I want to see him," I repeated.

I tried to get out of bed, but I was so weak I couldn't even sit up.

"You're not strong enough. If his condition changes we'll tell you," Ortiz promised. Then he turned to Mrs. Hale and ordered, "Give him another shot."

I was shaken awake by Jelly Roll. After a moment to clear my head, he asked me who shanked Doc. He said Muscle Jaw wanted to know.

"Was it Railroad and Latcheye?" he asked. "Or the black Muslims?"

"The Road and Latch," I said weakly, and he patted me on the shoulder.

"You be better now, Super Honky."

In the midst of my depression, Mrs. Hale brought Jimmy to my bedside to cheer me up. But I couldn't even muster a smile when he came into the room.

"Here's someone who wants to see you," Mrs. Hale said cheerily.

Jimmy plopped down in a wheelchair beside my bed.

"Hey, monkey," he said.

I nodded at him, but that was all. I knew that his mother had told him what had happened. We sat there for a long time, neither of us saying a thing. Jimmy came to visit me several times after that. Once when he was there Ortiz finally agreed to let me go see Doc. But he said that Jimmy had to push me down the hall in the wheelchair so that I wouldn't pull my sutures out by walking.

Doc looked like he was dead. He was breathing shallowly and was connected to a respirator. Wires ran under his shirt and tubes ran out of his arms.

Jimmy tried to be hopeful, "Hey, don't worry. He's gonna make it."

But instead of sounding hopeful, it sounded sad because he and I both knew what was far more likely.

As one day turned into the next I began to feel better. My parole hearing was coming up, and I spent my days reading and sitting up in bed with a pencil and a pad of paper trying to piece together a speech that would convince the board to free me.

"You're looking much better this morning," Doctor Ortiz said as he examined me. "Ready to get out of here?"

"The hospital or the prison?" I asked, smiling. "My parole hearing is three days away."

"Well, then we'll try and get you out of here in time for that," Ortiz said.

After I was released from the hospital, I went down to the intensive care ward. Doc's face was drawn and shiny. Still attached to a respirator, his breathing was labored and his chest rose and fell slowly. I took his hand in mine.

"Well, Doc, my parole hearing is tomorrow. I been working on what I'm gonna say. I sure wish you'd wake up so I can run it by you."

That night I slept in my own bed again, but I couldn't rest. Doc's empty bunk haunted me, knowing that he risked his life for me. The color of one's skin doesn't matter, only the purity of one's heart.

The next day as I was waiting for my hearing with a long line of nervous prisoners, an angry white inmate stormed out of the hearing room and declared, "I got some advice for all of you idiots! Escape if you can! 'Cause you're in a whole lotta trouble!"

After waiting all day with about 350 other inmates, I was the last man to be interviewed. The board was composed of five members and sat behind a long table. They each had a copy of my file. There was a single chair in the middle of the room, but I knew not to sit down until I was asked to.

"Sit down," the chairman said gruffly, moving right to the point. "Mr. Morris, I'm Bud Johnson, chairman of the parole board, and these are the other members. You have two life sentences for armed robbery and murder. In the seven years you've been inside you've completed all the programs this prison has to offer. You've done well. You're not the normal inmate. I see you still maintain your innocence."

I drew breath to speak, but before I could the chairman continued.

"But we have a problem: you are a murderer and a robber and society has not had your body long enough. And since you have never admitted to committing these crimes, quite frankly, I see no remorse. We feel that you might be in prison for the rest of your life. What do you have to say about that?"

My speech went right out the window, along with my heart. I had fostered a hope that he would pat me on the back and say that he believed in me. I didn't know how to respond.

"I'm told since you've been in here you've also turned your life around, that you've got religion," the chairman continued. "I don't believe in jailhouse religion, that foot-of-the-cross syndrome. And I don't believe in you. Do you have anything to say?"

My mouth was as dry as the desert, and my thoughts were all jumbled up with my emotions. But I knew I had to say something.

"You're not God," I blurted out. "And you can't know my heart. I stand before you today because a black man took a knife in my place. He knew my heart. And I'll die in here before I plead guilty to a crime I didn't commit. Sir, you may have my body, but you don't have my mind. And if God wants to open that door you can't stop Him!"

"You'll find out who controls your life," he growled. "Captain Tucker, see if you can open that door so he can go back to his cell."

Lying in my cell, I wept, realizing that I would probably spend the rest of my life in prison. Even so, I hadn't begged for freedom. My case could be reviewed in a year, but what would change in a year? The severity of the crime would never be altered; a man had been killed. The length of the sentence would never change; the judge had declared two life sentences. The counseling situation would never be any better; most of the counselors were former shotgun guards with no professional training or insight into rehabilitating inmates for a return to society.

I was convinced nothing would change, parole would never become a reality, and I would die in prison.

PART V
1976-1978

Twenty-six

One day the warden came to Doctor Ortiz's office on the hospital floor to visit me.

"Your little buddy, Jimmy Hale, did a real convincing number on his principal and me," he said. "He and his father came to see me. He seems to think you're just the person to talk to his high school about alcohol, drugs, and prison life."

"There's no way I'll speak in public wearing these prison clothes with a number stamped on my behind," I objected. "I have a mother out there, and I wouldn't embarrass her for anything. I'm not going."

"Well, I have arranged for you to go," the warden said, "but I ain't gonna force you. You've already done enough. We got this place integrated. And I believe you and Doc had a lot to do with it. I know y'all saved lives. What you and Doc did, it wasn't all for nothing."

The next morning Mrs. Hale came to my desk and informed me that Doc had come out of his coma and was asking to see me.

"You had better hurry," she said with a note of urgency in her voice.

Suddenly, I began to understand the seriousness of the situation. I ran down the hallway and into the intensive care ward. I knelt next to Doc's bed, and I took his hand and squeezed it. With tears streaming down my face, I told him how sorry I was for him and just how much I loved him.

"Please don't die," I begged. "I owe you my life. I'd take your place if I could."

"What day is it?" he asked.

"Friday. Guess what? I had my parole hearing."

"And?"

I smiled bitterly, "Held over by popular demand."

"I'm sorry, Harold."

"Jimmy came with me to visit you a couple of days ago."

"How's he doing?"

"You know what? He wants me to go to his school and talk to the students! Can you imagine that? Me making a speech!"

"Do it," Doc said. "They need to hear what you got to say."

"What? Go on a stage in front of hundreds of kids, with prison clothes on, and say, 'Don't do as I do, do as I say!'"

Doc started to laugh, but then he began coughing violently. He squeezed my hand, and tears filled his eyes, too. He grimaced as a jolt of pain wracked his body.

In a low, soft whisper he said, "I love you, Super Honky. You're a true friend."

It was the highest compliment I have ever been paid.

"I won't ever forget you," I said. "I won't let anyone forget you. I'll spend the rest of my life trying to teach others what you have taught me."

Doc nodded weakly and squeezed my hand, and I put my head down on his bed and wept.

As I left the intensive care ward, I saw Mrs. Hale walking down the hall towards me.

"You really care about him, don't you?" she asked.

"Yes," I nodded. "He's the only true friend I've ever had in my whole life. The first night we were in that cell the whole prison was taking bets on which of us'd kill the other. And the sad thing was I was willing to kill him because of the color of his skin.

"So what changed you?"

"I guess being on death row with no hope, and when they put me in that cell with Doc - that's when my life really began. He taught me so much about the true meaning of life and loyalty. And that's why I'd take his place if I could. The sad truth of it is I'll never be able to help anybody."

After thinking all night about what Doc had said about speaking at Jimmy's school, I realized I couldn't refuse. The next day I met with the warden and informed him that I had second thoughts. The following morning two guards drove me to Jimmy's high school. As I stepped out of a prison van handcuffed and wearing a prison uniform, I looked up to see Jimmy and his principal standing on the steps of the high school. Jimmy came running up to me and threw his arms around me.

The bleachers were packed with faculty and teenagers as Jimmy stood behind the podium to introduce me, "I have asked my convict friend Harold Morris to talk to us today. He has helped me with a lot of my problems, and he can help you if you will just listen. He cares about young people."

I took a deep breath as the guard unlocked the handcuffs. After a few moments to gather myself, I walked out onto the stage.

Seeing the gymnasium packed with teenagers frightened me so much that I honestly thought about trying to escape. A hush fell on the students as I started to speak.

"I would like to talk to you about making the right choices in life," I began. "Today, let's look at the negative forces that ruined my life: the alcohol, the drugs, wrong association, always running with the wrong crowd, and racism.

"Never sacrifice your ideals or your potential to gain acceptance in the wrong group. Now, don't feel sorry for me, I didn't commit the crimes I have been convicted of - armed robbery and murder - but I got what I deserved.

"You see, I had every chance in life to be everything I wanted to be. But I chose to run with the wrong crowd, and it wrecked my life. I ended up not being prepared for the game of life, and that's the most important game of all.

"Please don't let anything in this world rob you of the greatest years of your life. You can be anything you want to be. You can make a difference, just as Jimmy Hale has made a difference in my life. Young people, what did I learn through all of this? That the measure of a person's life is not in its duration but in its donation. It's all about caring and loving and giving. And in this world of give and take, there aren't enough people willing to give what it takes. I'm so thankful I found two.

"One was a twelve-year-old boy who came to a prison fence, and told me that he loved me when the whole world had turned its back on me. And the other was Doc Odomes, a black man who taught me the true meaning of life, of commitment, how to share love, and - most important of all - how to be color-blind.

"Doc Odomes was willing to lay down his life for me. He was knifed by men who wanted to kill me. And on his hospital bed, he squeezed my hand and in a very painful, low, soft voice, he told me he loved me and that I was a true friend. Then he issued a challenge to me that will go with me to my grave.

"Doc challenged me to be here today to tell you what we learned together - that we must expose the pain of racism. When racism raises its ugly head we must do something about it.

"It's time for all of us to come together and fight for social and economic justice for all people regardless of color. We must learn to communicate, to know, to teach, to learn from each other just as Doc and I learned in that prison cell.

"You can never right the wrong of violence with more violence. Yes, Doc Odomes was willing to give what it takes. He was willing to give his life for me. The sad thing in life, young people, isn't that people die. The sad thing is that they never live. Do you want to live? Do you want to live? In a few minutes, I'll be handcuffed by those guards, and I'll be taken back to Georgia State Penitentiary, the door will be slammed shut, and I'll be there for the rest of my life. It's real young people. It's real."

My talk was a mixture of my life story and warnings to the young people about alcohol, drugs, wrong association, and racism. They listened intently to every word I spoke. I illustrated every point with stories from my many years in prison to show how the decisions they make early in life can directly affect the rest of their lives.

I went on to say that one of the saddest experiences of prison is seeing potential wasted. Doctors, lawyers, athletes, and ministers joined with common murderers, robbers, and rapists to share the wreckage of life.

When I returned to the prison I learned that Railroad and Latcheye had been killed that very afternoon at yard call by a group of black inmates led by Muscle Jaw. As I heard it, a group of about ten black inmates had unearthed a sack of shanks that they had buried under the bleachers on the softball field. As they marched onto the east side of the yard, unarmed whites scrambled to get out of their way. Railroad and Latcheye ran, but the blacks chased them down and quickly closed around the two men in a tight circle. Words were exchanged, and then the blacks butchered them. Muscle Jaw admitted to the crime and said he'd done it to avenge the attack on Doc. The court convicted Muscle Jaw of the crime, and another life sentence, to run concurrently with all of his other life sentences, was added to his time.

Twenty-seven

Six months after speaking at Jimmy Hale's high school speaking requests were coming from so many schools that the warden decided to charge a fee, hoping to discourage invitations.

One day the warden sent for me and said, "I don't know what we're gonna do with you. In the past six months we've been flooded with requests for you to go speak. I wish you'd made parole. I need a secretary to keep up with all these letters and speaking engagements. What do you tell these kids that they keep inviting you all over creation?"

"Sir, I just give them my longhorn speech."

"What is that?"

"Sir, it's where you've got a point here and a point there and a whole lotta bull in between."

The warden leaned back in his chair and roared with laughter.

"Actually, I just tell them how wonderful this prison is and how nice you are, sir," I said.

The warden just shook his head and smiled.

Teenagers characteristically support the underdog, and they immediately rallied for me . . . and against the guard who waited offstage. He naturally became the butt of my jokes.

Many times after the principal introduced me to the packed gymnasium, I asked the students to indicate if they thought I really looked like a convict.

"Suppose I had on a three piece suit like this principal. If you didn't know I was a convict, which one of us would you think was sentenced to two life sentences in prison? Me?"

The students yelled, "No!"

"How about this guard?" I said, pointing to the guard.

"Yes!" they shouted, laughing and clapping as the old guard winced.

Later he warned, "Don't do that. I don't like it."

"Young people, I've done you a big favor today. I've gotten you out of class for an hour. Now all I ask is you return the favor, that you listen to me. You see, not that many years ago, I was sitting where you are. I had all the potential you have, but I blew it. I was an all-state athlete in high school. I was captain of the football, basketball and baseball teams. I had numerous scholarship offers, but I couldn't accept them because of my poor grades.

"So I said, 'I'm not going to college, I'm going to drink beer, chase girls - that's the life.' So that's what I did for a period of time.

"Finally, my dad told me I had to go to work. I got a job. I got married. I enrolled in college. Everything was going great. But my senior year, I dropped out of school, divorced my wife, and said, 'Now I'm free to do as I please.' I began to go to nightclubs, and there I met prostitutes, drug addicts, and ex-convicts. Young people, it took one year to destroy my life."

I told my story about meeting two men at a nightclub and going with them to Atlanta to party for a week. I explained how, as we were leaving Atlanta, my friends held up a grocery store and in the process shot an innocent bystander. One year later, I said, the F.B.I. arrested me, my two friends testified against me, and I was given two life sentences for armed robbery and murder.

"Young people, don't feel sorry for me," I told them. "I got what I deserved. I consorted with the scum of the earth, and I became what they were. I tell you today, the people you associate with will determine the outcome of your life, good or bad."

The students gave me a standing ovation and wrote me scores of letters in the week that followed. For the first time in many years, I realized that I could live a productive life behind bars. During the next two years I spoke to thousands of students in schools throughout southern Georgia.

When I finished my message, I said that any teachers who wanted me to visit their classes that day could sign up at the office. And then I fielded questions.

"Feel free to ask anything," I said. "You can even ask me why I'm so handsome."

Everyone laughed, and several hands went up, including the principal. I immediately acknowledged him.

I called on one little girl who asked, "Mr. Morris, why are your two little fingers so crooked?"

"You like these?" I asked.

I held up my hands to show that my pinkies were indeed bent at forty-five degree angles.

"These are so handy. They're great for picking lint out of my navel. Or how about cleaning ears? Or even picking a guitar?"

I stuck my little fingers in my ears and rotated them a couple of times for the howling crowd.

"You want to know how I got these?" I continued. "My right one was bent in a fight during a prison basketball game. The left one was broken when I got hit with a board during a fight. The prison hospital didn't set it right. So I got a matched set."

When speaking to students I demand respect, and I give it. If students are noisy and inattentive, I grab the microphone and say firmly, "Let me tell you something. You shut your mouth, or I'll run you out of here."

The gym grows quiet, and they can hear me say, "I love you, and I'm sorry I have to speak so firmly. I care about you and don't want you to turn out like I have. Thank you for listening."

Invariably, the students who were out of order apologize later. Students need discipline, and I'm convinced they want it.

With black students I have an especially good rapport, because they know my background. They realize I spent three years in a cell with a black inmate who became my closest friend and was willing to give his life that I might live. They know I understand them, because I was once an underdog, too.

Many times on speaking trips outside the prison I thought about escaping. In fact, I found it very difficult not to escape when faced with such tempting opportunities. But I had given the warden my word.

Speaking to young people brought me peace and joy I had never known before. It gave my life purpose and meaning: I was having an impact on others. I committed my life to helping young people. Although I didn't realize it at that time, I was preparing for the future.

Still, requests to speak poured in, along with letters from thousands of young people and parents. Imagine teenagers and parents writing to a convict for advice!

Some asked about dating and parent relationships. Others told of drug and alcohol abuse. A number of girls confided that they were pregnant out of wedlock. Their problems touched my heart, and I devoted all my free time to answering the letters.

I received a letter from a sixteen-year-old girl who said she was a drug addict and dating a married man.

She pleaded, "Mr. Morris, you're the only person I can trust. There's no one else! Please help me."

I wondered why a teenage girl would think that a man doomed to die in prison was the only person she could trust. Where were the parents? Teachers? Christians who knew her? After we corresponded for about six months, she wrote that she was no longer taking drugs or seeing the married man and had started going to church.

After class one day, several student leaders escorted me to lunch. As I got in the cafeteria line, I saw the student body president, two cheerleaders, and several of the top athletes jockeying for positions near me. They didn't know I had other plans. This was my favorite time of the day. I knew there were some kids I needed to talk to who would never have the courage to approach me. My eyes scanned the room, and I quickly located the perfect table. Sitting there were two very lonely-looking girls. Beside them was an even lonelier-looking pimple-faced boy. They were all looking at me, unaware that I had struggled with the same inferiority complexes they did when I was a teenager.

As I walked over and sat down across from the pimple-face boy I said, "Yo, bro, you bad!"

The boy started laughing. To the two girls, I said, "Hey there foxy mamas!" and gave each of them a kiss on the cheek. They squealed with delight, and we were off on a wonderful half-hour of fun and talk.

As lunch period was about to end, I looked at the young boy across from me.

"You know, you're special," I said for all to hear.

His eyebrows raised.

"We're just alike," I said. "People tell us that we're nobodies - that we're not as good as them. But they're wrong. Don't ever let anyone tell you different." Then, I hugged him and told him that I loved him.

A thirteen-year-old seventh grader approached me after I finished speaking at her school.

"Could I talk to you before you leave?" she said.

She was one of the most beautiful girls I had ever seen.

"What you said really meant a lot to me and my friends," she began. "One of my friends is thinking about taking her life."

"Honey, go get her," I urged. "I've got to talk to her before I leave."

"I can't," she said.

"Please! I must see her."

She hesitated and then quietly said, "You're talking to her."

"You? You're so beautiful! Why would you ever think about such a thing?"

"Nobody understands," she said. "Nobody listens to me. My parents give me everything I want. We're wealthy, but I don't need anything - except love."

I put my arms around her and held her close to me, and with a soft voice I said, "I love you, and I'll listen. Honey, your whole life is ahead of you. You can be anything you want to be. These are important years of your life. You've got to make something of them. You have every reason in the world to live. Promise me you'll call before you try to take your life!"

Her letters indicated that she was doing well, but her story wrenched my heart.

Many parents wrote to me. One said, "After hearing your story, my kids promised they would never use drugs. I never dreamed that a convict could help my children. I really appreciate your courage, and I will always be in your debt."

After speaking to 5,000 youths in several schools in one day, I returned to the prison. A few days later a letter arrived from a seventeen-year-old high school senior.

"I would have given anything to have heard your story years ago," she said. "I use drugs, I drink alcohol, and I'm pregnant. I have to drop out of school. My mother has rejected me. I want to die!"

I wrote immediately, advising her to go to a church for help. Her mother, after recovering from the initial shock, became supportive. And when the baby was born, the girl sent a joyful letter.

"He's the prettiest baby! I love him, and I'm going to bring him up the right way."

Later she informed me that she had finished high school and gotten involved in a church. Because she had followed her heart, she has a productive life helping young people with problems similar to hers.

That special day was typical of the days I spent in schools. It was an exhilarating time of speaking, encouraging, and counseling. My reward was not financial. My reward was seeing the response of so many young people who were hungry for love. It was also frustrating that there wasn't more time to spend individually with them. That is why I encouraged them to write. And many of them did.

When Doc was fully recuperated, the warden asked him to join me in speaking to high schools. Both Doc and I enjoyed the opportunities to travel outside the prison and share our experiences. Naturally, the teachers and students we spoke to were very curious about prison life, and they had many questions.

During one assembly, a young man asked, "How in the world did you get out of prison to come here?"

I quickly made up a response, "Yesterday, this guard was standing on the bank with a shotgun while we were digging a ditch. A little frog came hopping along, and I grabbed it and said, 'Frog, I'm going to squash your guts out!'

"The guard heard me and said, 'Go ahead, convict, but whatever you do to that frog I'm going to do to you.'

"I smiled and said, 'Frog, I'm going to kiss your behind and turn you loose!' And that's how we could come here today."

The kids loved the story, but the guard was fuming afterwards and threatened to send me to the hole. Later, he went to the warden and complained, but the warden just laughed and told me, "Go ahead and use that. It's the best prison story I ever heard."

One afternoon, after we had finished speaking at a high school, a young man asked Doc, "Prison sounds like the most horrible place in the world, and you've said you'll probably die there. Tell me, how do you manage to make it from one day to the next?"

"My first three years in prison I lived off of hatred," Doc explained. "I hated everyone and everything, and I had no hopes for my future."

Then Doc sidled over next to me, slipped his arm around my waist, and lisped in a high voice, "But the last four years I've survived off of love!"

I jumped back like a snake had bitten me.

"Get away from me!" I shouted as the packed gymnasium exploded in laughter.

Humor was an important part of our speeches, because it helped the students to relax and open their minds and their hearts to our message. Once Doc and I won the students and teachers over with laughter and our genuine loyalty to one another, it was much easier to open a real dialogue where we could discuss race or drugs or peer pressure or any of the other pressures that affect teenagers.

Often, troubled kids - those from the court system or youth detention centers - would be brought to the prison for a tour, and the warden would ask us to speak to them. Many of these youngsters were cocky and thought they were tough, but once Doc and I got tough with them their demeanors changed. They sat quietly as we told them how we had ruined our lives and landed in prison with two life sentences apiece. The warden called this his "Get Smart" program, and many of those kids took our words to heart and thanked us for setting them straight.

Several colleges sent students from their criminal justice departments to tour the prison, and Doc and I discussed prison and the prison system with them at the warden's request. We were even allowed to travel to local colleges and give the criminal justice students and professors there the benefit of our first-hand knowledge and experience.

In gratitude for our influence in the schools, the citizens of Douglas, Georgia, made arrangements with the state authorities in order for Doc and me to participate in their bi-centennial parade, July 4, 1976. We rode in the sheriff's car that led the parade. Although dressed in prison clothes, we felt good realizing that we had done something worthwhile with our lives, even under unfortunate circumstances.

As the years slipped by, I was no closer to freedom than I was the day I entered Georgia State Penitentiary to die. However, my family and friends believed in my innocence and continued to fight for my release.

They organized a committee to explore every possible avenue to freedom. The group met with Jimmy Carter, who was governor of Georgia at the time. They went to the scene of the crime and interviewed witnesses, who stated they had never seen me. They spent thousands of dollars and enlisted people all over the country to pray for me.

On September 1, 1976, the warden sent for me to come to the lobby. My two attorneys were on their way to see me, he said. I'd been in prison for eight years and had no money to pay expensive lawyer's fees.

I sat across the table from two men in dark suits. The men introduced themselves as Will Farlow and Eric Stone, attorneys from Georgia. We met privately in a prison visitation room.

"Each year we take on a case that we believe in pro bono," Mr. Farlow said. "We've talked to your brother and your mother, and we want to see what we can do to help you."

"How should we start?" I asked.

"Just tell us your story," Mr. Farlow said.

As I told my story, Mr. Farlow asked most of the questions, and Mr. Stone took most of the notes. I gave them details about the crime, the trial, and the prosecutor.

Farlow said, "I know the D.A. that convicted you. We went to college together. I bet I can get him on our team."

"He hates me," I said. "I was smart with him."

"Smart how?" Mr. Stone said.

"He offered me twenty years for both counts, and I told him I'd do ten if he'd do ten."

A look of outright shock crossed their faces as they fought back laughter.

"You didn't," Mr. Stone said.

"Yes, I did."

"Also, I know the governor. You haven't smarted off to him, have you?" Mr. Farlow asked. "I helped get him elected. And I'm going to get the parole board to review your case again."

"They just denied me for the second time. They're not gonna turn me loose."

"I'm not going to ask them to turn you loose. I'm going to ask them to justify why you're in prison. And if they can, I'll turn around and walk away. Now, I haven't met a lot of prisoners, but if there are a lot of them in here like you, then we've got a serious problem. Eric, do you have anything you want to say before we leave?"

"Yeah, I've got one question," Mr. Stone answered. "If we could open that door today and let you walk out with us, what would you do with your life?"

"Sir, I don't even have to think about it. I'll spend the rest of my life trying to keep young people from living the life I've lived and coming to a place like this."

These godly men became a part of my life. They visited me many, many times. Joining the fight for my freedom, they contacted the prosecutor. Although he did not favor my parole, he finally said he would not oppose it. My lawyers then asked the governor for a hearing. I am so grateful for these men and the faith that they had in me.

Twenty-eight

Winter melted into spring, and as summer gave way to autumn, I supplemented my speaking by participating in a Christmas toy project for underprivileged children. Several prison guards were members of the Jaycees in Reidsville, Georgia, a little town seven miles from the prison. The guards collected broken toys and brought them to me to be repaired. They purchased the mechanical parts I needed. Doc and several of the inmates helped me with the painting and refurbishing of bicycles, tricycles, dolls, small trucks and toy cars.

When Christmas Eve finally came, the guards loaded the toys into trucks and drove away. How I wished I could see the faces of those happy boys and girls! The joy of completing a worthwhile task made me feel good about myself. The local newspaper even carried my picture and a story about the Joy Toys project.

As I lay on my bunk that Christmas Day, I remembered an earlier Christmas when I was a newcomer to Georgia State Penitentiary. At the time I owned nothing but some loafers I had worn coming in, and I traded those for six Pepsi-colas. I no longer wanted beautiful women and fancy cars. A Pepsi would make my day!

I set the drinks on the window hoping they would be chilled by the freezing air outside. Lying on my bunk, considering how low I had come in life, I sipped those tepid drinks and moaned, "What a Christmas . . . what a Christmas!"

What a Christmas indeed! Soon the holiday season faded into the routine of prison life. About 7 p.m. on January 6, 1978, a guard came to my cell and unlocked the door.

"Get ready," he said. "You're going outside the institution."

In the lobby, I was met by one of the counselors.

"You're coming with me," he said, offering no further explanation.

Leaving the prison at night was highly unusual, and I wasn't even handcuffed. The counselor drove to Reidsville, parked at a restaurant, and escorted me inside to a banquet room. I recognized the sheriff, the mayor, and several prison guards who were members of the Jaycees. Their wives were also there. I had no idea what I was doing at the banquet, and I wasn't excited about wearing my prison clothes. After a while, I thought I'd figured it out.

"The counselor brought me to clean up!" I surmised. "After the banquet, I'm expected to wash dishes and sweep the floor!"

He showed me where to sit and told me to take a plate.

"Boy, this in nice," I thought. "At least I get to eat."

During the meal, many of the townspeople came by the table to speak with me. After several presentations were made to various men, I realized this was the Jaycee Awards Banquet. Finally, the counselor who brought me addressed the group. He discussed the Joy Toys program, mentioned the hours spent preparing the toys, and the delighted children who had received them.

"Ladies and gentlemen," he said, "in recognition of his contribution to the youth of this community, we are presenting the Jaycees Presidential Award of Honor to Harold Morris."

The crowd burst into applause as I tried to grasp the reality, wondering if I would awake in my prison cell and discover it was only a dream. As the applause died, the counselor asked me to speak. I looked into the faces of prison guards. It was a rare thing for an inmate to have a good relationship with guards and rarer still to be honored in the presence of their wives and dignitaries of the community. They accepted my thanks without knowing all that was going on in my heart.

Imagine, such an honor for a convict! There's hope for me! Everybody was wrong - I can be somebody!

But realizing that I was somebody did nothing to diminish my desire to be released from prison. I was very distraught, longing to be free yet unable to hope. Finally, I made a decision: if I didn't make parole by April 6th - Easter Sunday - I would escape.

The warden had promised me a sixty-hour pass for the weekend. This was given under the governor's furlough program. I would be free for the first time in nine years. I told no one of my plan to escape except the two people to be involved in the drama - my brother, who would pick me up at the prison, and a friend, who would give me enough money to leave the country. Both wanted me freed by legal means, but they were convinced, as I was, that my chances were running out. Rather than see me die in prison they were willing to take a risk.

Using a phony passport, I could travel anywhere in the world before being missed at the prison. I knew it was wrong, but there seemed no other alternative. Fortunately, before I had the chance to implement my plan, I received some wonderful news. On the first of March, a letter arrived from the State Board of Pardons and Paroles. Trembling, I opened it. I would be paroled on March 14th! At last! Freedom!

I was allowed a five minute phone call to share the good news with my brother Carl.

March 14th - it was two weeks away! But it seemed like two years. I was afraid to leave my cell. I might get into trouble . . . or be killed. Not wanting to take any chances, I stayed in the cell with Doc.

I was excited yet frightened about going into a world I didn't know. A job awaited me at the Brookland Boys' Home in Orangeburg, South Carolina. My parole officer explained that I would be assigned to another officer in Orangeburg, and many rules accompanied my free-dom. I would not be allowed to leave the Orangeburg city limits; I couldn't even leave my residence before 6 a.m. or stay out past mid-night. It seemed I needed permission from my parole officer for everything except breathing! To buy a house or car or to marry required approval. Because I had been convicted of a felony, the rights of U.S. citizenship were not restored. That didn't matter to me . . . I'd be free!

State Board of Pardons and Paroles

JAMES T. MORRIS
Chairman

J. O. Partain, Jr.
Member

Mrs. Mamie B. Reese
Member

March 1, 1978

ROOM 610
800 PEACHTREE STREET
ATLANTA, GEORGIA 30308

Floyd Busbee
Member

Mr. Donald Harold Morris; D-7739
Georgia State Prison
Star Route
Reidsville, Georgia 30453

Mobley Howell
Member

Dear Mr. Morris:

After careful investigation and deliberation, the Parole Board has tentatively decided to release you under parole supervision. This means you will be allowed to serve the rest of your sentence, minus credited good time, outside of prison where you may earn your own living and lead a normal life.

Your Certificate of Parole will be delivered to you soon by your warden, who will explain the conditions of parole which are found on the back of the certificate. These conditions will be explained to you again when you first contact your parole supervisor. Pay attention to all of these conditions and make sure they are explained to you fully. Remember that the only way you can go back to prison is by violating one of those conditions. The only one who can send you back is you!

The name and address of your parole supervisor will be found on the back of the certificate. Report to him immediately as required by the conditions of parole and follow his instructions. You will find him to be a friend and advisor.

You have our best wishes in your efforts to begin a new life. You went to prison because you failed to abide by society's rules. We think you are ready to abide by those rules and be an asset to your community instead of a liability. This is why we grant you parole.

You are scheduled for release on parole on March 14, 1978. This release date is tentative until actual release.

We wish you success and happiness.

Sincerely,

STATE BOARD OF PARDONS AND PAROLES

JAMES T. MORRIS, Chairman
J. O. PARTAIN, JR., Member
MRS. MAMIE B. REESE, Member
FLOYD BUSBEE, Member
MOBLEY HOWELL, Member

FOR THE BOARD:

Robertson Haworth
Executive Officer

ymh

cc: Warden

State Board of Pardons and Paroles
ATLANTA, GEORGIA

Parole Certificate

KNOW ALL MEN BY THESE PRESENTS:

It having been made to appear to the Georgia State Board of Pardons and Paroles that

_____MORRIS, DONALD HAROLD_____ , Serial No. ___D-7739___ ,

convicted of the following offense(s) in the court(s) indicated:

MURDER: ROBBERY   FULTON COUNTY SUPERIOR COURT

is eligible to be PAROLED, and that there is a reasonable probability that said prisoner WILL REMAIN AT LIBERTY WITHOUT VIOLATING THE LAWS, and it being the opinion of the said State Board of Pardons and Paroles that the release of this prisoner is not incompatible with the welfare of society, and it appearing further that the Board is satisfied this prisoner will be suitably employed in self-sustaining employment or will not become a public charge on release:

It is therefore ORDERED that said prisoner be paroled effective ____14th____ day of ___March___ , 19 _78_ , pending good behavior under supervision subject to the specific conditions of parole as listed on the reverse side of this Order, until the expiration of his maximum sentence, minus good time earned.

This parole shall not prevent the delivery of the prisoner to authorities of the Federal Government or any State otherwise entitled to his custody.

In witness whereof this Certificate bearing the Seal of the State Board of Pardons and Paroles is issued the ___28th___ day of ___February___ , 19 _78_ .

STATE BOARD OF PARDONS AND PAROLES
JAMES T. MORRIS, CHAIRMAN
J. O. PARTAIN, JR., MEMBER
MRS. MAMIE B. REESE, MEMBER
FLOYD BUSBEE, MEMBER
MOBLEY HOWELL, MEMBER

FOR THE BOARD:

Order No. __39,750__   B. YOUNG

On March 13th - my last day in prison - I went to see several old friends. I visited with one man who had spent forty-seven years in prison. Oh, the tragedy of a wasted life! There were many hugs along with prayers that I would have a successful life on the outside.

That afternoon, I looked up to see Jimmy approaching me. He had heard that I was to be paroled the following day. He reaffirmed his love and thanked me for being the brother he'd always wanted. Then he promised to visit me at the Boys' Home. We were both emotional when we shook hands and said our good-byes.

There wasn't much sleep for either of us that night as Doc and I talked and swapped old stories until, finally, morning came. Fully awake at 5 a.m., I lay in bed thinking about what was ahead. In just three hours, I'd be leaving the prison. At 8 o'clock, a guard would unlock the door, and I'd be a free man - for the first time in about ten years. I was frightened to death. I knew that supportive family members and friends would be waiting. More than anything in the world, I wanted them to see my changed life.

Through the window, I could see the sunrise. I held those cold, unfriendly bars and watched the earth take on a golden glow as I tried to remember when I first came to the prison. It seemed so long ago!

Suddenly, I heard footsteps and the sound of keys.

"I wish I could take you with me," I said.

"I wish I could go!" Doc shot back.

I turned and grinned at him.

"Doc, you know I love you, and I won't ever forget you. You have taught me so much - to love, to care, to give - you've changed my life."

"I love you, too, Harold," Doc said.

"And I'll be back, I promise you that." I looked him in the eye and said, "Thanks for risking your life to save mine."

Tears streamed down our faces, and we hugged and I kissed him on the cheek. The guard who unlocked the door said nothing as he led me to the building where the final paperwork was done before inmates left the institution. Also being paroled were two inmates whom I'd never met. Even though I'd been in prison for many years, there were inmates I had never met. The three of us talked of our plans as we waited for the process to be completed.

"We've got some clothes for you," said an old guard, handing each of us an outdated polyester suit and a pair of white socks.

He then offered each of us a bus ticket to our destination and a check for $25 - meager wages for better than nine years of work.

"I don't need any of that. My family is coming," I explained.

"Ain't nobody coming to get you," he snarled. "You'd better take this bus ticket and these clothes and get out of here."

"My family's coming," I repeated. "They care about me. They'll be here."

The other two inmates changed clothes and boarded a bus for a little town seven miles away. As I watched them leave, I began to imagine what would happen if I were the typical inmate: I accept the suit, the $25 check, and the bus ticket. Arriving in a strange town, I have no identification. After all, I'm not a citizen of the United States. Cashing the check proves to be very difficult, but finally it is approved. After buying three meals, I'm almost broke - just enough left for a couple of beers. A beer joint is the one place I should never be! Now, I'm high but broke. I sleep on the sidewalk and start the day looking for work. When the prospective employer asks for three references, I name the warden and two inmates. He threatens to call the sheriff to lock me up.

In my imagination, I continue the scenario . . . I turn and look at the man who could have been me - without friends, without money, without hope. How long would it be until I hurt someone? At that moment, I understood why men return to prison. They can't manage their lives.

Living is hard on the outside, and a life of crime is all they have known. At least in the institution they are among men who profess to be friends, and they receive free meals. No wonder the return rate is eighty-five percent.

As the mental picture of "Harold Morris, the typical inmate" faded, I began to pace the floor . . . 8:15 and my family had not arrived.

"I told you nobody cares," the guard reminded me. "You'd better take this suit and get out of here. There ain't nobody coming to get you, you animal."

"At least I'm free," I shot back. "You'll never be free. You'll die here."

By 8:30, my family still had not come, but I wasn't worried. Some problem had caused the delay. I knew they would come; they had invested five years in my life.

Finally, at 8:45, a van pulled up in front of the prison bringing my brother Carl and other members of my family, along with several friends. I thanked God for them, knowing that no other inmate had ever been met by more caring, supportive people.

Carl hurried through the prison door, explaining the motel where they had stayed in Savannah had failed to make the wake-up call as requested. He handed me a pair of pants and a shirt. The average man attaches little significance to changing clothes, but I was hardly average. I was convict 62345 becoming a free man!

I accepted the $25 check for nine-and-a-half years of labor, representing less than a penny a day. At 8:52 a.m., after a 3,500 day interruption in my life, I walked out of prison a free man!

The warden had joined Doc and several guards and inmates at the prison fence. "I'll keep W-8 cell empty for you," he said. "You'll be back."

I nodded and looked at Doc through the fence.

He said, "I love you, Harold."

"I love you, too, Doc, and I'll be back. I won't ever forget you."

A brilliant sun peeked through the trees as I stepped outside and looked around. That gorgeous day was unlike the morning I had arrived at Georgia State Penitentiary. The earth was bursting with overtures of spring, and my heart was bursting with immense gratitude as I knelt in the shadows of the guard tower, thanking God for a new beginning. Stepping into the van, I wondered if the prison nightmare really had ended or if parole were only a dream.

Seven miles from the prison in the town of Reidsville, a parade happened to be under way.

"A parade! You've over done it!" I teased, knowing it was merely a coincidence. The laughter of many hearts was like medicine healing my tattered soul.

When we reached Claxton after travelling just twenty miles, I suggested that we stop to eat. I've never had a better meal than the breakfast I ate at Mrs. Rogers' Restaurant. I don't know if it was the taste of the food or the taste of freedom.

After eating, I turned to my brother. "Where's the rest room?" I asked. "For nearly ten years, I haven't gone to the john without someone watching!"

I asked my brother if he wanted to watch.

He said, "You've lost your mind."

We drove on to South Carolina for the highlight of my release - holding my dear mother in my arms and telling her I loved her. This time I didn't hear the trained dogs barking in the distance or feel the shame of wearing prison clothes. When I looked into my mother's face, I finally understood how much she had suffered because of my suffering. I realized that her prison term ended with mine.

Within twenty-four hours after my release from prison, I had to check in with my parole officer in Orangeburg. To my surprise, the officer was a stunning lady.

"Ma'am, I haven't seen a woman in nine-and-a-half years," I said. "You're beautiful! I don't know the rules, but I'd be glad to report to you every day!"

Laughing, she said, "We're going to get along just fine."

She explained that I would report to her in person once a month as well as submit written reports monthly. She gave me permission to spend a week with my family before starting to work at the Boys' Home. As I left, she reminded me that I was not a citizen of the United States, that I couldn't vote, and that I couldn't own property without her permission. Those restrictions didn't discourage me. I knew I could survive. Besides, I only had $25, and I didn't think you could buy much property with that.

I had never been to the Boys' Home, but some of the youngsters had sent letters to the prison. When I arrived, the boys were waiting for me. Large yellow ribbons were tied around the pecan trees, and a big sign announced, "Welcome home, Mr. Morris." I cried, realizing that there I would be loved and needed.

My responsibilities included coaching and counseling the boys who were ages eight to sixteen and from varied backgrounds. Some were orphans, some had been abused and neglected by their parents, some had been kicked out to roam the streets, and some were from broken homes. They were exactly what I needed. Being outcasts themselves, they wouldn't look down on me. I learned a great deal as those kids worked their way into my heart.

I was unprepared to return to the society that I had left a decade ago. Times had changed, but I had not changed with them. In the area of politics I was well informed, having read a great deal while in prison. Most inmates don't bother.

Contact with high school students through the speaking program in prison had kept me informed about their problems and attitudes, but the change in moral values came as a surprise. I had not expected to find such widespread immorality. In the area of male-female relationships, it was a whole new ball game.

The openness of homosexuals gave me another jolt. Although I had lived with them in prison, I was not aware of the rights they had gained on the outside.

Freedom gave me an appreciation for the things that many people take for granted. What a joy it was to talk on the telephone! During my first four years in prison, I did not make or receive one phone call, and for the last four-and-a-half years my calls were limited. In the free world I could pick up the phone every day and tell someone, "I love you!"

At first people seemed to have a problem communicating with me.

"What do you think?" they would ask, in an attempt to draw me into the conversation.

They didn't realize that in prison I didn't grow as they had grown. My life had stopped many years earlier, leaving a tremendous void. I could contribute only memories.

Making decisions proved very difficult for a while. In prison, my life had been managed for me. I was told when to go to bed, when to get up, when and where to work, and when to eat. Even the amount of food had been predetermined and served on my plate. Ordering from a menu in the free world was a frightening experience. Salad bars were terrifying!

I happened to be with friends in a shopping mall in Charleston, South Carolina, when I found something unbelievable - rows of restaurants! I went door to door, ordering a little at each. After sampling the fare at half the restaurants, I decided to wait until the next day to try the others. I'd already made a pig out of myself! To be able to eat anything I wanted seemed overwhelming. I ate every meal as if it would be my last. The result was a weight gain that eventually affected my health before being brought under control.

Inflation offered another big surprise. Fifty cents for a Pepsi-cola. One cost fifteen cents when I went to prison. All I wanted was refreshment. I wasn't interested in buying stock in the company!

My employer signed a bank note so I could purchase an automobile. Designs had changed so drastically that I hardly knew a Volkswagen from a Cadillac. Passing a junk yard, I marveled at some ten-year-old models I'd never even seen.

Buying clothes embarrassed me because I knew nothing about styles. The sales clerks really had a field day.

Occasionally, a very simple thing proved to be a large challenge. Some friends hosted a party for me, and I went to the kitchen for a drink of water. I twisted those fancy knobs in every direction, but the water just wouldn't come. When I heard their laughter, my friends worried that I might be embarrassed.

Someone whispered, "He doesn't even know how to turn on the faucet."

I really wasn't embarrassed.

About six months after being released from prison, I decided to try to find the men who had betrayed me. One of the parole rules stated that I was never to have contact with an ex-offender, and I had intended to honor it. Knowing the kind of men Frank and Al were, I feared they might try to kill me.

Nonetheless, I felt it was important to bring closure to the problems between us. After numerous phone calls to mutual acquaintances, I finally located Al in North Carolina. His wife answered.

When Al came to the phone he said, "Who is it?"

"Don't you recognize my voice?"

"No, I don't think I do."

"Does the name Harold Morris mean anything to you?"

"Where are you?" he gasped in fright.

On the day of my conviction, I had promised to kill him, and I'd sent word from prison that I intended to keep my word.

I thought about saying, "Turn around and look through the window. There's a gun pointed at you." Instead, I replied, "Don't worry, I'm in South Carolina."

"Harold, I'm sorry! Forgive me! They said if I tried to help you I'd go to prison forever!"

"Listen," I interrupted his explanation. "I just called to ask you to forgive me for wanting to kill you."

He asked me to come and see him. I'm afraid I had to decline that offer.

I asked how to reach Frank. Al gave me a Florida number, but when I called it had been disconnected. I called Al again and asked him to tell Frank that I tried to contact him to say I had forgiven him.

Several times I took troubled kids from the Boys' Home to the prison to see Doc. He often pulled up his shirt to show the boys where he had been stabbed seven times, and this had a tremendous effect on the boys as did his stories about life behind bars.

When we got back to the Boys' Home, the children who had visited the prison couldn't wait to tell the others about what they'd just seen and heard.

"Inside that prison I saw the meanest people in the whole wide world," one would say.

"They're not even people - they're animals," another would cut in. "They'd rape you in a minute if they could get at you."

"I'd kill myself right now before I'd go back there," a third would promise solemnly.

I remember one little boy, desperate for some of the attention, vividly describing Doc, "You should've seen him - he had big hands like road scrapers, and when he pulled his shirt off he had fifty stab wounds on him."

Meanwhile, I didn't forget my promise to Doc. In the first two years after my parole I visited him fifty-five times. I made sure that he didn't want for anything. I brought him food, spending money, everything that the prison would allow him to receive.

Doc was paroled a few months later, and I went to pick him up even though one of the conditions of his parole and mine was that we couldn't associate with ex-cons. I drove him to a small Georgia town where he had a job and a parole officer waiting for him.

During the next few years I lived in four different states, but any time I was nearby I'd drop in for a visit. We both struggled to find our way in the world. While I decided to return to college, Doc got married and had two kids. I knew that he longed to leave the South and that as soon as he was released from parole suspension he would move to the North, where his wife was from. We talked by phone for six years, but my constant moving around made it difficult to keep in touch. Then one day my world was turned upside down - my doctors told me that I had throat cancer and it was terminal. I was in for the fight of my life. Month after month, I was confined to my apartment, leaving only to receive radiation treatments that left me mentally and physically drained.

After a year, I finally regained my health and tried to get on with my life. I tried to contact Doc but found that he and his family had moved and left no forwarding address. So many times I have regretted that I didn't let Doc know about my illness, because I know he would have been there for me. But I didn't want him to see me sick and dying when there was nothing he could have done for me. I didn't want him to suffer because of me. Again, as it had in prison, my pride had shut me off from the ones I loved. To me, pride is the worst sin in the world - it will destroy your life.

I have thought about Doc often since then. I will never forget him or the lessons he taught me. He will forever live in my memory.

PART VI
1978-1997

Twenty-nine

Meanwhile, I made the decision to go back to college, and I enrolled at Southeastern in Birmingham, Alabama. After much convincing, my parole officer granted me permission to leave South Carolina and to report to a parole officer in Birmingham. Going to college after nearly ten years in prison can only be described as a growing experience. I was twice the age of most of the students on the campus. However, they accepted me immediately.

I had heard of William Russell Moore months before we met. In almost every class someone requested prayer for him, because he was hospitalized with cancer in Houston, Texas. I wrote to him saying I'd heard many good things about him and promised to pray for him. I also added a few notes about myself.

In the fall of 1979, six months after his left leg was amputated below the hip, Russell was back on campus wearing an artificial leg and the warmest smile I'd ever seen. He carried his textbooks and Bible under one arm and a black walking cane in the other hand. I introduced myself to him.

"So you're Harold Morris!" he exclaimed. "Thanks for your encouraging letters. They helped." He smiled, cocked his head, and stared at me for a few seconds. Then he nodded and said, "You've gone through quite a bit yourself."

Encouraged by his warmth, I found myself spending a lot of time with him. We shared our deepest dreams in the days that followed,

and I marveled at the young man's courage and determination to fulfill his dreams.

"Harold, I have a deep love for the Jewish people, and I want very
much to spend the rest of my life in Israel," he told me. "Before I got
sick, I had planned to enroll in Hebrew University in Jerusalem. I
worked hard to earn the money, and then the very day of the trip, I
got sick." He thumped his artificial leg. "Cancer in my left knee. But
the doctors think they got it all, and as soon as I'm strong again, I'm
going to Israel. And I want you to come with me."

I shared Russell's dreams of traveling to Israel, and I had a passport.
My problem was that as a convicted felon I was not supposed to
leave the country.

One day Russell returned to the doctor for a routine check-up,
and X-rays revealed a suspicious spot on one lung. Two weeks later
he saw the doctor again, and afterwards he came straight to my
apartment.

"What did the doctor say?" I asked as he stood in the doorway supported by his walking cane.

"If the doctors know what they are talking about, I have no more
than twelve days to live."

I stared at him, unable to absorb the news. Receiving two life
sentences was nothing compared to this. Twelve days to live!

What does one say to someone who learns he is dying when he
has just begun to live? Finally, I found my voice.

"Russell," I asked softly, "what are you going to do?"

"I must go to Israel. I want to fulfill my dream. I want to die there."

Russell attended classes for another week. Growing weaker each
day, he asked me to see if the college president would arrange for
him to speak to the student body before returning to the hospital. The
chapel was packed with students and faculty as Russell challenged us
never to forsake our dreams.

When he finished, every student and faculty member stood with
tear-stained faces. His mother and I helped him leave the stage, and
that night he entered the hospital to die.

Each time I visited him in the hospital I did something crazy, such
as feel around his bed and exclaim, "Good night! There's a leg missing!

Russell, where is it? Your doctor has told you to take your medicine
and get plenty of rest. But you're not following his instructions,
because your leg's missing!"

One time I felt his leg, and I said, "I see the rustlers have been
here."

He said, "What are you talking about?"

I said, "Your calves are missing."

Russell burst out laughing. "You're crazy, Harold," he said.

He was right; I was crazy. But I believed my warped humor helped
him. Once he told me he especially liked my visits because I wasn't
quiet and self-conscious around his hospital bed as were most of his
other friends. Perhaps by accident I'd learned that joking and laughter
was a healthy way to face the problem honestly, and it opened the
door for Russell to discuss his feelings.

That's not to say the visits were easy. I watched him spit up blood
and parts of a tumor, and the sight made me nauseated. I saw him
shrivel to half his original weight and struggle for every breath. But
he never wavered. To the end, he was determined to live his dream.

Sometimes in the middle of the night he'd call saying, "Harold, I
need help. Please come see me."

Twelve days passed, yet he clung to life. His mother stayed by his
side as he underwent chemotherapy and suffered the notorious side
effects. He lost his hair and a great deal of weight. At times, visitors
were restricted when his white blood count dropped, leaving him
susceptible to infection. One day as I started into his room, he
stopped me.

"Hold it! My white blood count is down to 800. Please, before you
take another step pray that it will double. I believe it will happen if
we just pray."

The next morning he called me, "Hey, you won't believe it, it didn't
double - it tripled!"

During the next few weeks Russell was in and out of the hospital
many times. Although he struggled with pain, he never lost his faith
or his sense of humor. I was already grieving for him, and one day
as we drove through Birmingham, he teased me out of my somber
mood.

"Why are you so quiet? Don't be glum. Listen, so what if I die? Just think, I'll be in heaven! If you have a flat tire down here, and you're too lazy to change it, I could send a couple of angels down to help. And another thing, I'll have seniority over you when you get there."

Hardly a day went by that he didn't beg me to go to Israel.

"Russell, I can't go. You know I'm on parole. Get your dad or someone else."

"You're it," he said. "You're the only one who can pull it off."

On one of my visits to the hospital I met Russell's physician.

"How's he doing?" I asked.

"Not very well," he said. "The right lung is completely gone, and only one-third of the left one remains. I don't know how he's breathing. I'd give him no more than four days to live."

I walked to my friend's bedside and asked him, "Russell, if you knew you only had four days to live, what would you do with your life?"

"I'd go to Israel. I want to die in that country."

"Let's go!"

"I love you, Harold!" he said, reaching up to hug my neck. Immediately, his health began to improve. He called for the doctor and bargained, "If you'll let me go home, I'll eat vegetables and get strong. I'm going to spend Christmas in Israel!"

The doctor loved Russell as a son and reluctantly agreed to his making the trip. "People will call me a fool for letting him go," he sighed as he looked into my eyes. "And they'll call you a fool for going."

"They've called me a fool all my life, but I don't care," I said. "I've made my decision."

He gave detailed instructions about Russell's medical care and asked if I could administer the injections every five hours. I assured him that I knew how to use needles. He typed a letter authorizing me to carry the drugs and syringes.

"Give this to the captain of the plane and to any authorities who question you," he said. "If a problem arises, tell them to call me collect."

Not all my friends at the college endorsed our plans.

"You will violate parole by leaving the country," a professor pointed out. "And Russell is not physically able to make an eleven-day trip. If that boy dies, you'll be locked up. We don't want that to happen."

The next morning Russell's parents drove us to the airport. Although they realized that they might never see their son alive again, they understood the desire that consumed him, and they did not try to discourage him. As I pushed his wheelchair up the ramp at the Birmingham Airport that sunny Sunday morning December 16, 1979, his mother hugged us both and said, "Take care of him, Harold."

"We'll be back," I said, trying to appear confident.

We flew to New York and then eleven hours on to Israel on El Al Airlines. Most of the passengers were Jewish, and they were drawn to him, curious about his reasons for travelling while so obviously ill. Even flight attendants knelt by his side and asked his reasons for going to Israel. At one point during our trip I felt a nudge on my shoulder and turned to find a flight attendant in tears.

"Sir, I'm so thankful that you and that young man were on this plane," she said. "I was ready to divorce my husband, but because of that young man I'm going to try to save my marriage. I had to thank you. Please look after him."

We rented a car as soon as we arrived in Tel Aviv. The doctor had cautioned me that the slightest exercise would exhaust Russell, decreasing his chances for survival. He had stressed that driving was out of the question. But as soon as we rented a car, Russell announced, "I want to drive."

"Take over," I said, and he headed towards Jerusalem, forty miles away. We were barely a mile out of Tel Aviv when we passed two young hitchhikers - girls dressed in military uniforms. Russell stopped, and the soldiers climbed into the backseat. One spoke English fluently, having graduated from Boston University. When we reached her home in Jerusalem, she gave us her phone number and suggested we have dinner together after we had toured some of the cities.

Russell and I found a room at the Moriah Hotel and planned our sightseeing so he would have adequate rest and receive his injections on schedule. Every five hours he filled the syringe and brought it to me, waking me during the night at the appropriate hour.

Wherever we went, people were attracted to Russell. Many approached him on the streets. After two days in Jerusalem, he suggested we return to Tel Aviv. From there we drove to the beautiful city of Haifa, arriving in the late afternoon. The strenuous trip had drained Russell's energy, and he seemed to take a turn for the worse. But after resting through the night and eating green vegetables he began to regain strength.

On the sixth day, Russell woke me at three in the morning and asked me to give him an injection. Handing me the syringe, he said, "Harold, this is the last of the drugs."

"What?" I asked, stunned.

"I was supposed to take one vial every five hours, but the pain was so bad I've had to double the dose. There's no more morphine."

I was frantic. By morning Russell was trembling with pain again, and he was spitting up parts of the tumor. I went to see the local druggist. He read the letter from Russell's doctor and said he could not give us the drugs. When I begged him to call Russell's doctor collect, he refused.

I returned to the hotel to call the doctor myself, and when I arrived I could see that Russell was deteriorating rapidly. When I reached Birmingham on the telephone, the doctor was in surgery. I left a message with Russell's mother to get in touch with the doctor.

By late afternoon, Russell was bleeding from the mouth, spitting up dead tissue, and slipping in and out of consciousness. Desperate, I telephoned several doctors and pleaded for help, but none of them understood the urgency of our situation. I thought of robbing the drugstore, then shoved the thought aside. Desolate, I fell to my knees beside Russell's bed and prayed.

Moments later, the telephone rang. It was the druggist, who said that Russell's doctor had called. If I could find a doctor to write a prescription, he would fill it. The druggist gave me the number of a physician who spoke English. He came to the hotel right away.

After examining Russell, the doctor said, "He's dying. He may not live through the night. What are you doing in Israel at a time like this?"

While the doctor gave Russell a series of injections, I repeated the story. The doctor shook his head in amazement.

"Here is enough medication for the night," he said. "I will check on him at eight in the morning. If he is alive, I will see that the druggist gives you all the medication you need."

Through the night I administered Russell's shots. About 3 a.m., he opened his eyes. I ran to the bed and squeezed his hand. He was thirsty and asked for an orange drink. I hunted the streets of Haifa and finally returned an hour later with the drink. In the morning, I bought vegetables for him and bathed him before the doctor arrived. Surprised to find the patient much improved, he went to see the druggist and returned with enough medication for the remainder of our stay in Israel.

After resting for two days, Russell was ready to go again; we headed for the coastal city of Nahariya. Russell phoned a family who had recently moved there from Great Britain, and we were invited to visit. Russell had been given their number by a friend in Birmingham prior to our trip. While Russell rested, our host's nine-year-old son, David, came to me. His eyes were dark with sorrow.

"Why is he dying? It's not fair!"

"Son, there are many things I don't understand," I said. "Right now I can't tell you why this is happening. One day we will understand."

"Will you do me a favor?" he asked. "When you go back to the United States, will you call me if Russell dies?"

"I promise," I said.

They were a very poor family and couldn't afford to feed us. David and I went shopping for food, and that night we had a feast.

On the way back to Jerusalem we hit a rugged stretch of road going about thirty-five miles-per-hour. In the middle of nowhere the car left the road and rumbled into a rocky area, nearly turning over, before finally coming to a stop. Russell was thrown to the floor. I visualized the headline: Ex-convict Kills Boy Dying of Cancer in Israel. The engine had stopped, and I was certain the car had sustained heavy damage. But I turned on the ignition, and to my surprise the motor started. After backing out of the rocks, I looked the car over. There wasn't a dent, and it ran as well as it had before the accident. Again Russell offered an explanation: "Angels, Harold, angels!"

The next day, we attended an outdoor worship service. I bundled Russell up in a blanket to shield him against the early morning chill.

The following day, we were invited to the home of a girl named Esther, whom we had met at the worship service. There were about twenty-five guests, and we had a wonderful time of fellowship. All of them just fell in love with Russell. As soon as we returned to our hotel, she telephoned.

"You will not believe this," she said. "But tomorrow you and Russell have been invited to the Knesset to visit Yechiel Kadishai. He is the second most powerful man in the country - Prime Minister Begin's top aide and closest friend!"

How had such an unlikely meeting been arranged? It seems that Esther - an ordinary girl with courage reminiscent of the Biblical queen - recognized in Russell such love and compassion that she called Mr. Kadishai. When she explained that Russell had come to Israel because of his great love for the Jewish people, he agreed to meet with us.

We stayed awake most of the night we were so excited. The next day - Christmas Eve - Esther drove us to the Knesset, where we were welcomed warmly by Mr. Kadishai.

"Come in. I've been expecting you," he said, shaking our hands. As we walked into his office, I noticed a door to the left. Mr. Kadishai pulled a chair close to Russell and sat facing him.

Russell could speak a little Hebrew, and they had a great time trying to communicate. Mr. Kadishai seemed mesmerized by Russell.

Then he presented me with an autographed copy of a book he had written, *Myths and Facts of 1978*, a Concise Record of the Arab-Israeli Conflict.

"So you were in prison?" Mr. Kadishai asked. "Menachem Begin was in solitary confinement in Russia. He wrote a book, *White Nights*, detailing his experiences. Mr. Begin chose the title because the desert nights viewed from his prison cell were never dark."

Mr. Kadishai rose and disappeared through the door I had noticed when we entered the room. In a moment, he returned with Menachem Begin!

"May God bless you, young man," Mr. Begin said as he shook my hand. Then, turning to Russell, his warm expression changed to shock at the severity of Russell's condition. He walked over to Russell and extended his hand in friendship.

"May God be with you, young man," Mr. Begin said.

Without a moment's hesitation, Russell reached into his pocket and pulled out a letter that he had written the night before. He handed it to Israel's Prime Minister. Mr. Begin placed the paper in his pocket and talked with us for a long while.

Finally, I said to Mr. Begin, "Thank you, sir, for the gifts and for letting us come today. It is a day we will never forget. But I must share one thing before we leave. When Russell was told he had perhaps only four days to live, I asked what he wanted to do with his life. He said he wanted to come to Israel and to die in this country. He loves you and your people enough that he has come here to die."

Mr. Begin wrapped his arms around Russell as a father would embrace his son, and I saw tears in his eyes as he spoke, "May God be with you, young man, because you are a winner. And one day you will return to Israel."

He turned and left the room.

Russell and I returned to our hotel, thrilled that we had met such important men. We spent Christmas Day in Bethlehem.

Russell's health continued to decline daily, and he seemed satisfied that he had lived his dream. I arranged for an earlier flight home. Our journey had surpassed our greatest expectations. Although we had no advanced reservations, we always found a room and Russell never got diarrhea, which the doctor warned would be deadly in his weakened condition.

Having lived his dream, Russell no longer smiled. On the plane, all of his energy seemed to have been expended. His suffering intensified hour by hour. I couldn't understand why this was happening. The closer we got to New York, the more distressed I became.

In New York, I carried him through the airport like a rag doll and laid him down on a couch while I called his mother; he fell asleep. As we arrived in Birmingham at 3 a.m. Russell squeezed my hand and said, "Let's pray."

I'll never forget his words:

"God, thank you for letting me live my dream. Thank you for bringing me home to see my mother once more. And, please bless those who are less fortunate than I am."

I saw that he was crying, and I knew he was praying for me. Russell faced his death with calm serenity while I was distraught.

Russell lived forty-two days after our arrival back in the United States, and I saw him every day. On the morning of February 7, 1980, Russell had been scheduled to speak at Georgia State Penitentiary. When he realized he didn't have the strength to make it, he urged me to go in his place. I called the hospital that morning and spoke with him.

"Russell, I love you, and I want to thank you for the impact you've had on my life. I've lived many years, but you are so young. If I could, I would take your place and die with honor."

"I know that," Russell whispered. Struggling for breath, he added, "You're a loyal friend, Harold, but never forget this: it's loyalty to God that counts."

That was our last conversation. A few hours later, Russell passed away. Through his friendship, I learned that it isn't the length of one's life that counts, but the quality of one's years.

I called David, the little nine-year-old boy in Israel, as I had promised him. I told him that Russell had died, and we cried together.

In the end, Russell's life was woven into the fabric of my being, a continued reminder of what mighty things can be done by a person who is faithful. I shall never forget Russell Moore. He shall always live in my memory.

I am so thankful for my time with Russell, because four short years after he died I used every lesson he taught me. You see, Russell didn't just teach me about how to live; he also taught me something about how to die. Little did I know how soon I'd need to use those lessons.

Thirty

In February of 1984, I noticed a swelling on the left side of my neck, similar to that caused by a bee sting. A fever and a sore throat had plagued me for six months, but a physician diagnosed the problem as simply a virus, which improved with medication.

The swelling lasted just a few days, but it left a small knot and the fever and sore throat recurred. I saw physicians in South Carolina, Ohio, and Colorado as I continued my speaking schedule. After each exam I was given medication and assured there was no reason for concern as the knot did not appear to be symptomatic of any serious disease.

Returning to Atlanta, where I was living, I consulted a physician and underwent another thorough exam. He also believed the knot to be insignificant but advised me to have it removed. The surgeon whom he recommended agreed. The surgery would require only one day of hospitalization and about three days of recovery at home. Since the problem appeared to be minor, I told only a few close friends.

On a Monday in April of 1984, at 9 a.m., I entered North Fulton Medical Center in Atlanta. When I awakened from surgery around 3 p.m., the room was very dark, and I was terribly hazy from the anesthesia.

"Can you hear me?" the surgeon asked.

I nodded. He began to talk, but what was he saying? Bad news.

Cancer. Three lymph nodes. Did he have permission to talk to my friends who were there?

"Yes, tell them anything," I said, sinking into a deep sleep.

When I awakened two hours later, my friends were crying. The doctor was there again. He explained that three lymph nodes on the left side of my neck were malignant, but he didn't know the extent of the cancer. Biopsies were ordered of suspicious tissue. These tests along with numerous others confirmed malignancy behind the left ear, sinuses, and tongue, as well as in my throat. Physicians agreed that with proper treatment, I might live three years.

I left the hospital after a week, and for the first time I was alone. The trauma finally hit with full force. As I lay in bed fighting the pain and the effects of medication, I could see outside the brilliant sun and the trees blowing in the wind. It was a beautiful day, but a feeling of dread draped my being. If the doctors were correct, this was the beginning of a long, hard road for me.

A cancer specialist at Crawford Long Hospital recommended two months of radiation therapy, but he didn't paint a hopeful picture.

"You need a lot of luck and prayer," he said.

It was the most depressing day of my life. How could a tiny lump change things so drastically? Alone in my apartment that night, I tried to sort out the puzzle.

My experience with illness was minimal; I couldn't ever remember being sick. I'd spent some time in the prison hospital after an inmate split open my head, and it took thirty-nine stitches to sew me back together. I was in the hospital again after being stabbed. The pain of cancer didn't scare me, but there were so many other unknowns. How would my friends react? What would I look like after the treatments? Could I continue my work speaking to kids and prisoners? How much would the cancer treatments cost? How long would I be sick? How would I react to a slow, painful death? Would I have to die alone?

The cancer specialist had referred me to an outstanding oncologist at St. Joseph's Hospital. After looking over the medical reports, he pointed out that the primary tumor had not been found, although it was believed to be in the head area. He explained that radiation fights cancer cells by blasting them with high-energy rays. Unable to repair the resulting damage or to reproduce themselves, the malignant cells die. While this sometimes leads to immediate shrinkage of the tumor or relief from symptoms, he said, often results are not evident until weeks or months after the treatment has been completed.

Radiation would be aimed at several areas of the head in an attempt to destroy the hidden primary tumor, along with the cancer tissue that had been found. My face and neck would be painted with a solution to mark the target areas. Treatment was scheduled for 10:15 a.m. Monday through Friday for the next eight weeks.

"We're going to fight this thing," the doctor said, although he gave me only a 32% chance for recovery.

I told him things were looking up for me. Those were the best odds I'd ever had.

"Let's go for it!" I said.

My face and neck were painted with colorful crosses and other markings, which would remain throughout the treatment period. Stopping by a hotel to make reservations for friends, I realized the clerk was self-conscious and trying not to stare.

"Ma'am, are you wondering what's wrong with me?" I asked.

"Yes. Please tell me, are you a clown?"

"That's right," I said. "I'm an entertainer, and I'm looking for work."

After leading her on for a short time, I explained I had cancer.

"I'm so sorry!" she said.

"Please don't be sorry," I said. "The death rate is one apiece. We all die. Every day brings each of us closer to death. I might die of cancer, or perhaps be crushed by a car as I leave here."

"I've never met anyone like you," the clerk said. "I can't believe your attitude. You handle your illness so well."

Following the first radiation treatments, I looked like a lobster. My skin turned pink and darkened. Then it peeled.

After each treatment, I drove the eleven miles from the hospital to my apartment and went to bed. The radiation burned calories, draining my energy. Daily I grew weaker. My throat was swollen and unbearably sore. Swallowing became so painful I could no longer eat. Through a straw I sipped water and special liquid nutrients, which provided barely enough energy to keep me going.

That period was the most difficult of my life. It was an agonizing, lonely time, yet I was never alone. Always there were my loyal friends standing with me. I'm so thankful for my many special friends - people whose love was displayed in many different ways. I'm so thankful for their steadfast loyalty.

Several times at the point of collapse, I was rushed to the hospital to receive intravenous feeding before the radiation could continue. At times the pain was so acute I thought I was dying. There were days when death would have been a relief. The nurses, so kind and caring, shared my hurt. When I flinched at having tape removed from around my I.V. tube, they understood my pain.

The lonely years in prison - particularly the time in solitary confinement - helped me accept the discipline of being confined to an apartment for five months. However, I was not prepared for the emotional trauma or the physical anguish.

The radiation destroyed good cells along with the cancer cells. My taste buds were damaged as well as my saliva glands, but these were expected to return. Other side effects were diarrhea and vomiting. Through the night my body was racked with dry heaves, and every ten minutes, phlegm had to be cleared from my throat. The dry heaves were so bad that the doctors finally gave me marijuana in pill form, because nothing else would work.

A blood sample was taken each Tuesday to determine if the cancer had spread. My weight dropped steadily, twenty pounds in a matter of days, and eighty-five pounds in six months. Being overweight, I had the pounds to spare, yet before long I felt like a skeleton.

The final seven radiation treatments were shot directly into my mouth, turning it into one giant blister. I was unable to speak, and the pain was unbearable. Wet cloths cooled my neck and face for only a moment before absorbing the intense body heat.

In my apartment one day, I fainted. I was used to having dizzy spells whenever I stood up, but suddenly, as I sat, the walls began to spin. I squeezed the armrests of my chair, but the walls and pictures kept spinning. I felt like I was on a fast merry-go-round that had slipped a cog and was about to rocket off its axis. It was as though I was caught in a horror movie. Suddenly my head crashed against my desk and everything went black.

When I regained consciousness, my head was lying on some envelopes scattered across the desk. Opening my eyes, I saw only a blurry darkness. Several minutes passed before I realized where I was and who I was. But my world remained black. My hands groped across the top of the desk, sending envelopes flying. Suddenly my heart began lurching out of control in my chest, and my arms started shaking violently. The shaking spread across my entire body. My heart felt ready to explode. My pulse galloped in my head and slammed against the inside of my chest like a rapid-fire cannon. Sweat poured off my body. My hair was soaked. Streams of perspiration coursed down my back.

With great effort I grabbed my chest, unsure of what to do next. Then the thought struck: I am dying! As my heart bucked and lurched, I slid out of my chair, got on my hands and knees and began to crawl towards the bathroom. My brain screamed for water. Somehow I had to cool down my head. Still unable to see, I crawled across the living room, through my bedroom, and into my bathroom. I pulled myself across the linoleum and leaned over the commode. Fortunately, a towel was lying nearby; I sloshed it around the toilet and plastered it over my face.

Then, I crawled to my bed, pulled myself up onto the mattress, and sprawled across it on my back. My chest was heaving, and the perspiration continued pouring. I was blind to everything. I knew my heart had to burst. I tried to hold it, to take deep even breaths, but that didn't help.

This was it. Death was just moments away. The only thing I could think to do was reach out to God in prayer.

After praying, I closed my eyes and waited for my heart to lurch one final time. Instead, at that moment, an amazing thing happened. My heart stopped pounding and returned to its normal beat. The breaths I'd struggled for came easier. I still felt incredible pain in my head and chest, but a peace surrounded me, which surpassed my understanding.

My body continued shaking, and my vision remained black. As I kept perfectly still, I began to see pools of light swim before me, presumably coming from my bedroom window. Within the light pools, I slowly began to differentiate colors. Splashes of greens and blues circled in front of me. I adjusted the wet cloth on my head but was careful to keep movement to a minimum.

I tried to sit up, but the room started swimming. If I kept still, I could see a little bit, but the minute I moved, I was blinded again. So I kept perfectly still. Then I closed my eyes and didn't wake up again until after sundown. My eyesight returned and eventually the dizzy spells went away.

The treatments were completed close to schedule, and I returned to the cancer specialist to learn if the radiation had been effective. If it had not been, there was little hope. Because of the location of the cancer, surgery was not an option, and further radiation treatments would not even be considered. After completing the exam, the doctor sat down in a chair and looked at me.

"This is a miracle," he said. "There is not a trace of cancer. It's the most amazing thing I've ever seen. I can't believe it."

I could believe it. I had expected it. However, the radiation damage to my throat would require months of healing. The physician expected me to be eating soft foods very soon. I didn't attempt anything but liquids for several more days, and by the end of the week my throat had closed completely. I couldn't even swallow water. Suddenly the miracle began to tarnish.

My throat muscles had contracted from lack of use, and scar tissue had filled the opening. The dilation procedure was very painful, requiring general anesthesia. A rubber tube two-and-a-half feet long had to be inserted regularly for several weeks in an attempt to stretch the opening to forty-eight millimeters - the size of a normal throat. But each time my throat closed again. Finally, the physician prepared me for the worst.

"We might have to insert a tube in your throat to feed you for the rest of your life."

"Doctor, you can't say that," I said. "You gave me hope! I'd rather die than have this happen!"

I wouldn't be able to talk, and if I had a craving for a hamburger and fries, I'd have to tear them into little pieces and cram them down the tube without tasting a thing.

"Can you imagine me telling my girlfriend, 'Hey, kiss my tube?'" I asked the doctor.

"Harold, you're crazy," was all he could manage.

"I won't let you do that," I said. "That's no way for a person to live."

He mentioned the possibility of surgery to rebuild my throat using tissue from the colon. But after further consideration, he felt that this would not be successful because of the amount of scar tissue.

One alternative remained: stretching my throat daily myself. The first attempt was so painful it took one hour to insert the two-and-a-half-foot tube. But I eventually became so proficient that I could insert it twice in seven seconds. Surely that was a Guiness record! If anyone challenged me, I was prepared to better my time!

After being warned that I likely would lose my teeth as a result of the radiation, I resorted to the daily gum massaging that had worked so well in prison. Again my teeth were saved!

My taste buds returned gradually, but doctors said my saliva glands would probably never function again. And after thirteen years they haven't returned. I still insert a two-and-a-half-foot tube in my throat twice daily and have been doing so for thirteen years. I was forced to sip water constantly to alleviate the leather-like dryness of my throat . . . but I could live with that. One might say that when I spoke, it was an instant message - I just added water.

The cancer went into remission. All visible cancer cells were killed, but the doctors have advised me that the malignancy could recur, especially since the source was never found. While I lived with the reality that it could return, I didn't awake each morning and search for swelling or knots. I just thanked God for the day and lived it to the fullest. Every day was Christmas!

It is amazing what a brush with death will do for one's perspective. I have learned to appreciate the small things in life much more than before.

I didn't realize how precious my taste buds were until I couldn't taste. I didn't know how wonderful my eyes were until I blacked out and wondered if I would ever see again.

I was most thankful for my voice. At first thought, it seemed impossible that I could be grateful for my rubber tube, but then I realized that it enabled me to speak, swallow, eat, and lead a fairly normal life. There were additional benefits. The tube was very humbling. It kept my feet on the ground and enabled me to relate with hurting people. It was a daily reminder of how healthy I was, how blessed I was to be able to walk, see sunsets, breathe the sea air, and feel love. I would take that all for granted were it not for my tube. Today, I wouldn't trade it for anything in the world.

Through all of this, I have found that we must persevere, especially when we are suffering. By overcoming our weaknesses and trials, we can gain the strength necessary to lead a full and meaningful life.

Thirty-one

When I think of tough faith, I'm reminded of a young lady I met during the darkest hours of my life. One day during my radiation treatments at St. Joseph's Hospital, my doctor told me about a young twenty-eight-year-old woman named Linda O'Malley who had the same type of cancer I did. He said she was just starting her treatments and was feeling depressed.

"Would you mind speaking to her?" he asked. "She's in the waiting room."

When I first saw her, I was struck by her beauty. She weighed a petite 110 pounds, and her long brown hair curled atop her shoulders. Her eyes were bright and her smile warm.

After a moment of small talk I learned she was a flight attendant. "I'm told we have the same type of cancer," I said. "And since I've been at this a few weeks longer, I want you to know the treatment is a piece of cake. You can lick this thing." Wanting to cheer her up, I said, "I only have one thing to say. It says in the Bible that woman was made from man's rib. If this is so, then you are most definitely a prime rib."

She smiled but was too choked up to talk. I understood. When you're young, death isn't something you've thought a lot about. The prospect of dying before you've really lived can be terrible.

"If I can do anything for you please let me know," I said.

"Thank you."

When I came out after the treatment, Linda was gone. I looked for her on subsequent visits as well, but we never crossed paths. Finally, I asked the doctor about her. He said Linda had lost so much weight that treatments had to be stopped. She had gone to Birmingham, Alabama, to be with her parents. I understood, without the doctor having to say it, that Linda had gone home to die.

Two years later, shortly after the release of my first book, *Twice Pardoned*, I walked into a bookstore in Atlanta. During a conversation with the couple that owned the store, the woman said, "There's a young woman who comes in here, and her story is a lot like yours. She went to the same cancer center you did, but her cancer has come back and she's very depressed. She struggles with bitterness towards God!"

"I understand the feeling," I said. "Tell me more about her."

"Well, she says she's seen you before. She came in, picked up your book and said, 'I've seen that man before.'"

"What does she do?"

"Said she was a flight attendant."

Suddenly I remembered the girl I'd met in the St. Joseph's waiting room one day.

"Wait a minute. How old is she?" I asked.

"About thirty."

"Linda Somebody?"

"Linda O'Malley."

Linda was living in the apartment complex behind the bookstore. The couple gave me her phone number, and I left a message on the answering machine, reintroducing myself.

"I'd love to talk to you," I said. "Please call. It's important."

Linda called back and agreed, after some hesitancy, to let me take her to lunch. I was excited about our date, remembering how I was struck by her beauty the first time we met. When Linda opened the door, my anticipation turned to shock. She was so thin and had a scar like mine on the left side of her neck. Her hair was short, and she wore a sleeveless dress that hung on her frame like a pup tent. Her left shoulder was dark, like badly cooked steak.

Noticing my stares, she said, "I've started radiation again. The cancer came back to my shoulder. The dark spot is where they accidentally burned me with the radiation."

As we ate lunch we compared our experiences. We'd had the exact same cancer treatment. We'd both had lymph nodes removed, and both of us had our saliva glands burned away. Like me, Linda carried a glass of water wherever she went. The only difference was that her cancer had returned; mine remained in remission.

"Oh, there's one other difference," I said.

"And what's that?"

"My scar is prettier than yours!"

Linda tried to smile, but it had been so long since she laughed that the smile looked awkward. Then I got serious.

"I'm told you're struggling in your relationship with God."

She nodded and quietly said, "I've questioned why God would allow the cancer to come back."

We talked for a long time, and I was amazed how open we were, considering how little we knew each other. For the first time, I found myself telling someone my deepest fears, anxieties and gripes, because I knew Linda understood.

"The radiologist never told me what to expect," I said. "He just said the radiation would destroy my teeth, but I've yet to lose one."

Linda nodded knowingly.

"It bothered me that some of the nurses seemed so calloused," she said. "I had trouble sleeping, and one morning a nurse woke me up at four o'clock just to weigh me. Another told me, 'If the cancer doesn't kill you the chemotherapy will.'"

I told Linda about my throat problems, and how for weeks no one seemed willing to take my complaint seriously. She shook her head as my recitation brought back memories for her.

"I started spitting up blood last August," she said. "The doctor x-rayed me and found they'd fried the top of one of my lungs. They were treating my shoulder but went too low with the radiation."

I looked at her and felt intense empathy. Having suffered as much as she had, it was tragic that she should endure further pain because of a technician's error.

As I drove Linda back to her apartment after lunch, I asked about her future plans. She sighed heavily.

"It's been two-and-a-half years since I worked," she said. "I don't know what I'm going to do. I'll probably lose my apartment. My money's all gone."

I realized Linda needed more than just words of reassurance. I understood her situation, and I had recently been blessed with financial resources.

"Linda, don't worry about losing your apartment," I said. "I'll be over tomorrow to make the mortgage payment."

During the next few weeks we went out to eat frequently. She told me about how she was taking a sewing class and thought she could accept small sewing jobs to earn a little income, as soon as she could afford a sewing machine. The next day I bought her a deluxe sewing machine that she had picked out.

"You go ahead and sew," I told her. "It will be good therapy."

For the first time since we met, I saw her smile. The glow in her face was all the thanks I needed. I was just grateful that God allowed me to help her.

Our favorite restaurant was a little place Linda found called "Eat Those Vegetables". That became her frequent exhortation to me as I reverted to my old pattern of gorging myself. I quickly put on weight, but she encouraged me in a kind way to let the air out of my "spare tire" by improving my eating habits.

The restaurant had outstanding vegetable dishes, and we'd sit for hours, eating, drinking our water, and talking. "This is a five glass conversation," I joked to her one day. She quickly pointed out that she'd had more water than me, and we laughed to think we sounded like two kids vying for the upper hand.

On another occasion I told her, "I knew I was in trouble on my first visit to the doctor. He put his hand on my wallet and said, 'Okay, cough!' And after surgery the doctor came to see me and said, 'I have bad news for you. You only have one year to live.' I went to four other doctors, and they all said the same thing, so I figured I had five years to live! That same doctor came to see me another day. He said, 'You've been here one year, and I've noticed that you haven't paid your bill.' I said, 'I'm not going to pay it.' He said, 'Then I'm going to give you one more year.'" The more we joked about our illness the better we felt.

One of the hardest aspects of our illness was losing people whom we had considered close friends. Linda told me how she and her boyfriend had talked of marriage before she had cancer.

"He dropped me as soon as I got sick," she said. "Another guy was afraid our kids would be born with the disease, so he bailed out."

"The same thing happened to me," I said. "I haven't told anyone about it, but I was dating a woman and we'd talked about marriage. But then I got sick, and she changed. She actually asked whether my cancer was contagious and if I'd be able to father children. It was as if I'd become a leper to her."

The more we talked, the better I felt. Just discussing our shared experiences and feelings was extremely therapeutic. "You're helping me understand myself better," I told her.

It was encouraging to see Linda gradually regain her strength over the months. Color returned to her face, and she put on some weight. Before long, she began thinking she was healed. She talked about some long-range goals - to return to college and perhaps go into the missionary field. In the meantime, she decided to return to work with the airline.

In November of 1987, shortly before I left on a long trip, Linda called. She was just weeks away from going back to work with the airline. I expected her to sound excited. But her voice was hesitant, and I got a sinking feeling in my stomach. There was a silence on the other end of the line, and I thought she was crying.

"Linda, are you okay?"

"Harold, I need you," she said.

"What's wrong?"

"The doctor wants me to go to Chicago for some special tests."

"Oh, Linda. I'm sorry."

"I don't have money for the trip."

"I'll cover the expenses and the medical costs on one condition: that you call me as soon as you return. I want a full report."

A week later, she called. "The cancer has spread to my pelvis," she said.

She didn't need to say any more. We both knew what that meant. Within a short period of time her doctor discovered the tumor had spread to the stem of her brain and was growing bigger. It caused her double vision and incredible headaches, but the doctors told her that they couldn't operate and that additional radiation therapy would kill her. The only possibility, they said, was chemotherapy. But it would only provide temporary relief and would cause such intense sickness that she'd wish she was dead.

One night she called to ask my advice, but as gently as possible I told her that a decision about continuing a temporary treatment was one that only she could make. A few days later she called to say that she would decline the chemotherapy, because it would just postpone the inevitable. Then she announced that she was going to fly home to Colorado to be with her parents, who had recently moved there.

"They need me," she said quietly.

It was painful to realize how attached I'd grown to this godly woman. I didn't want to lose Linda, yet I knew that any day could be her last. That only reminded me of my own mortality. I had to constantly remember that tomorrow my cancer could also return.

I suppose it would be normal to want to retreat from a relationship like the one I had with Linda. Why should I open myself to more pain and suffering? Why should I love her if I'd only lose her? But that wasn't my perspective. No matter how painful, I would stand by her until the end.

Linda called me every day from Colorado. She was so sick, and it was obvious she was failing fast. One night she shared with me about this beautiful white horse.

"I would give anything if I were well enough to ride him," she said. "I love horses so much!"

"Ride him," I said. "I think it will do you good."

The next night she called. She was ecstatic!

"I rode that sucker!" she said. "I hurt all over, and I can hardly walk, but I rode him!"

It was so good to hear her laughter! Before she hung up the phone, she told me that she loved me. If only I had known then that that would be the last time I would hear her soft, sweet voice.

Three days later I received a phone call from a friend. He said that Linda was in the hospital in Atlanta and that she was in a coma. Linda awakened just long enough to talk to her family and plan her funeral. She requested that I speak at her funeral.

At her funeral, I shared that the Linda that I would always remember in my heart was not a person who was sick, but a person who was beautiful, joyful, loving, caring and giving. She was a person of hope who had tremendous faith.

Through knowing her I learned to reach out and help hurting people. And I am determined that as long as I live, I will love the Lindas that come into my life.

Thirty-two

During my illness a radio station with a nationwide listening audience made an announcement about my illness, asking people to pray for me. That produced an avalanche of mail - letters full of "get well" wishes and encouragement. Unfortunately, I was too sick to even read, much less answer, the majority of them.

One day when I was feeling more energetic than usual, I sorted through a pile of mail. My eye caught a pink envelope from a young woman in New Jersey. Inside was a warm and cordial message written in clear script on flowery stationery. The writer said she shared my burden for young people and that the radio program had made a big impact on her life.

"You've suffered more than anybody I know," she wrote. "You were in prison on false charges for nearly ten years, and now you are fighting for your life from cancer. I don't know what the future will bring, but I want you to know that I am praying for you. Harold Morris, you are my hero."

It was signed, Crystal Lavelle. I sensed that this woman, whoever she was, really cared, and in appreciation I managed to jot her a brief note of thanks. A few weeks later I received another encouraging letter from her, and again I sent a brief note in return. After several more letters, she wrote, "If you'll send me your picture, I'll send you mine."

I followed up on the request and waited expectantly for Crystal's next envelope. When it arrived the following week my heart raced with expectation. I knew nothing about her other than what I'd learned from her letters. She lived in New Jersey. She was twenty-eight years old. She loved young people. She prayed for me daily. Her relationship with God was the most important thing in her life. I did my best to read between the lines, and in my mind I pictured her as having long blond hair and blue eyes.

I held my breath as I slit open the envelope. Slowly, I pulled out the picture. I took one look, and instantly my eyes welled up with tears. I held the picture in front of me and cried as hard as I've ever cried. Crystal Lavelle was nothing like what I'd envisioned. She didn't have blond hair and blue eyes. She was not a full-grown woman with an all-American figure. She was sitting in a wheelchair, her body twisted by cerebral palsy. In an accompanying note, Crystal explained that she had been born with the disease and had spent virtually all of her life in institutions.

"My parents gave me up at birth," she wrote matter-of-factly.

I stared at her face, which bore the most joyful expression I'd ever seen. Her mouth was crooked, but her teeth gleamed. She seemed to be laughing through a smile that beamed from ear-to-ear. All I could think about were the lines from her first letter. She said I'd suffered more than anybody she'd ever known. She said I was her hero. But compared to her, I had never suffered.

As soon as I regained my composure, I wrote a note to her, "Please call me collect as soon as you get this letter."

Two days later, I was sitting in my living room contemplating my future. I had completed the radiation treatments and was trying to recover before my visit to the cancer specialist. I wondered if the cancer was gone. I wondered if I could ever speak again. I was practically broke and increasingly concerned about finding a way to earn some money. Suddenly the phone rang, and the operator asked if I would accept a collect call from Crystal Lavelle. I authorized the reversal of charges.

"Harol'? Harol', is that 'ou?" she shouted; her voice was fragile but loud. I battled my emotions as I listened to her struggle to enunciate each word.

"Yes, it's me," I said, and I thanked her for calling and told her how much her letters meant to me.

"Thank 'ou!" she practically squealed. "I pray for 'ou every day!"

Her voice was so cheerful, so positive. I had to learn more about her, but it was hard because she wanted to ask all the questions and her voice was difficult to understand.

Finally, I managed to tell her, "Crystal, you don't know how hard I cried when I saw your photo. Compared to you, I don't know what suffering is. You make me feel as if I've never been sick a day in my life. My prison was nothing compared to yours."

We continued writing on a regular basis, she with the help of an attendant named Donna, which explained the beautiful handwriting. We also talked often to each other by phone. Whenever I called, the attendant on duty would set the phone down and go find Crystal. Then I would hear, far off in the distant halls of the home, a guttural scream of excitement.

"Harol'!" she would yell, not quite able to mouth the final consonant. "Harol'!"

I pictured her racing through the halls in her electric wheelchair, trying to reach the phone as fast as possible. Our phone calls, I knew, were one of the highlights of her week. She talked with exclamation marks in her voice. The first thing she generally said was that she'd been praying for me. The last thing she said before we hung up was that she loved me. It took a while to piece together her life story.

"Crystal, do you go to church?" I asked.

"Sure I do! Harol'! I've written some songs! Would 'ou 'ike to hear them?"

"I'd like nothing more."

A few days later I received a cassette. As I played it I cried as she sang. I'd noticed that when she got very excited, it was hard to understand her. And as she sang, I tried to imagine how she strained her mouth and stretched her neck and body trying to express the love she felt so deeply in her heart.

I didn't know what her financial situation was, but since she was institutionalized, I figured she could probably use some help. So, I mailed her some money. She immediately called me, telling me not to send any more.

"Crystal, I want to give it to you," I told her. "You can do anything you want with it. It's yours."

"No, I can't take it!" she protested.

"Isn't there anything you'd like to buy?" I asked her.

She was quiet for a moment.

"It's not right for me to take it."

"Crystal, I want to send it to you. Are you going to rob me of that blessing?"

She said she would accept my gifts on one condition: " 'ou have to let me send 'ou gifts."

"Honey, the money is yours to do with as you want," I said with a chuckle.

"I will also tithe to my church," she announced.

Shortly thereafter, I received a small package in the mail. It contained a painting she'd done on a six-by-eight-inch piece of cardboard. The picture consisted of hundreds of lines of bright red, orange, yellow, green, and blue paint, and in the far right corner were her initials, CL. I don't know much about art, but I keep the painting on my desk and look at it every day. To me, it's more valuable than a Picasso, and I wouldn't trade it for any price.

As I got to know Crystal better, I learned that she had endured two operations that totally fused the vertebrae in her back, and she'd spent a year immobilized inside a body cast. Meanwhile, her parents had become wealthy through business. She told me that for years she was bitter towards them for having abandoned her in an institution, and that the bitterness grew to hatred by the time she was twenty-five. She also hated the world for giving up on her, for not loving her.

The hatred finally grew so intense she knew she had to do something. She even thought of taking her own life, but instead she rolled her wheelchair into a dark corner of her room and cried out for God's help. She told me the hatred was replaced with a new love and understanding for her parents.

Crystal spent six hours every day at "workshop". That was her job, and during those six hours she screwed nuts and bolts together. It was hard work for Crystal, and she was paid by the piece. All year she saved her nickels and dimes, pooling the money she earned to buy a plane ticket to visit her parents in California.

Through my assistance she was able to visit her parents on several occasions. I even paid an attendant at the institution to travel with her and look after her. For her the trips were well worth it - just to tell them she loved them.

I talked to her after she returned from one of those trips and asked how it went.

"It was okay," she said, without her typical enthusiasm.

"Did you do anything fun together?"

"We went shopping. But Harol' I couldn't wait to get back home to my friends. My parents don't understand me."

"I can imagine that you're a painful reminder to them," I said.

One day she told me that my love for families and young people touched her so deeply that she arranged to be transported to a near-by high school where she spoke to the entire student body about how I'd landed in prison because I hung around with the wrong crowd. She urged them to pick their friends carefully and to avoid drugs and immoral sex. Then she told them how even in our own prisons of a wheelchair and a state penitentiary, we were freer than most people.

"Harol', they gave me a standing ovation!" she said excitedly. "And they've asked me to come back and speak again!"

I was stunned. Here was a person with incredible physical limitations going out and speaking to kids. I couldn't help thinking of all the excuses I'd heard from others about why they didn't try to help others. But Crystal didn't know any excuses or acknowledge any limitations. She was an inspiration.

For two-and-a-half years, Crystal and I carried on our long distance correspondence and conversations. She was always there to encourage me when I felt down, to offer a kind word of hope, to ask me about my most recent speaking tour and how the audiences had responded, and to tell me that she loved me. Then one day she shared with me something very private.

"Harol', there's one thing I want that only 'ou can give."

"Crystal, there's nothing I would deny you. You've given me far more than I can ever give back."

"Harol', before I die, I want 'ou to come and spend a day with me in New Jersey."

"I promise you I'll come, and you'll be my date! We'll go to the park, and I'll take you shopping at the mall."

"Would you really do that, Harol'?"

"Crystal, I promise you I will. Not only that, but I'm going to push your wheelchair, and I'll grease up the wheels so they won't squeak. We're going to have ourselves some kind of fun!"

In the spring of 1987, I finally had the opportunity to fulfill my pledge. I flew to New Jersey, rented a car, and drove to the institution. I arrived two hours earlier than expected, but she'd been ready since the crack of dawn. When told she had a visitor, I heard her top-of-the-lungs scream from the back of the home.

"Harol'! Harol'!"

She came rolling around the corner in her motorized wheelchair, her face lit with a thousand-watt smile.

"Harol'!" she beamed.

I bent over, put my arms around Crystal's twisted little body, and for a long time we just stayed that way, holding each other and crying. Finally I stepped back to get a good look at her. She was wearing her best satin dress with a matching cream-colored ribbon braided through her hair. Around her neck was a beautiful gold crucifix hanging on a gold chain and in her ears were diamond earrings.

"My you are a beautiful woman," I said, and never had those words carried more meaning.

It was a vacation day for Crystal, so she didn't have to go to "workshop". We sat in the front room of the home and for two hours reminisced about our two-and-a-half years of letters and phone calls.

"Harol', I pray for you every day," she said.

"I know, Crystal. And God honors those prayers."

"Every day after lunch, I have one hour to pray. It's hard sometimes to keep that up because of the other things that I do, but it's the most important hour of my day."

There were several other residents in the room, and I noticed many were in pretty bad shape. Several of them eased their wheelchairs close to where we talked. One boy in particular kept looking at

Crystal with a twisted grin on his face. I found out his name was Ralph, and later I asked Crystal about him.

"Ralph's all right," she answered. "He used to be my boyfriend!"

One of the other residents heard that and added, "Ralph flirts with all the girls. He's got another girl now."

I shook my head in amazement. Even in this little world of twisted bodies and unimaginable affliction, there was a need for courtship.

Crystal asked if I'd noticed her earrings. I nodded.

"Are they real diamonds?" I asked.

"They sure are! I bought them with money 'ou gave me."

"They're beautiful."

"I like nice things!" she beamed. "Harol' thank 'ou for the money."

"Crystal, it's a joy to send it to you."

" 'ou know something? 'ou always send the right amount. 'ou always send just what I need. Always!"

At that moment, I felt a great satisfaction. How wonderful to know that Crystal could buy nice things and not worry about whether she could afford them. She had also asked me to send her two cases of my books. She gave them to everyone who visited the home.

As we talked, a large black woman with graying hair walked over and sat on the edge of an armchair. Crystal introduced her as Mary Sue, and said that she was in charge of the kitchen.

"Me and Crystal, we go back a long time," Mary Sue said, fingering a curl in Crystal's hair.

They looked at each other and smiled. In that glance was more love than I'd ever seen displayed in all my life.

Most people would not have given Mary Sue a second look. Her clothes were worn, and a lifetime of service was displayed in her tired feet. She was wearing a pair of inexpensive vinyl sandals that exposed a collection of bunions and calluses that covered her toes. Her feet themselves were broad and worn, and on them you could see the miles. And when she walked, she shuffled slowly. I knew every step was taken in pain.

I asked Mary Sue to tell me about her life. She said she was one of fifteen children and had lost her mother when she was young. So Mary Sue became the mother to seven of her younger brothers and sisters. Then came a bad marriage, the birth of a handicapped son, and a continuing life of non-stop work and sleepless nights. She supported her family and extended relatives by doing the same thing she did at home - caring for people. She'd served Crystal for twenty years, becoming the mother that Crystal never had, loving her day by day as she grew from a small child into an adult of thirty.

Mary Sue said she arrived at the institution early each morning and worked all day, preparing breakfast, lunch and dinner for fifteen handicapped residents, plus staff. Then in the evening, she returned home to prepare dinner for her grandchildren and severely handicapped son - a son whom she'd been loving and serving for forty years. I knew it was love that drove Mary Sue. She didn't do all that work for money, because there wasn't much financial payoff.

"Mary Sue, it would mean a great deal to me if you did not have to cook lunch today," I said. "I want lunch to be my treat. I'll go out and buy food for the entire home and all the workers."

"No, no, Mr. Morris. You will be our guest."

"Mary Sue, I insist. I want to buy lunch for everybody, to give you a break, and to-"

"No, I-"

I turned to Crystal.

"What's your favorite food in the whole world?"

Crystal leaned her head back to her shoulders and burst out laughing.

"Chinese! Chinese! Chinese!" she chortled.

"Can the other residents eat Chinese food?" I asked Mary Sue.

She nodded reluctantly.

"Then I'll be back in a half hour with enough food for an army. Is there anything else you want, Crystal?"

She leaned her head back again and laughed with excitement.

"Milk shake! Milk shake!"

I returned with a huge cardboard box filled with just about everything on the Chinese restaurant's menu. Waiting in the dining room were Crystal and most of the other residents seated around a sprawling formica table. They were in wheelchairs, and all of them were severely disabled.

Crystal's right hand was completely useless, and she could only move the two small fingers of her left hand. A fork was placed between those fingers so that she could eat. I couldn't help noticing that her feet, which had never taken a single step, were wrapped in thick socks of wool.

I looked at some of the others eating with her. Susan not only had cerebral palsy, but she was also blind. Her food was mixed into a large bowl, and an attendant put a fork in her hand and then moved the hand to the bowl. Brian looked to be about twenty-five and had a Stephen King paperback beside him. He wore a pair of binoculars around his neck. As he ate, he took short breaks to watch birds outside the window. Terry was in her sixties and talked a mile-a-minute during the entire meal. But I didn't understand a word she said. Joseph had a small body like Crystal, but his head was oversized. He told me that he'd read my book. Little Mary, with a urinary drainage bag strapped beside her on the wheelchair, wore most of her food on her blouse before lunch was over. It was a circus of excitement presided over by Mary Sue.

After the meal, I obtained clearance to take Crystal shopping at the mall. But there was one contingency - an attendant from the home also had to accompany us. Mary Sue agreed to go along, providing she was back in time to prepare dinner. I carried Crystal to the car, my hand braced against her knotted back. I gently set her in the seat and fastened the belt around her waist. After loading her wheelchair in the trunk, the three of us set off for the mall on what was a post-card perfect afternoon. We started in one of the large department stores.

"Pick any dress you want," I told Crystal as I wheeled her through the racks of the women's clothing department.

She giggled and rolled her head as we scavenged about for a petite size six. Dozens of dresses were held out for her and dismissed with a shake of the head and a few summary words: "Too blue." "Wrong neckline." "Not soft enough." "No thanks."

Then Mary Sue held up a shimmering sky blue dress, the bodice of which was covered with little spangles that glinted in the light. It was the type of dress a young woman might wear to a senior prom. Crystal rolled her head and screamed with excitement. Other shoppers turned and stared.

"She likes it," I said. "I'll buy you another," I told her, and she screamed again.

We found her a cotton-candy soft pink dress that had Crystal's name and Sunday morning written all over it. She would wear it to church.

As we headed to the cash register, I followed behind Mary Sue. I thought about how she'd stood faithfully by Crystal and probably hadn't bought anything for herself in years.

"We forgot something," I said.

Mary Sue turned around.

"I want you to pick out a dress, too," I told her.

She looked at me like I was crazy.

"No, Mr. Morris, I couldn't."

"You find yourself something pretty, Mary Sue."

"I wouldn't think of doing such a thing, Mr. Morris. You've already been so good to us all."

"Either you can pick it out, or I'll pick it for you. And if I pick it I can guarantee you'll be sorry," I said, draping my arm around her shoulder and gently nudging her back towards the racks.

Within ten minutes, she was trying to decide between two gorgeous dresses, both size twenty-two-and-a-half. She asked Crystal which one she liked best. I shook my head.

"They're both yours," I said, taking the dresses from her and heading for the cash register.

Five other women stood in line before me. When my turn came, the clerk took the four dresses and gave me a funny look.

"It was hard to find something in my size," I said, placing my hand on my hip. "But if I lose a few icky pounds, I think I can squeeze into them. Of course, they're not exactly my color. I'd wanted something more lavender."

The clerk rang up the purchase as fast as he could, without looking up, and the three of us laughed all the way out of the store.

Again I was walking behind Mary Sue. Her calloused feet looked like they hurt, and I knew she probably didn't have a comfortable pair of dress shoes in her closet. I also knew she couldn't afford to buy a pair for herself.

"One more stop," I said. "Mary Sue, let's find you a nice pair of shoes to go with your dresses. And a purse to match."

She stopped dead in her tracks and turned around in shock.

"Don't even bother protesting," I said. "It's something I want to do for you."

"But Mr. Morris-"

"Mary Sue, there's a store up ahead."

We stopped there and at two other stores, but nobody carried her size. Her feet were too broad and wouldn't fit into the narrow confines of a pair of pumps. We were running out of time, but there was one other shoe store in the mall. I waited several feet away as she approached the clerk and inquired if the store had her special size. As she talked, the woman looked her up and down and then glanced at another customer and rolled her eyes. Mary Sue was not the typical customer. She had no purse and no pockets, which in the woman's mind probably meant no money. Her clothes were wrinkled; her hair unkempt. She was black, and all of the other customers in the store were white.

"I'll be with you in a minute," the woman said and proceeded to help everybody else in the store first. We waited patiently until the store was empty. Finally the clerk turned back to Mary Sue, scowled at her feet, and then disappeared into the back room to check for her size. She returned a minute later with one box.

"It's all we have in your size," she said. "One pair of off-white pumps."

"That's what I need," Mary Sue said, easing herself slowly into one of the narrow chairs. The woman stood opposite her, again looking down at her feet.

"Do you have a pair of stockings or hosiery?" she asked.

Mary Sue shook her head.

"You'll need something on your feet before you try these on."

I watched from a distance, prepared to offer her the socks off my feet if the woman didn't come back with something herself. The clerk disappeared again into a back room and returned with two plastic trash bags, which she held out to Mary Sue.

"For your feet," she said gruffly.

Mary Sue shook the bags out and, without complaining, slipped them over her feet. The woman handed her one of the shoes. Mary Sue squeezed one foot in and then held her hand out for the other. Mary Sue put it on and stood up. She looked pitiful walking around in the trash bags and fancy shoes, and my heart broke knowing the humiliation I'd have felt if I was in her place. But if she was feeling anything, the only emotion that showed on her face was pure joy. The shoes fit, and her face beamed.

After purchasing the shoes and a purse to match, we finally headed for the car. No doubt about it, I was accompanied by two of the happiest women on earth. I also felt I was in the company of two of the holiest women as well.

Crystal had arranged for me to speak in her church that night. I was tired, my throat was sore, and I didn't feel like going. But I had promised Crystal that I'd speak on one basis: that she introduce me. I didn't know quite what to expect, because I'd never before been to a church service on a Friday night. It was the end of the week, and people would be tired. They'd drag home from work, eat, and land in front of the television. Or they'd grab some dinner and catch a movie. Maybe they'd read a good book or flip through a magazine.

I expected thirty or forty people, but when we pulled up to the church the parking lot was packed. A couple of hundred people were inside warming up with the help of three musicians playing piano, bass guitar, and drums. Before long, a bongo player joined in, and the church was rocking with music.

When I pushed Crystal through the door she was immediately surrounded by church members. People stopped their conversations and walked over to hug her. Others gave her little chicken-peck kisses on the cheek. One little girl had drawn a crayon picture on construction paper and gave that to her. Another little boy had made a ring for her out of aluminum foil. I knew instantly that this was a church that loved people. Though I was a thousand miles away from home, I felt surrounded by family.

When the service started at eight o'clock, Crystal was sitting in her wheelchair in the front row. The first few minutes were devoted to singing of praise and worship, which Crystal belted out at the top of her lungs. Looking at the joy in her face, I realized how important praise was to her. She couldn't read the Bible or comprehend complex sermon outlines. Her outlet for worship was singing and making a joyful noise.

After a brief welcome, the pastor turned the microphone over to Crystal to introduce me. She rolled her head back, and in a little sweet voice that you had to struggle to understand, she simply said, "I want to introduce 'ou to my friend Harol'. He loves me. Please listen to what he has to say."

I had tears in my eyes when I stepped up to speak, and I found it difficult to think about anything other than the day I'd just spent with two incredible women. So I did something unusual. I scrapped my planned talk and spoke instead about what I considered to be one of the most meaningful days of my life.

My message was a living illustration of faith and commitment - the faith of a young handicapped woman who supported an old ex-con through a serious illness, who prayed an hour a day, and who worked all year just to buy a ticket to visit the very people who abandoned her to an institution as a child. And I spoke about the commitment of an aging black lady who raised seven of her brothers and sisters, who supported an extended family when her husband deserted her, who cared for a handicapped son for forty years, and who worked all day in a hot kitchen to make life a little easier and a lot brighter for fifteen handicapped people.

"Today I saw more love displayed than I've ever seen before in my whole life," I said in closing. "It's the love of God lived out in very ordinary everyday ways by two individuals whom most people would dismiss with hardly a glance. I know there is a special corner in heaven waiting for them."

After I finished speaking there wasn't a dry eye in the church. It was well past midnight when I finally crawled into bed. I could think of no better way to have spent the night. I lay awake for a long time, thinking, remembering. As I finally drifted off to sleep, I thought about how one day I wanted to be greeted in heaven not by an angel, a choir, or a preacher wearing a clerical robe, but by a young woman in a blue-spangled dress, her body no longer twisted by the ravages of cerebral palsy. And right beside her would be a big-hearted black woman standing tall in a brand new dress and a pair of off-white pumps.

I continued to talk to Crystal frequently on the phone, and she constantly encouraged me in my faith. She didn't even realize how many people she was touching. One afternoon I called her from my motel before I was to speak to a large rally of some three thousand teenagers.

"Crystal, will you pray for me tonight?" I asked after I told her about the rally.

"Of course!"

"I'm going to tell them about you tonight, Crystal. Is there anything you want me to say?"

"Harol', tell them to stay out of trouble. Tell them to 'isten to 'ou. Tell them to 'isten to their parents. And tell them to put their faith in God."

"I will tell them," I promised.

That night as I brought my message to a close, I talked about peer pressure and the importance of following positive role models. And then I told them about one of my heroes, Crystal Lavelle.

As I finished my story, I said, "Young people, I talked to Crystal tonight, just before I came here. I asked her if there was anything she'd like to say. Can I tell you what she said?"

Perhaps it was my imagination, but it seemed like each of the kids leaned forward to catch the special words.

After I repeated her message, I challenged them: "Are you going to do that?"

It was a powerful evening all because of a thirty-year-old woman imprisoned in a twisted body who had tough faith. I'd heard some people say that if she really had faith she'd be healed - she'd jump up out of that wheelchair and walk. What they didn't realize was that faith was what kept her in that wheelchair day after day, year after year, with enough love for God to speak to an entire student body about her faith, enough love to fly to California to tell her parents she loved them, and enough love to pray daily for a friend who was told he would die of cancer. That's faith!

One night Crystal called me about eleven o'clock, which was unusual because she was normally in bed by nine. She told me she'd been out to a special church function and had just arrived home. But she wasn't the same cheerful person I normally talked to.

"Crystal, is something wrong?" I asked.

"Harol', I'm not doing well physically."

In the years since I'd first known her Crystal had never complained about her condition. I knew she had to be hurting bad to say even this.

"Crystal, there's something you're not telling me. What's wrong?"

"I'm just not doing well, Harol'."

There was no way I could get her to say any more about her problems. We had talked at times about how she believed that she would not always be in an institution.

"You know how much I love you Crystal, I'm so thankful you came into my life. You know my heart; I can take the wheelchair. I would give you my legs right now, if I could, so you could walk."

Crystal interrupted me, "Harol', I don't want 'our legs."

"But Crystal-"

"Harol', I am freer in this wheelchair than most people who have complete use of their bodies. I don't have 'egs, but I have loyal friends like you. And that's all I need."

That night I knew I'd witnessed genuine faith. Here was a woman who had never experienced the love of her parents, never climbed a tree or pedaled a bicycle, and never known the love of a man. But she knew how to love. Yes, Crystal had true faith that could move mountains, and she'd learned it through suffering.

It's been more than eleven years since that special day when I visited Crystal and Mary Sue. We kept in touch by phone and through letters, and I helped them financially through the years. Mary Sue, due to poor health, had to move back to her home state of Alabama so that one of her daughters could care for her. We kept in touch after she moved for a period of time, and then the phone was disconnected and my letters were returned. I've thought of her so many times and will never forget the impact she had on my life.

It's been fourteen years since I received Crystal's letter. We still talk on the phone, I still send her letters and gifts, and I have visited her numerous times. I remember her on her birthday and on special occasions, and I'm so thankful that she came into my life.

To me the measure of a person's life is not in its duration but in its donation. It's about caring, giving, and loving. I learned this great truth through battling terminal cancer and watching many loved ones suffer. Cancer changed me. It changed my perspective on life. When I was up against the wall fighting for my life, I discovered what was really important.

When I think about what is really important in our lives, I'm reminded of a story I heard about. There were two men sharing a hospital room. Both were extremely ill. One was confined to the bed 24 hours-a-day and was in traction and couldn't move.

The man closest to the window was allowed every afternoon to prop up on his elbow and look out the window. He would describe to the other gentleman what he saw - the beautiful trees and the beautiful lake. There were ducks and swans, and the little children fed them with breadcrumbs. There were softball games and picnics. There were little girls wearing their summer dresses. Lovers walked hand in hand in the park beneath the beautiful city skyline above the lake and the trees.

The man in traction couldn't understand this. He said, "Why does he get to see all of the beauty? Why do I have to suffer like this? It isn't fair. Why can't I look out the window?"

One night the gentleman next to the window began to cough. Later that night he died. The next morning they rolled his body away.

After a reasonable length of time the man in traction asked the nurse if he could be moved to the bed next to the window. She said yes and moved him. After the nurse left, very slowly and painfully he began to prop himself up on his elbow. He couldn't wait to look out that window. But when he looked, there was a blank wall staring at him.

I have known many people whose lives have faced a blank wall. William Russell Moore, Linda O'Malley, Mary Sue, and Crystal Lavelle are four of those people. Yet they somehow managed to convey hope and joy to those around them. They managed because their joy was not dependent on circumstance. Their joy was soul deep and seemed to radiate even when there was nothing to smile about.

Well, what have I learned through all of this? I have learned that victory comes through defeat, healing through brokenness, and that you can only truly find yourself through losing yourself.

Through all of this suffering I have also learned this: we are all born in darkness, and it's up to each of us as individuals to turn on the light - just as Crystal did. She was freer, despite her physical handicap, than I ever was when I received my parole. Her example was further motivation for me to go back to Georgia State Penitentiary to fulfill a dream.

Thirty-three

One sultry day in the summer of 1997, I was returning home to Atlanta after vacationing in Florida. As I came through Savannah, Georgia, something kept pulling me to go by my old prison seventy-five miles away.

A massive renovation program had brought many changes to the prison. I parked near the building that used to house death row and looked up at the window in the cell where I spent six lonely months.

The broiling summer sun glinted off rows of chain link fences topped with barbed wire and blanketed with coils of razor wire. It was a menacing barrier - seemingly capable of tearing and slicing anyone who even dared to look at it. And for good reason, because behind it rose an imposing cement structure, home to one thousand of the world's most violent men: murderers, robbers, and rapists with spine chilling nicknames such as Phantom, Shotgun Kelly, Big Mac, Scar Face, Big Money, Mad Dog, Monkey Man, Lug Wrench, Double Ug, and Hog Barn Shorty.

Six towers, each manned by a rifle-toting guard, loomed above this fortress otherwise known as Georgia State Penitentiary. Occasionally an inmate would challenge the odds and attempt an escape. If the fence didn't stop him, the ever-vigilant patrols would pump him full of lead. For a fleeting moment as I stood in the shadows of the prison, I thought of the many inmates who had caught a bullet while trying to vault the fence on a rainy Georgia night.

For those very few who might through some ingenious plan or incredible happenstance penetrate these initial lines of defense, the surrounding countryside formed another barrier. In three directions lay ten thousand acres of farmland that produced food for most of Georgia's prison population. The fields provided easy hunting grounds for posses and thin bloodhounds. The only other escape route was into a serene-looking forest that hid a swamp populated by man-eating mosquitoes, snakes and alligators. Men who entered that jungle inevitably surrendered - willing to return to prison after two or three miserable days experiencing the worst Mother Nature had to offer.

As I surveyed the knife-like fencing before me and the pastoral scenery behind me, memories of my years on the wrong side of life flooded my mind. Despite the unbearably hot and muggy weather, I shivered as I recalled my first view of this setting. Shackled in handcuffs and leg irons, I was transferred to Georgia State Penitentiary in 1969. As I stood at the gate a guard instructed me to take one final look over my shoulder.

"Double elbows? You can forget about it," he snarled. "They're gonna carry you outta here in a pine box!"

Against all odds, I walked through the gate to freedom nine years later. So why was I now drawn back to this desolate prison? Certainly not to admire the picturesque landscape. And definitely not for a slug of nostalgia, because this had been the scene of innumerable nightmares. Here a man had beaten me over the head until I nearly died. Here I'd seen men die by murder and suicide, their bodies carted past my cell.

But this was a different prison from the one I'd suffered in all those years. Since my release it had been totally refurbished to the tune of 60 million dollars. The renovation was certainly overdue. Originally built for 750 men, the prison population had swelled to 3,200 by the time of my release. I'd seen as many as seventeen men crammed inside an eight-foot by ten-foot cell. Violence and murder were a way of life. Drugs flowed like water into the institution. Riots were ignited over real and perceived injustices. Racial tension was always present and hung in the air like summer humidity. Health and cleanliness were virtually impossible due to the filth of plugged up toilets and the disease-carrying insects and rodents that freely roamed every inch of the prison. Simply put, the penitentiary was a place you wouldn't want a dog to live, if you cared about dogs.

During the reform era the government spent millions of dollars to upgrade the main building, construct individual cells, improve medical facilities, and install surveillance cameras. Most of the inmates had been shipped to other prisons. Of the approximately 36,000 men imprisoned in Georgia, only the one thousand most dangerous criminals were still housed at Georgia State Penitentiary.

With all of the changes complete it was still an awful place. After several requests, the warden finally permitted me to again visit the men in their cells.

Stepping through the doors of the prison vestibule, I stated my intended business to a uniformed woman, who was shielded from me by an inch-thick pane of bulletproof glass. Without a twitch of a smile, the guard took my driver's license and phoned the main office. She nodded curtly, then punched the button to release an electronically-controlled steel door. I passed through a narrow walkway lined with ever-present razor wire and entered the main prison building - a giant block of concrete that had withstood the elements and untold coats of paint since its construction in 1936. It looked like a low budget city hall, minus the manicured lawn and statues.

Inside the rotunda, I asked for a cup of water to soothe my throat, which was dry because cancer killing radiation treatments had also burned away my saliva glands.

"Super Honky!" one of the guards suddenly yelled. "How are you doing?"

It had been years since I'd heard that nickname, bestowed by black inmates because of my athletic prowess.

"You haven't changed a bit," the guard said as he stood there smiling.

"Got better looking," I responded.

The guard laughed, took my pass, and stamped my wrist with a light sensitive ink. He then had me step through a metal detector. Next, he summoned the deputy warden, Darren Fields, who welcomed me to the institution and offered to give me a tour before I visited the inmates in their cells. I accepted the invitation and followed him through a thick steel door which slammed on our heels. The clang of metal on metal sounded like the collision of two diesel train engines and reverberated in my head even after the noise had died in the cement hallway.

The other sounds of prison were equally harsh. There was constant yelling and swearing, rattling of cell doors, and the clanging of utensils and pots in the mess hall. And then there were the bells. As they rang, I recalled how they had ruled my life for so many years. They woke us up, called us to meals, and ordered lights out. Every two hours the bell blasted to signal the time for inmates to be counted and then sounded again when the guards had accounted for all the men.

There were more clanging doors to pass through, and with each it seemed like I was descending deeper into the infernal regions. A repulsive odor, worse than a crowded locker room after a big game, invaded my nostrils. I'd forgotten how bad a prison could smell. In the free world, people bathe daily, use deodorant, wash sheets and clothes, and flush toilets. When I was in prison, most inmates seldom used deodorant, rarely bathed, changed sheets and underwear once a week, if that, and intentionally plugged up toilets for entertainment.

I was also struck by the absence of color. I'd forgotten how plain my world had been without bright shades of red, blue, orange, and purple. The prison walls were painted drab green to cover previous coats of drab brown, drab yellow, and drab ivory. The concrete floors were unpainted, and not even the government's millions of dollars in renovations could correct the depressing sight.

My first tour stop was the morgue. At one end of the room, rising off the floor like an altar, stood a large stainless steel table upon which autopsies were performed. As I surveyed the room and its bright lights and cadaver drawers, I thought back to my first year in the penitentiary. I'd been assigned to clerk for the doctor, and one day I reported for work to the morgue. There I saw a black man stretched out on a table with his arms raised in the air.

"What you doin'?" I asked. "Taking five?"

It seemed like a strange place to nap, but then there weren't many quiet spots where a man could catch a few minutes of peace. When the man didn't answer, I asked what was wrong with his arm. Again he didn't respond, so I repeated the question. When he still didn't speak, I turned to the guard by the door.

"What's with this guy? He doesn't want to talk."

"By God, I guess he doesn't!" the guard said with a laugh. "He was stabbed all to pieces."

I thought he was joking. But when I stepped around the table, I saw the man's guts were lying in front of him, his knee was sliced up, and the muscles had been cut out of his arm. Evidently he'd thrown up his arm to defend himself against attack, and rigor mortis had frozen his body in this pose of death. It was my job to take pictures of the body and measure the wounds for the doctor, who in turn wrote up a formal report. I counted fourteen stab wounds in his chest, any one of which, the doctor told me, could have killed him.

I was told that after I saw a few bodies I would become callous. Maybe death didn't bother most inmates because it was so "everyday" and because life had little value in prison. But I never became desensitized to such butchery. Even all these years later, I couldn't rid my mind of the men whose bloody corpses had lain on that shiny table.

The next step was death row, where I'd spent six of the worst months of my life. As we walked down the dimly lit corridor, I could still hear the words of Sly growling in the cell beside mine, "Hey, next door. When I get out of this cell I'm going to kill you!" That was my welcome.

I stepped into a little holding room beside the electric chair where condemned men had spent their final minutes on earth. I looked up at a small bar-covered window cut high in the wall, through which inmates got their last look at the sky before they were executed. Some unexplainable emotion gripped me, and I felt tears cloud my eyes. A total of 484 men had stood in this same spot, looking up for their last view of the world, and most of them died without any hope.

That's what bothered me. And that's what drew me back to the penitentiary. Just a few cells away, in 1973, I'd lived here without hope.

As the deputy continued the tour, I wondered how I would be received by the inmates after so many years. Many of my old buddies had gone, either paroled or transferred. Many were no doubt dead. A few might recognize me, but that didn't mean I would be welcomed. Inmates had a strong "us versus them" mentality, and I was now a "them". I represented something they might never attain and preferred not to talk about - freedom. Once you'd been released, it didn't take them long to forget you. Misery loves company, and I was guilty of having deserted their world. I'd become an outsider. I could visit; they had to live here.

On March 14, 1978, I left Georgia State Penitentiary on parole. Three years later the governor of Georgia and the pardon and paroles board issued me a commutation, taking me off all supervision. The crime was never to be used against me again, and my rights as a citizen of the United States were restored. Nevertheless, no one could take the prison out of Harold Morris.

The undeniable fact was that this penitentiary remained part of my everyday life. It affected the way I talked, the way I hurt, the way I loved. I'd seen men bleed from the inside out because no one cared for them. Knowing they were desperate for love, and remembering the years when no one loved me, I often went overboard to express my love for people. It also affected how I dealt with perceived injustice. Instinctively, I could back someone into a corner if I believed I was right. Sometimes I forced people to face unpleasant facts that they did not want to face.

The deputy interrupted my thoughts by asking me if I remembered Muscle Jaw. I stopped and looked at him funny.

"Sure," I answered. "He was one of the meanest cons I ever knew. I was told he was killed in an escape attempt."

"Shot, but not killed," he said. "He survived and is still here."

I stopped in my tracks. "Then I'd like to see him," I said.

The guard shook his head. "That may not be possible. Nobody has to tell you about ol' Muscle Jaw. He's the most dangerous man here, and anything could set him off. He'll never get out of prison. He'll die here."

As we resumed our walk, I couldn't help thinking about the fear Muscle Jaw instilled in inmates and guards alike while I was in prison. He hated whites, and he'd attack them at any time, without reason. And of course, I knew that he had avenged Doc's stabbing. He had

State Board of Pardons and Paroles
ATLANTA, GEORGIA

ORDER OF RESTORATION OF
CIVIL AND POLITICAL RIGHTS
COMMUTATION

WHEREAS, _____Donald Harold Morris_____ , Serial Number __D-7739__
was convicted in the court(s) indicated below the following offense(s) for which he received the sentence(s)
hereinafter set forth:

OFFENSE	COURT OF CONVICTION	DATE SENTENCE BEGAN	SENTENCE
Murder	Fulton Superior	6-18-70	Life
Robbery			Life concurrent (c/f 3-3-70)
			Parold 3-14-78

and,

WHEREAS, an application for restoration of civil and political rights has been filed by the above
named individual; and

WHEREAS, it further appearing from proof satisfactory to this Board that said applicant has been
fully rehabilitated and is now a law abiding individual, now,

THEREFORE, in compliance with the constitutional and statutory authority vested in this Board to
remove disabilities imposed by law, it is hereby

ORDERED that time remaining to be served on the sentence(s) described above, if any, is hereby
commuted to present service, and it is

ORDERED that all disabilities resulting from the above stated sentence(s) and any prior thereto, be
and the same are hereby removed; and

ORDERED FURTHER that all civil and political rights lost as a result of the above stated offense(s)
and any prior thereto, be and the same are hereby restored.

It is directed that copies of this order be furnished to the said applicant and to the Clerk(s) of the
Superior Court(s) in the County(s) where the above sentence(s) were imposed.

GIVEN UNDER THE HAND AND SEAL of the State Board of Pardons and Paroles, this __17th__
day of _____April____ , 19 81

STATE BOARD OF PARDONS AND PAROLES

(SEAL)
dsm

JAMES T. MORRIS, CHAIRMAN
J. O. PARTAIN, JR., MEMBER
MRS. MAMIE B. REESE, MEMBER
FLOYD BUSBEE, MEMBER
MOBLEY HOWELL, MEMBER

FOR THE BOARD:

D. S. Moore

killed Railroad and Latcheye.

"How about letting me see Muscle Jaw, even for just a few minutes?" I asked again.

"We can't let him out of the cell," the deputy said. "He'll kill somebody or start a race riot. All the inmates, even the guards, are scared of him. He might attack you."

. It sounded as if nothing had changed. He was a man who'd find a way to kill with his fist, a board, a spoon, possibly even a Q-tip, without batting an eye. I'd met many killers in prison. Deep inside, most of them had cowardly personalities. You could go to sleep at night with them around and not worry too much. But Muscle Jaw was pure killer, and you didn't dare close your eyes when he was awake.

"You don't have to let him out," I said. "Just let me talk to him through his cell door."

"I don't know. I think it would be better if you didn't."

"It's very important," I persisted.

"I'll check with the warden," he said, stepping by one of the guard stations to use the phone.

As I waited, I wondered about my persistence. Why should I force myself to see a man no one cared about? Who would criticize me for letting this opportunity pass? It seemed like I was constantly putting myself in the toughest situations. However, for some reason, I felt compelled to visit Muscle Jaw.

When the deputy returned, he looked serious.

"It's cleared," he said. "Let's go see Muscle Jaw."

Security surrounding Muscle Jaw was tight. We passed through several doors on our way to his cell, which was monitored around the clock. The cell was no bigger than a walk-in closet, and the sink and commode took up most of the space. He was standing inside with his back to me as I approached. The deputy hung back to give us some privacy. I took a gulp of water, mouthed a quiet prayer, and then said, "Muscle Jaw?"

He turned around, revealing a hard, wrinkled face that reminded me of a rabid dog. He was a stout six-foot-one with a scarred complexion. He had a long scar across his muscular face and on the side of his neck. It was obvious someone had tried to cut his throat. His real scars, I knew, were beneath his shirt, and he had a significant collection. He'd occasionally taken a knife in the gut, but he'd always come out of fights on top. Even when he looked bad after a brutal attack, the other guy always looked worse.

During my years inside the penitentiary, no one frightened me more than Muscle Jaw. And now, his canine-like face resurrected that feeling of dread.

"Muscle Jaw, how are you?" I ventured, trying to keep my voice even.

He eyeballed me for a long moment before a look of recognition crossed his face.

"Super Honky," he said, slowly. "Super Honky."

His voice sounded like it had been dredged up from his stomach.

"I was just visiting, and I found out you were here. I begged the warden to let me come see you."

"You came back."

I tried to read his inner thoughts. Muscle Jaw had ice water in his veins, and fifty of the most dangerous men in the world could not scare him. This man couldn't be reasoned with, shouted down, or bullied. His eyes seemed to glow and looked right through me. I recalled how those eyes always glowed just before he plunged off the deep end.

Standing outside Muscle Jaw's cell, I hoped he would not remember our old disagreements. I tried to keep the conversation upbeat by talking about his life and how others perceived him.

"I was surprised you were around. I thought you were finished after being shot."

"They knock me down, but they can't knock me off," he said with pride.

"The warden says he's afraid to let you out into the population."

"They got me locked up on a bum rap," he growled. "They think I'm gonna kill somebody, but I only kill somebody when I got to. But people, they misunderstand me. Honky, you know I never killed nobody who didn't deserve it."

I nodded sympathetically but felt at a loss for what to say.

"Muscle Jaw, how old are you?" I finally asked.

"Sixty-four."

"That so? Muscle Jaw, I know you've been here a long time, but how long's it been exactly?"

"Forty-two long ones."

"That's a lifetime."

"I'm on my last leg, Harold. The last leg."

I told him I knew the feeling. "Two years ago I found out I had cancer," I said, showing him the scar on my neck. "They cut out my lymph nodes and have operated numerous times on my throat. I've been blasted with so much radiation that I've lost all of my saliva glands, and that's what this water is all about. I have to drink it all the time."

"So you're on your last leg, too?" he asked.

"They say they got it all, but I never know when it might come back."

"You sure look good," he said.

"You know, Muscle Jaw, there are three stages to life. There's the youth stage, middle age stage, and the 'you sure look good' stage."

He laughed and shook his head. "Everything changes. Ain't the same anymore - not like when you was here."

"How's that?"

"They's a different breed of con today. Ain't like our day. They's younger. They's drug heads. Nobody gives you no respect no more. Integration didn't work. There's more hatred and racial tension here today that there has ever been. You and Doc didn't make any difference in this place."

I knew Muscle Jaw was referring to the prestige certain inmates received for their crimes. Murderers and armed robbers got the most respect in the prison hierarchy. Child molesters were on the very bottom rung. In between, men generated varying levels of respect based on their crime, sentence, and ability to defend themselves. But things were changing; many of the young inmates were not willing to abide automatically by the unwritten convict code. I also knew that Muscle Jaw, despite what he said, got plenty of respect. At age sixty-four, he instilled fear in men forty years his junior.

I realized we didn't have much time, and I couldn't leave without addressing the heavy burden I felt.

"Muscle Jaw, there is something I want to tell you," I said, looking him square in the eye.

"Yeah, what's that?"

For once I wished the bars did not separate us.

"Muscle Jaw, I've got to apologize for being afraid of you. I was always afraid of you in prison, and I could never let you know my true feelings. But let me tell you, Muscle Jaw, you can spit on me, you can hit me, you can do anything you want to, but I've come today to tell you that I love you. And please know that Doc's sacrifice wasn't meaningless. It's because of his courage that I can come here today and say I love you. I'm so thankful he came into my life and for the impact he's had on my life. I won't ever forget him."

There was a tenderness I'd never heard in his normally sludge-thick voice. When he reached through the bars and grabbed my arms tears were streaming down his face. All these years he'd been killing people without blinking; now Muscle Jaw was crying!

"Thank you! Thank you for coming. I'll never forget this day," he said.

He squeezed me again through the bars, and I could feel a desperation in his grip. He didn't want to let go.

"Is there anything I can do for you?" I asked.

The ice seemed to melt from his eyes, and for the first time I realized that Muscle Jaw knew fear.

"I'm on my last leg, Harold," he repeated. "Before it's all over, I want to smell the roses again. I don't have nobody, no family, nobody to sponsor me. Ain't no way they'll parole me without no sponsor or no plan. But I want to smell the roses, Harold. Just like you. You understand, don't you?"

"I understand Muscle Jaw," I said solemnly.

He was dying. He needed help. He wanted somebody to care.

"Harold, please don't let me die here. All I'm asking is that they give me a proper burial. Don't let 'em bury me in Pissant Hill."

"Muscle Jaw, I promise I won't," I said. "Don't you worry about that."

Muscle Jaw wiped away a tear with the back of his hand and

looked at me with a crooked smile, "Super Honky, you came back. You remembered us."

"Yes, Muscle Jaw. I remember."

"I see something about you is different. You've changed. Me, nothin' changes. Day after day, until I die. But I want to thank you for coming back, Harold. I want to thank you for not forgetting us."

I told him I would write him and send him some reading material and some money. And I assured him I'd return again. Then I turned and walked slowly down the hall, back through the twelve doors that kept Muscle Jaw isolated from the world.

My mind was a blur for the next few days. The whole experience seemed incredible. But somehow Muscle Jaw seemed too hardened, too violent, too set in his ways to respond to love and caring. Never in my wildest imagination could I have anticipated such a response.

Three days after my visit, I received a letter from Muscle Jaw. "I thought about you all night," he wrote. "The minute I saw you I knew you was different. You wasn't the same Harold Morris. I'm sorry you got cancer. I'm on the last leg of my life, Harold, and I pray that one day I get to smell the roses before I die. Like you. I want to also grow a garden and live in a house." He thanked me again for visiting him. Then he closed with these words, "Harold, you're the only one that's ever told me that you love me."

I put Muscle Jaw's letter down and cried. They were tears of joy and sadness. For decades, he'd suffered in a prison of his own making. I knew what that was like; the same thing had happened to me. If it hadn't been for family and friends visiting me and sharing love with me, who knows how many more years I might have languished in a cell?

What would it take for Muscle Jaw to break from his violent anger? He had spent two-thirds of his life in prison. He'd known nothing but violence and hatred and might never leave the confines of Georgia State Penitentiary.

Nevertheless, Muscle Jaw could change - by learning to love. Love is the key that can open any prison - the physical penitentiary as well as the private cells that bind much of society. For Muscle Jaw, the bars and razor wire were visible reminders of his incarceration. But people all around me are just as trapped by their past or present hurts. And without love, their futures are equally bleak.

As I left the penitentiary that day, I made arrangements with the prison authorities to assure that Muscle Jaw would never be buried in Pissant Hill.

Thirty-four

The rain slammed down with a fierceness I had rarely seen as I walked towards the prison graveyard, named Pissant Hill by the prison inmates. If an inmate's body is not claimed within twenty-four hours after death, he is buried in the prison graveyard in a wooden coffin built in the prison carpentry shop. Inmates on work detail dig the grave, and the prison chaplain offers the final words. A small numbered cross marks the grave.

I came to a special marker. Suddenly a memory surfaced, and I was surprised both by its poignancy and by the fact that I had forgotten it. Suddenly I was back in prison. The year was 1972, and I was helping with the burial of an inmate friend.

My heart was heavy as I thought aloud, "He doesn't even have a tombstone; he's just a number."

"That's all you are, a number! A bunch of animals!" snapped the guard. "You're not even a citizen of the United States. Society doesn't care. Your own family doesn't care. Nobody cares!"

Boiling rage inside drove me to action. The men who died here would have a memorial. Several of us made arrangements through the chaplain's office to purchase a marker, and other inmates helped me collect money. The inscription was carefully worded:

"Georgia State Penitentiary cemetery. The first burial was on December 20, 1937. The state provides a Christian burial for all deceased inmates for whom private or family burial arrangements are not available. The Savior said, 'Come unto me, and I will give you rest.' These men lie here in peaceful anonymity. Ezekiel 18:22 reads, 'None of the transgressions which he has committed shall be remembered against him. Because of the righteousness which he has done, he shall live.' This memorial marker was provided by inmates July, 1, 1972."

Grief flooded my spirit as I read the inscription. Most of the inmates buried here suffered violent deaths. Did they have a Christian burial and lie in peaceful anonymity? It was a comforting thought, but it was a farce.

As sheets of rain poured from above, I wept for these poor souls in the prison graveyard who never experienced the true meaning of love.

Shouldn't society care? Shouldn't people care about these unwanted and unloved men?

Everywhere we look we can see people locked inside their private prisons: a girl trapped by cerebral palsy; young people driven by peer pressure to have illicit sex because they so desperately want love; a man caught in alcohol addiction; a woman forced to endure an unwanted divorce. Peer pressure, poverty, broken families, drugs, illness, and loneliness - these prisons are every bit as real as the cells that once confined 3,200 men inside Georgia State Penitentiary. Our reason for living should be to try to free as many of society's inmates as possible.

At the time of my arrest, I was bent on self-destruction, and there is no doubt that, had I continued in that direction, I would have become a drug addict and an alcoholic. Ultimately, mine would have been a life of crime. I'm convinced that if I had not been arrested, I would have fallen to such a low point physically and mentally that I could not have overcome my problems. I might have even killed somebody.

But it took those years in prison - living with the most powerless people in society - to realize there was more to life than what I had.

Prison. It is forever a part of me, for in that decade, I lived a lifetime.

I've relived that experience a million times. The anger. The hatred. The racism. The terror. The utter hopelessness.

To lose everything, to be reduced in life to nothing, to be among the most powerless people on earth, then suddenly to be given everything! The anger, the rage and hatred being replaced with love for those who hurt, and hopelessness being replaced with hope.

But the underlying factor, the one that drove me back to Georgia State Penitentiary, was the fact that God had reached through the bars of a filthy, roach-infested cell in this very prison and touched my life. And He used a man called Marcus "Doc" Odomes, who helped me become free not only from my physical prison, but from the shackles of sin and despair. He shared love with me when I had no one else, stood with me when I needed a friend, taught me about faith and prejudice. And finally, he was willing to give his life that I might live. His life challenged mine. I shall never forget him. He will forever live in my memory.

As I slowly walked to Pissant Hill, my face was solemn. The tears streamed down my cheeks, and my heart was filled with sadness but at the same time joy. As I stood at Pissant Hill in the driving rain, I said, "You were right, Doc. I'm unshackled. I'm free. Freer than I've ever been in my life."

PART VII
THE LAW OF THE HARVEST

HAROLD MORRIS SPEAKS TO PARENTS AND TEENS ABOUT THE LAW OF THE HARVEST

The Law of the Harvest

There is a law that God has written into the physical universe and the spiritual universe, and this is the law: you always reap what you sow in life. If I want to pick tomatoes three months from now, then I have to plant tomatoes. I can't plant something else and expect to get tomatoes. That's the law of the harvest.

The law of the harvest says this: you reap what you sow, you reap later than you sow, but you always reap more than you sow. By planting a tiny acorn you can grow a mighty oak. Now, the law of the harvest applies to the spiritual universe as well as the physical universe. If you plant one evil seed, you will reap evil a thousand-fold in return. And if you plant one good seed, you will reap good a thousand-fold in return. But you always reap what you sow.

You can't sow disrespect, hatred, ignorance, dishonesty, and racism, and expect to reap honor, love, wisdom, truth, and understanding.

Young people, I don't know what kind of life you want, but whatever kind of life you want, pick it out right now. You see, every day you can sow good or evil in your life. You have to choose. And if you are not careful, some of the things you choose to do today can cause you a terrible heartache tomorrow.

I am a perfect example of this. What did I sow into my life? I associated with the wrong kinds of people, I drank, I did drugs, I had immoral sex, and I was proud to call myself a racist. What did I reap? Two life sentences at Georgia State Penitentiary for armed robbery and murder. And I almost died there.

Growing up in South Carolina, I was an all-state athlete in high school. I captained the football team, the basketball team, and the baseball team. I had numerous scholarship offers, but I couldn't accept them because of my poor grades. So I said, "I'm not going to college. I'm going to drink beer, chase girls - that's the life." I began to go to nightclubs, and in there I consorted with all of the worst kinds of people: prostitutes, drug pushers, drug addicts, ex-convicts - you name it, they were there. And, young people, it took me one year to destroy my life. One year.

I met two men in a nightclub. I envied their fancy clothes and free-spending ways. It seemed to me that they lived life in the fast lane, and I wanted to be a part of that so I became friends with them. We decided to go to Atlanta, Georgia - where I now live - to party, to smoke dope, and have fun. We hit all the night scenes for one week. We checked out of the motel to go back to North Carolina, but before we left my friends wanted to go by and visit these girls that we had met. So, we drove to their apartment complex, but the girls weren't there. My two friends left my car and went a block and a half down the street and decided to rob a supermarket.

They pulled guns on twelve people and told the manager to open the safe. He was getting ready to do that when an innocent bystander pulled a pistol out of his belt to shoot them - to become a hero. But one of them shot him first. And they ran back to where I was, a block and a half away, and they said, "Drive! Drive! We've shot a man!"

The worst mistake I've ever made in my life was driving them back to North Carolina. En route, I asked them what happened, and they told me.

I asked, "Well, did you kill the man?"

They said, "No, he was standing when we left. We're sure he'll be all right."

When they got out of my car, I didn't see them again for one year. In the meanwhile, I was arrested by the F.B.I. They charged me with armed robbery and murder. I learned that the man who'd been shot had died five minutes later.

I was driven back to Atlanta where I went on trial for my life. The district attorney promised he'd see me fry in the electric chair. You see, the district attorney had cut a deal with my two so-called friends, and they agreed to testify against me. They came into that courtroom and took the witness stand and told the jury that I had masterminded the whole crime. After my conviction, they were set free. I was given two life sentences but spared the electric chair.

Lying in a lonely prison cell at Georgia State Penitentiary, I reflected on the events that had led me to such a horrible place. And I cried that night as I thought of my wasted life.

It became clear to me that my problems really began at an early age. In retrospect, I saw that I had always run with the wrong kinds of people, and this had led to an immoral lifestyle fueled by drinking and, later, drugs. My life had been going downhill for a long time, and it wasn't hard to see how each choice I made in life had led me further and further down until I finally hit bottom - Georgia State Penitentiary.

Through that long night of relived memories, I came to understand the law of the harvest, even though I did not call it that then. Although I had been wrongly convicted, I realized that I had put myself behind bars.

I made it out of Georgia State Penitentiary after more than nine years, but the next person I would like to tell you about did not. His story also illustrates the importance of making the right choices in life. Randy Adams died young, but he still lives in my memory and I will never forget him.

On Christmas Day 1974, I promised all the inmates that if I were ever released I would return one day to give everybody there a real Christmas! I never forgot that pledge. Eight years and nine months after my release, along with eighteen of my loyal friends, I returned to Georgia State Penitentiary to fulfill my promise. We had over twenty-five thousand dollars worth of gifts with us - a gift for every inmate in the prison.

At 8:00 p.m., after all the gifts were handed out, my friends gathered in the prison rotunda before departing. As we were about to load up the vans, one of my friends handed me a note that an inmate had slipped to him earlier in the day. The name on it nearly took my breath away: Randy Adams. I hadn't seen him in sixteen years.

I went straight to the warden and said, "Everybody's got to wait. I must go back and see this man."

A deputy warden escorted me back to the prison block.

"You know how old Randy was when I first met him?" I asked. "Fourteen. I was in the county jail, and they put him in there with all the murderers, thieves, rapists and drug addicts. I tried to protect him."

"He's in pretty bad shape," the deputy warden said.

Finally, at the end of the long hallway, the deputy warden stopped and unlocked a cell door. Inside was a man who looked weathered. He took a good look at me and then hobbled over and threw his arms around my neck.

"I knew it was you!" he said in a voice choked with emotion. "I just knew it was you! If you only knew how many times I've thought of you and wondered what happened to you. After all these years . . ." he said, his voice trailing off.

"Randy Adams," I said, holding him at arm's length. "Let me get a good look at you."

The last time I'd seen him he was a pimple-faced fourteen-year-old kid. Sixteen years later, his face was prematurely wrinkled and covered with scars, and there were streaks of gray through his tangled mop of mud-brown hair.

Randy was about six-foot-two and skinny as one of the bars in his cell door. Every exposed part of his body had slash marks. Some had healed, others had festered. On his bony wrists were scars, obviously recent. He looked filthy and smelled like old hamburger.

I asked the deputy warden if we could meet privately, and he ushered us into a nearby holding room just outside the cell block, locking me in with Randy. During our short walk, I noticed that Randy hobbled badly on his right foot and dragged his left leg. I asked what the problem was.

"Leg's been amputated just below the hip," he answered. "Got infected from a dirty needle."

"How about your right foot, what's wrong with it?"

"Part of my toes are missing."

As I sat looking at him, I remembered him as a scared kid acting tough in a county jail. It was a terrifying place for a youngster, and I tried to help him. But he wouldn't listen to my advice. One night in a fit of anger, he'd stabbed me with a fountain pen. But most of the time he respected me, and I became his protector. I didn't see him again after I was shipped to Georgia State Penitentiary.

"Randy, tell me what happened in your life since we were together," I said.

"Got raped right after you were transferred," he said. "Wanted to kill the sorry convict, but then I got released. That was all right, being out again, but it didn't last long. In Florida I stole a car, and then I robbed a bank and did time in a Florida state pen for several years. Got released again and came back to Georgia, but they busted me for drugs and . . . well, here I am. The guards, they've shot me four times trying to escape. Now I got diabetes, and I'm going blind. They don't give me a long time to live."

"Randy, how about the slash marks?" I asked.

"I put some of them there. Others were from fights."

"What about your throat?" I asked, eyeballing the expansive purple mark that cut from one side of his neck to the other.

"Tried to kill myself. I just couldn't take it anymore." He paused. "You remember the time you took an iron pipe and beat that punk almost to death because he was messing with me? Grabbed that pipe and went after him. You looked after me. You protected me when anybody bothered me."

I felt a twinge of embarrassment when Randy spoke. This was a side of my life that I didn't want resurrected.

Looking at Randy, I felt a lump in my throat. He had a man's body, what was left of it, but in his eyes I saw a scared fourteen-year-old boy who'd never grown up. He was a shell of a man, the perfect picture of a wasted life. If the warden had told me to take Randy home with me, I couldn't have. Randy simply could not have survived on the outside. What could a man do who was missing his left leg and part of his right foot, who was going blind, and was popping all kinds of pills to medicate the last months of his life? Without insurance, who would pay the medical bills? What company would hire him? Where would he live?

But escape was all Randy could think about.

"Harold, you got to help me get out of here," he suddenly pleaded. "I don't want to die here. I don't got long to live, you see. I'd try to go over the fence, but they've already shot me four times. And now I can't even run."

I nodded without saying anything. It was tragic, but I realized that Randy was better off in prison, though I couldn't tell him that. I didn't know what to say.

His eyes studied my face before he finally broke the silence, "Harold, I don't understand. You used to be so full of hate. I remember that."

"Yeah, Randy, I remember that, too," I said.

"But you come here and do something no one has ever done. You give us stuff. You remember us on Christmas."

"I finally learned that hatred is not the answer, Randy."

When I started to leave, Randy threw his arms around me. I could feel the desperation in his fingers as they dug into my shoulders, and he didn't let go for a very long time.

The results of our Christmas visit were better than anything I could have dreamed up in my wildest imaginings. As we drove to a motel for the night, one of my friends handed me a note from an inmate he had visited. The note was brief and to the point: "Harold, thanks for the Christmas gifts. Love, Sly."

I couldn't believe it. "Love, Sly"? It was written plain as day by a man who'd killed at least three people. He was the neighbor who'd snarled to me my first day on death row, "Hey, next door, I'm going to kill you." Somehow in the intervening years, he had changed.

My amazement didn't stop there. A week after our visit, I received a thank-you card signed by 190 inmates. Others wrote individual letters to say that my book gave them new hope. Of course, there were a few con artists who wrote to say they were innocent, too, and asked me to speak to their judge or call their parents or help them find a job or send them money.

The most precious letter was from Randy.

"It's four o'clock in the morning, and I just finished reading your book, *Twice Pardoned*," he wrote. "You will never know what your visit has meant in my life. But I am not going to live long, and I know it. Before I die, I'd just ask one favor. I got a fourteen-year-old nephew who doesn't live far from you. He is on drugs and is going down the same path that led me to prison.

"Please, Harold, don't let him become what I am. He's the same age I was when I got into trouble. In the last sixteen years, I've been outside prison for less than one year. I don't want anybody to have to repeat my life, but I'm afraid he might if something doesn't happen to change things. My sister has done all she can to help him, but he won't listen and they'd never let me speak to him. Please, Harold, help my nephew. Tell him about me - how I ruined my life."

As I read Randy's letter I was heartened to see a man who wanted to reach out and help somebody else. Though his own life was wasted and almost over, he had a burden for another person who was following in his footsteps towards disaster. I did meet with his sister and his nephew and did my best to help him.

We continued to correspond, and I sent him some money and visited him when I could. I thought often about Randy, and how, in a sense, his life represented my work. He is a vivid picture of the toll that alcohol, drugs, and wrong choices can have on a teenager who follows the wrong crowd.

In one letter Randy wrote, "I wish I could do what you are doing. I wish I could tell young people the importance of making the right decisions. I wish they could see my body, all chopped up and scarred, because then they might understand. My life has just been a very long, slow, painful process of dying."

After many discussions, the prison authority transferred Randy to a prison hospital in Milledgeville, Georgia, where he could get better medical attention. On March 17, 1988, fifteen months after my Christmas visit, I received the phone call I had been expecting. Randy had died. I was true to my word and saw that he had a proper burial in a cemetery in Milledgeville. What a tragedy!

Wrong Association and Peer Pressure

A problem that I faced as a teenager, and a problem that teenagers face today is handling peer pressure and dealing with acceptance. Young people will do a lot of things to gain acceptance. Many times they make mistakes to gain acceptance into a group that's not going anywhere and these mistakes hurt them and haunt them for the rest of their lives.

Why do young people crave acceptance? I think it's because many don't like themselves the way they are. They have low self-esteem, and they desperately want the approval of others. They want to be liked and loved more than anything on earth, and the sad thing is many of them will do just about anything in order to gain this approval and acceptance. And it's different with the boys than it is with the girls.

One of the ways the guys gain acceptance is through material possessions. You have seen the guy in the flashy clothes, the fancy car. He wants the attention of others, and he'll do anything to get it. But what he doesn't know is that anyone who accepts him just because of his material possessions, because of what he owns, is not really his friend. Don't be fooled into believing that you can buy someone's friendship with material possessions. Those people who pretend to be your friends are playing you for a sucker, because they're more interested in what you have than who you are.

Some boys will turn to athletics to gain acceptance. That was the route I chose. Now, athletics are good. They've meant a lot in my life. I think athletics teach character. But athletics are not the most important thing. Being a good student academically is far more important. I look at my life today, and I realize that even though I excelled on the athletic field, I would have done better to excel in the classroom. When I was in school I was always prepared for the next ball game, but I never studied and prepared myself for the game of life, and that's the most important game of all.

Other boys will pull the chair out from under someone or put chewing gum in the teacher's chair to get a laugh. Still others boys will brag about how great they are and all the exciting things they've done, but, in reality, they haven't done anything. And finally, there are the boys who will drink the booze, smoke the dope, do other drugs, pop the pills, and smoke the cigarettes. All of these boys have one thing in common: they desperately want the attention and the approval of others.

But you stay away from the boys who get mixed up in alcohol and drugs, because they are on the same path I chose as a youngster. They're headed for trouble and possibly for prison.

With the girls, it is totally different. To girls, beauty is the most important thing. Appearance is so important. I think it's partly because our society has put a premium on physical attractiveness. And the number one problem girls have is keeping up with that girl who gets all the attention, all the dates.

Well, let me tell you about her: because of all the attention and all the pressure she's under, many times she'll get married at an early age. She won't go to college. She will have one child after another, and she stands a greater chance of her marriage ending in divorce. When you see her coming down the street she's got a cigarette hanging in her mouth and so much make-up all over her face that you could write your name in it. And she is miserable. You'll say, "Look at that hag."

Now, when I was in high school I was the meanest student there. One day I told this girl, I said, "You ugly."

And she looked at me and she said, "Well, beauty is only skin deep."

And I said, "Honey, with you, ugly goes all the way to the bone."

She was so ugly her boyfriend took her to the beach and the waves wouldn't come in. Not only was she ugly, she was skinny. She was so skinny she got a run in her panty hose and fell through the hole. She could stand sideways and stick out her tongue, and she looked like a zipper. She was so skinny she could stand under a clothesline and not get wet.

One of my friends said to me one day, "Be nice to her, Harold, look up her family tree, it will tell you a lot about her."

"Look it up?" I responded. "It looks like it fell on her."

I just saw that same girl not too long ago, and you know what she said? She said, "You're right. Ugly does go all the way to the bone. I'm looking at you!"

But let me tell you about her today. She's married, has two kids, and today she's beautiful. You know why? She always had a beautiful personality. She had character. She cared about her appearance. She always dressed well. She went to college and got a good education so she wouldn't have to depend on some sorry guy to support her. And she had compassion for others. To me she is indeed beautiful. So that equation, beauty equals happiness, does not always prove to be true.

Right now you may think that group acceptance is the most important thing in your life. But the most important thing you can do as a young man or a young woman is to stand up for what you believe in and not be swayed by peer pressure. Be a leader in your school, and you will give others courage to resist peer pressure.

Young people, never sacrifice your ideals or your potential to gain acceptance in a group that's not going somewhere. You can belong to the right group if you'll choose one that has the same ideals and the same goals as you have. But don't follow the wrong crowd.

How do you resist peer pressure? I'll tell you how: first of all, you be selective in who you associate with. You choose a group that's going somewhere. I promise you, if you choose the wrong group it will determine the outcome of your life, good or bad.

And secondly, take a stand and learn how to say a simple, two-letter word: "n-o".

Some of you have a problem learning to say no to those things that you know are wrong. If your friends shun you because you stand for what you believe in then they weren't really your friends.

At Georgia State Penitentiary I decided to quit doing drugs. One day two of my friends came up to me at my bunk and said, "Hey, man, you wanna smoke some dope?"

And I said, "I'm through."

They said, "Yeah, you'll be back."

For the first time I had taken I stand. I had said, "No." They left me alone after that, and if you'll learn to say no those that are trying to pull you in the wrong direction will leave you alone, too.

Thirdly, if you want to resist peer pressure, you must count the cost. Think things through. Ask yourself, "What happens if I give in and do this?" Even little things like cheating on a test or telling a lie can have unintended consequences. Remember, you always reap what you sow.

Young people, wrong association is so important. I'm living proof. One night of pleasure almost wrecked my life. But I was given another chance at life, and I'm so thankful for that.

Alcohol

Where did it begin for me? I began drinking alcohol as a sophomore in high school. When I got drunk for the first time I was with two seniors at a house party on the beach. They handed me a vodka bottle and said, "Take a drink."

I knew it was wrong, but I drank it. It was the most awful stuff I'd ever tasted in my life. I turned around and threw up. But when they passed it around again, I took another drink. Why? Because I wanted to be accepted. I wanted them to like me and think I was really a cool guy.

You see, I had low self-esteem. I didn't like myself or my family. I was ashamed of how poor we were. I was ashamed of the old run down shack we lived in and the fact that my father couldn't read or write. He had never been to school a day in his life. All I wanted was to be accepted and loved by everybody.

I drank throughout high school and later in college. I said, "Man, this is the thing to do." I always justified my drinking by saying "everybody's doing it". But everybody wasn't doing it then, and everybody isn't doing it now. That's just a cop-out.

Young people, I've been right where you are today, and I can tell you from experience that alcohol will wreck your life. So, why do so many teenagers drink alcohol? First of all, I think society promotes teenage drinking. All you have to do is turn on the television, and you will see some great athlete with a beer in his hand trying to entice you to drink alcohol. He would have you think that drinking alcohol gave him that tremendous body that God gave him. He is promoting drinking alcohol for the almighty dollar and no other reason. But he will never tell you about the dangers of drinking.

I was speaking in a school in Georgia one day, and I saw a teenage boy in a wheelchair in the front row start crying as I began to tell about the dangers of alcohol.

Later I asked one of the coaches, "What's wrong with him?"

He said, "Last year, under the influence of alcohol, he was out speeding in an automobile. There was an accident. His young friend was killed, and he's to be paralyzed for the rest of his life. He's one of the greatest athletes ever to attend this school. But he's through. Because of alcohol, he has wiped out his potential."

Another reason teenagers drink is that, frankly, their own parents promote it. A teenage boy once explained to me why he didn't feel there was anything wrong with him drinking alcohol or smoking cigarettes.

"You see, my dad drinks and smokes, and he told me, 'It's alright, son, to do that.' And so I did. If my dad says it's okay, then it must be okay."

A friend of mine shared an article with me that was in the local newspaper of the town he lived in. Two sixteen-year-old boys went out speeding in an automobile. There was an accident. Both were killed. The highway patrolman that investigated that accident found a liquor bottle in the back seat of the car. He then had the very difficult job of going to the parents and telling them that their sons were dead. At the first home, the father answered the knock on the door.

The patrolman said, "Sir, I regret to inform you, but your son is dead. And, sir, I also regret to inform you, but he was under the influence of alcohol. We found a liquor bottle in the backseat."

The father became hysterical, he raged, "I would kill the man that sold my son alcohol! I would choke him to death with my bare hands!"

The father became so emotional that he went over to the liquor cabinet to get a drink to settle his nerves. He opened the liquor cabinet; there was a note. It read, "Dear Dad, I took a fifth of liquor with me, because I knew you wouldn't mind."

That father had killed his son. That father reaped what he had sowed.

After I spoke in an assembly program in a high school one day, a teenage girl handed me a pack of cigarettes.

"I'm through smoking and drinking alcohol," she said.

"That's great, honey," I said. "I'm glad you won't be spoiling your pretty teeth any longer with those old cigarettes."

Then she handed me her matches.

"Take these," she said. "I'm serious."

"I'm so proud of you. You're taking a stand. Please know that you have the strength, power, and courage to overcome smoking, alcohol, or any other problem you have. And I will do all I can to help you."

It seems smoking cigarettes and drinking alcohol go hand in hand with so many of our young people. I addressed this one day in a high school assembly.

I said, "Now if you were intended to smoke, you would have been born with a little chimney on top of your head, or your nose would have been turned upside down so you'd go like a choo-choo train."

I was speaking one day to a group of people, and after my speech an old lady came up to me. She asked, "Young man, will smoking send you to hell?"

I said, "No, ma'am, but it will make you smell like you have been there."

She just turned and left without saying a word.

Young people, you don't need that garbage in your life. I promise you. You simply must realize how it will affect your health. So what's the answer? Why do so many young people continue to drink and smoke even though they know it is the wrong thing to do? Why do so many teenagers rebel against their parents' authority? I think the missing ingredient in so many homes today is love. And so many parents aren't even aware of it.

Many a father has said to me, "I work hard to make a living for my family. Somebody has to pay the bills. I do everything for my kids. I give them everything. And you're telling me my son is smoking cigarettes, drinking alcohol, and doing drugs. I can't believe this! Our home has love!"

So many parents do their best to share love, but kids see love differently. A new bicycle or a new automobile isn't always love in a kid's eyes. Giving a hug or a kiss, going to the ball game, the park or the zoo - in these a kid sees love.

If a teenager is prepared to stand on his own in a sick, hurting, dying world, it will be because parents have taken time to deal with his problems - taken time, that is, to love!

Young people want something real. They want and need and deserve parents who love them enough to set an example for them. They're looking for role models. They're tired of the double standard: a parent with a beer in one hand and a cigarette in the other preaching, "Do as I say, not as I do."

And then, finally, teenagers drink alcohol because they want to be powerful - to defy their parents, their principals, their teachers, their pastors. "Everyone else is doing it," they say. They want to be cool, powerful and gain acceptance in their little peer groups. Well, everyone isn't doing it.

At Georgia State Penitentiary I would see these young guys come in, and I'd say, "Son, tell me, why are you here?"

Did you know that practically all of them told me that their problems had an alcohol root to them? That's where it begins.

I heard a story about this football coach who wanted to teach his players about the dangers of alcohol. When they were all seated in the locker room, he called Fat up to the front of the room. Now, Fat was a 320 pound offensive lineman, and he lumbered up to where the coach was standing.

"I'm going to do an experiment here, Fat," the coach told him. "And I want you to watch closely. After I'm done I want you to tell your teammates what you have learned. Okay?"

Fat nodded. The coach put a glass on a stool and filled it with pure grain alcohol - 180 proof.

"Are you watching closely, Fat?" the coach asked as he produced an earthworm.

"I'm watching," Fat said, eyeing the glass of alcohol single-mindedly.

The coach dropped the earthworm into the alcohol, and it immediately flipped over on its back and threw its heels up in the air and died - graveyard dead.

"Well, what'd you think of that experiment, Fat?" the coach asked after a long silence during which Fat still wore an expression of studious concentration.

Finally, Fat said, "That's a great experiment, coach. I got a lot out of that!"

"Why don't you turn around and tell the rest of the players exactly what you learned?"

Fat turned around, and he threw out his chest. Wearing a self-satisfied look, he surveyed the faces of his teammates and said, "Now, what I got out of that there experiment is this - if you drink a lot of that there alcohol, you won't never have none of them worms."

After a high school assembly program a teenage boy came up to me and told me, "My dad would kill me if he knew I smoked dope and drank beer. What you told us is so true. First it's cigarettes, then alcohol, then marijuana and other drugs, and finally sex. Everything you said has happened to me. I want you to know I'm through with that dead-end lifestyle. Thank you, sir, I wish I could have met you a long time ago."

"It's never too late," I told him. "You've learned a valuable lesson. Now, you can help your friends with similar problems. Your whole life is ahead of you. I'm so proud of you! You can make a difference with your life, son. I admire you for taking a stand!"

Drugs

The best way to describe the dangers of drugs would be to share with you about Georgia State Penitentiary and many of the experiences I had there. I have seen men there inject drugs into their veins and develop serious infections from unclean needles. I've seen addicts with amputated arms and legs. I've seen addicts lose their eyesight, their hair, and develop hepatitis - all because of drugs. I watched a nineteen-year-old boy sniff glue out of a bread sack. He went into a coma and became a vegetable. He stayed that way six months until he died. They buried him in the prison graveyard, because no one claimed his body.

When I think of drugs and alcohol, I guess I think of marijuana as well, because marijuana is the second most preferred drug by teenagers. And the great danger about marijuana is you don't know what you're getting when you buy it. You see, you buy it from the drug pusher, and he's the scum of the earth. He would sell his soul for the almighty dollar. In prison we scored some marijuana that had been dipped in opium or some other hallucinogenic drug. It nearly drove us crazy. One inmate attempted suicide.

The most horrible thing I've ever seen in my life happened to a twenty-year-old inmate who slept in the bunk next to mine. I watched two men come up to his bunk and hold him down while a third guy stabbed his eyes out with a knife.

They thought that he had ratted out a drug transaction they were involved in. It was later proven that he was totally innocent.

The next day they said, "Why did we do it? He was our friend."

He is blind today. I promise you that you don't want to mess around with drugs or even associate with those who do. Those people are sowing all of the wrong things into their lives, and they will reap the addiction that leads to desperation and then to crime and eventually to prison.

I would give anything if I could take you to Georgia State Penitentiary and let you spend one day and go through the normal routine that I went through. Then you might have a different outlook on life and might even find it easy to say no to drugs.

There were 3,200 men crammed into a building built for 750. The dormitory where I was housed was built for 45 men, but I was crowded in with 115 of the meanest, most vicious, short-tempered men anywhere in the world - men who had committed every crime conceivable to man. In that dormitory there were two commodes and one shower for 115 men, and I once saw a man killed in an argument over a pair of shower shoes.

Violence is a way of life in prison, and only the strong survive. I must have seen over 50 men die in the nine-and-a-half years I was incarcerated. Do you realize that 85% of the inmates participated in homosexual behavior? That 75% participated in drug use? I promise you, you don't want that kind of life. So, be thankful for your school, your teachers, and your parents.

You may say, "Man, my school is a prison. A dog wouldn't eat the kind of food they serve us."

Let me tell you about a meal that they served us at Georgia State Penitentiary. I ate it for three years, and I liked it until I found out what I was eating. One day my buddy, Doc, was sitting next to me.

He said, "How do you eat that slop?"

I said, "Man, this is good. This is Brunswick stew."

He said, "Oh, it is, huh?"

He reached over in my bowl and said, "What is this?"

And there was an eyeball looking at me. Every Thursday they would chop up hog heads, throw them in these huge vats, throw vegetables in, and call it Brunswick stew.

The next time you eat lunch at school be thankful that you don't have to eat that kind of food, and give thanks for what you have. Young people, you have so much to be thankful for.

After I spoke to a group of high school students, a teenage boy gave me a handful of marijuana leaves used to wrap marijuana joints.

"I'm through with this stuff," he said.

"Where's the marijuana?" I asked.

"In the car."

"Go get it. I won't turn you in," I promised.

Minutes later he returned with the marijuana.

"Now I believe you," I said. "If you hadn't gone after the marijuana, your words wouldn't have meant much."

"I'm through," he repeated. "Thank you, sir. I will never forget you."

I went to the men's room and flushed that junk down the toilet.

How serious are drugs in this country?

I'm convinced that the drug problem in this country is one of the most serious problems this country has ever faced. And we don't seem to be serious about it. A solution must be found very quickly, because drugs are destroying the lives of too many of our nation's young people.

I'm also convinced that the adults that use and sell cocaine and other drugs are aware of the dangers and don't care. We need to take a serious look at cocaine because it's the source of crack, which is at the root of the problem of despair and bloodshed in our inner cities, especially among our young blacks.

How do we stop it? There is no way to keep people from wanting drugs. And we simply can't arrest our way out of it. Locking so many people up isn't the answer.

So what's the answer? We must stop the source, the cartels, the drug lords, those who are responsible for bringing most of the cocaine and other drugs into this country. We must use force. We are a powerful nation, and they are individuals. We have the troops and the man-power to stop them.

They should be arrested, brought to this country, and given a trial. They should be convicted and given the death penalty. In a short period of time, after the first one is put to death, they will be dealing elsewhere. They will take their business to other countries.

We could solve the drug problem in this country in a short period of time if we really wanted to. We have the power to stop them. But we don't have the courage or the guts.

Why is drug abuse so widespread?

I think drug abuse is so widespread in this country because of the desire of the people, because of the variety of drugs that are readily available to us such as cocaine, marijuana, the pills and other drugs, and because drug use is heavily promoted by the media. They seem to glorify legal and illegal drugs. Finally, I think drug abuse is so widespread because society tolerates it.

I would now like to give you some examples that will show you the importance of saying no to drugs.

I was visiting two friends in South Carolina, and I heard them talking about a young boy. He had broken in a drugstore and overdosed in an apparent attempt to kill himself. By pumping out his stomach, they saved his life. He was locked up in the local jail. He came from a wealthy family, but his family had disowned him. He had been in so much trouble that he had been kicked out of every school in the county. I went to that jail, and I asked to see that young boy. They locked him in a small room with me.

He was the most filthy-looking sight I've ever seen - you could smell him as he came up to you. He looked at me, and he said, "Sir, everybody thinks I smoked marijuana, but I've been snorting cocaine since I was thirteen years old. You see, I hate my dad. He gives me the money to buy it. He doesn't care about me. And I'd kill him today if I could get to him. I have no reason to live."

I looked at him, and I said, "Son, I want to tell you something. I don't know your father, but I care about you very much. And I'm going to get you turned over to me for twenty-four hours, and I'm going to take you to Georgia State Penitentiary. I want you to see the place you're going to spend the rest of you life if you continue the lifestyle you're living."

Well, arrangements were made with a judge, and he turned the boy over to me for twenty-four hours. I called the warden, and I asked him if I could see three inmates who were there. I called them the "unholy three."

The first man that came down was Big Head Yank. He had been there 19 years. It was August, and it's extremely hot in south Georgia in August. He had on a sweatshirt. He had a shirt over that. He had on a prison jacket, a prison hat, dark glasses, and a scarf around his neck. And he walked up and said, "Hey, punk, what's your name?"

And the boy almost forgot his name. He said, "M-m-m-m-m-m" and repeated his name.

He said, "Sit down, boy." He looked over at the boy, and he said, "Boy, how old are you?"

He said, "Sevent-teen, sir."

He said, "When I was your age, I'd done come to prison for murder. I done robbed a bank. I rented a motel, filled it up with women, and I've done come here and killed three teenagers just like you, boy."

Big Head Yank reached into his pocket and pulled out three indictments that he had carried around for nineteen years and showed them to the boy. Then, suddenly, the big man barked, "Get off my foot!"

The boy jumped back and piped, "Yes, sir!" even though he wasn't on the inmate's foot.

I called down another inmate, and he looked at this young boy and he said, "Son, I want to tell you about my life. You see, at age ten I killed my mother. I beat her to death with a baseball bat. I've been here twelve years. I've never received a letter. I'll probably never receive one, either. I've never had a visit from anyone. The only friend I have in the world is Harold. I have a life sentence, and I deserve to die in prison. Son, please, you don't want this kind of life. I want you to leave here today and never forget my face or this prison. Please listen to Harold. He cares about you." He turned and walked away.

I had saved the best until last. His name was Big Mac. He had been in prison twenty-four years. He weighed about two hundred-and-fifty pounds. He had tattoos all over him. He had scars from stab wounds all over his body. He was a drug addict. He was a homosexual. He walked up and grabbed the boy and said, "Punk, what's your name?"

The boy forgot his name again.

Big Mac looked at him and said, "Listen to me. I don't like Morris. I never have. And I want you to leave here today, and I want you to go out and I want you to smoke dope, I want you to shoot dope, drink alcohol, I want you to rob, steal and murder. Do it all, son, because then you're coming back here and I'm gonna make you my boy. You're cute."

And Big Mac lifted the boy off the floor, and he kissed him on the mouth. That young boy went crazy, he ran to the door, and said, "Let me out! Let me out!"

They let him out, and all the inmates and the guards were laughing. I was about to crack up myself. I went out to the car, and he was sitting there. I got in the car, but I didn't say a word for several moments. Finally, he looked at me.

With tears in his eyes, he wiped his mouth with his hand and said, "He kissed me. He's an animal." Then he said, "Mr. Morris, will you help me? Please, help me."

Well, I went to his family, and together we persuaded the judge to give him probation under certain conditions. He was to be tested for drugs once a week, and he was to continue his education. We got him back in school. Four years later, I was sitting in my apartment in South Carolina, there was a knock on the door, and there he stood.

He hugged my neck, and he said, "Mr. Morris, I'll never forget that day at Georgia State Penitentiary. And I'll never forget Big Mac. He kissed me!"

Then he took his hand and wiped his mouth as he frowned.

"But because of those men that day, my life had changed," he said. "I will never forget them. I just wanted you to know that I'm doing well in college, and I'm thinking about going into the ministry. Thanks for everything, Mr. Morris."

Drugs will wreck your life, young people, know that. Drugs are a one way street going nowhere. If you've started, stop. If you haven't started, don't start. Yes, you reap what you sow.

Sex and Dating

Many times when I finished speaking in a high school assembly, teachers would invite me to come to their classrooms. I enjoyed talking with kids in a classroom far more than in an assembly. In the gym, many of the kids were embarrassed to ask a question, but in the class they were among friends and felt more freedom to talk about the issues that affected their lives.

"I don't have all the answers," I said after the teacher introduced me and told the kids they could ask whatever they wanted. "I've come here today because I love you, and if you have a problem, you write me or call me collect. We'll work it out together."

I passed out a stack of cards with my name, address, and phone number.

In the first class, a group of giggling girls sat together on one side of the room.

"Will you look at these angels? They must be having a recess in heaven," I quipped. And turning my attention to the girls, I pointed at several boys and said, "Now you stay away from these sorry rascals, hear?"

All the girls started laughing and that naturally sparked a discussion about dating. One of the girls asked a question about sex. "It's like the guys have only one thing on their minds," she said. "And sometimes I wish we could just have a good time without getting, you know, physical and all."

"Honey, the problem with most teenagers is that they wait until they're in the back seat of an automobile to make a decision," I said. "You'll fail every time if you do that. Now girls, let me tell you what to look for with these guys when you're out on a date. See, these sorry rascals will take you out, and they'll park. And he thinks he's a cool dude in the groove. He thinks he's King Cool, and he'll look over at you and say, 'Baby, you know what you are?'

"And you'll say, 'What?'

"He'll say, 'You are a T.F.'

"You'll say, 'What in the world is a T.F.?'

"He'll say, 'You're a total fox.'

"And you'll say, 'Gollee, he's nice.'

"And then he'll look at you, and he'll say, 'Ain't gonna be long before you'll be a U.B.M.'

"And you'll say, 'What in the world is a U.B.M.?'

"He'll say, 'An Ultra Bad Mamma.'

"And you'll say, 'Gollee, he is King Cool. He's so nice.'

"But look out, the sorry rascal is setting you up.

"He'll look at you and say, 'If you love me, prove your love.'

"Listen to me. He doesn't love you. Anyone that'll ask you to prove your love doesn't love you. I used that line many years ago. He's taking you to be the biggest fool, the most gullible fool that ever walked this earth. You figure it out for yourself. What is he asking you to do when he says, 'Prove your love.'?

"He's asking you to commit immoral acts. He's asking you to surrender your virtue, throw away your self-respect, jeopardize your precious reputation, and risk getting pregnant or getting some disease. That's not love. Anyone who loves you wants what's best for you.

"You need to say no to those sorry characters. You see, he doesn't love you, he loves himself and wants to use you.

"Now, he might not ask you out again, but he's doing you a favor. You don't need a character like that. You see, he's a Romeo. He's a Don Juan. And that's not what you need. You see, all the girls want a macho man. And all the guys want a macha girl. But that's not what you need. You need a natcho man and a natcha girl. That's one who will take a stand and say, 'I'm natcho man' and 'I'm natcha girl with a lot of cheese on it.' These are boys and girls who will stand for what they believe in and never give in.

"So you start looking for a natcho and a natcha. 'Cause let me tell you about that sorry rascal, girls. After he gets what he wants, he'll move on to someone else and brag about his conquest. He doesn't care about you. Please, take a stand and never give in to immoral sex."

Too many girls feel that they have to play the dating game, and many will do anything to get a date. Many will even lower their standards. Please, never never lower your standards to get a date. You will regret it later if you do.

Girls, never be flattered that there are boys willing to use you. Listen, you could dress up as a parking meter and some of these characters would say, "Hey! Baby! What's happening?"

Please, don't look back on your life and say, "If only I had one more chance."

One day I was speaking at a high school assembly in Georgia. After my speech was over, one of the girls who'd sat quietly in the corner came up to me. She started to cry as she said, "I wish I could have heard this two months ago. I really needed it then."

"Well, it's better late than never," I said. I looked at her and asked the question to which I already knew the answer, "Are you pregnant?"

She nodded.

"Have you told anyone?"

"No. My parents would kill me if they found out."

"What's your name, honey?"

"Cynthia."

"Cynthia, there was a time when I thought it was too late for me. But it wasn't. It's never too late."

"I'd just like to get rid of this problem, to have it over with. No one would know."

"Honey, it's not a problem. It's a baby, a human life. I know this is a terribly lonely time for you, and I'm sure it's tempting to think about an abortion. But I hope you'll think not just about your life, but also about the life of the baby inside you.

"Please do me a favor. Tonight would you give this a great deal of thought? Do that, and then I want you to call me collect when we have more time to talk. Cynthia, I want to help you. Just promise you'll call. I'll talk to your parents. I'll stand by you all the way. I give you my word. It's not too late. Together we can work this out. Every day is a new day, and I care about you. You promise to call?"

"I promise."

I followed up with Cynthia. We had many, many phone conversations over the next few months. I even visited her and her parents. Finally, one day I received a letter from her saying she'd followed my advice not to have an abortion. She also stated that she was attending church.

"I want to thank you for loving me and caring," she wrote. "You were so right. That boy who got me pregnant has never spoken to me to this day. In fact, he laughs at me when he sees me. I dropped out of school for a term to have the baby, and now that I'm back, I've been able to help other girls with similar problems. That makes it all worthwhile. I've got the most beautiful baby on earth. Even though I've scarred my life and that of my child, I'm so thankful I listened to you."

Young people, why do I talk about getting out of the back seat of the car and taking a stand with your life and saying no to immoral sex? Because in a period of one day you can make a mistake that will affect your life forever.

I think teenage pregnancy is one of the most serious problems in our society. It's sad when the United States, the most powerful and wealthiest nation in the world, has the highest teen pregnancy rate.

And I think it's about time that we speak up on behalf of that mother who is no more than a child herself. Yes, we have children raising children, and in many cases children are running the home.

A recent study showed that children having children costs our society twenty-nine billion dollars a year. It has simply gotten out of control, and something has to be done.

Why are teenage pregnancies out of control? Simply because everybody wants to be loved, and so many of our children are living in broken homes where they don't feel loved.

And children born to a teen mother come into the world with three strikes against them. Sons of teen mothers are almost three times as likely to end up in prison as other young men. Daughters of teen mothers are eighty-three percent more likely to become teenage mothers themselves. Children born to teen mothers are more likely to repeat a grade in school, they perform significantly worse on development tests, and are twice as likely to be abused or neglected as children born to women twenty and older.

It's high time we take a serious look at this problem and do something about it, because it's affecting our society in a tremendous way.

Young people, don't sell out to immoral sex. Keep your body pure for one man, one woman, for a lifetime, and you will never regret it. Don't look back on your life and say, "If only I had one more chance."

Suicide

I think the saddest people I meet are teenagers. But it doesn't have to be this way. Young people, believe me, each of you has the potential to find real happiness in life. We are all born in darkness, and it's up to each of us as individuals to turn on the light. And we can if only we never give up hope.

Even so, thousands of desperately unhappy American teenagers committed suicide in this country last year. Hundreds of thousands of others attempted suicide. At Georgia State Penitentiary I watched three teenage boys commit suicide. They rolled their bodies right in front of my cell, and I watched them carry the bodies away. And I remember one of them, before he hung himself, he told me from his cell that he was going to take his life. And I've got to live with the fact that I didn't try to help that young boy.

But I cried the day they rolled his body in front of my cell. You know why? Because I was suicidal. I hung on the bars one night to see if my feet would hit the floor. I saw no reason to live. I said, "I can never endure prison life. I can never do these two life sentences. There is no hope for the future. My life is over."

But I'm so thankful that in the darkest hour of my life I made a decision. I made a decision that life is indeed precious. I was going to fight for my life, and that's the reason I'm free today and I'm so thankful for that, young people. You feel many times that there's no hope. No one cares. I know the loneliness you go through. I know the confusion you go through, I know the sexual pressures, I know your vulnerability to drugs and other problems. But no matter what the problem, suicide is not the answer. It is not the answer. And many young people have shared with me their frustrations because they can't communicate with their parents, their teachers, or those in authority. And many have shared with me that they have no one whom they can turn to, but I can tell you that there is someone. And you're going to find out just like I found out that if you'll give your teachers, your parents, and your pastors a chance that they care very much about you. They love you. They don't have all the answers, but they will try to help you. There are a lot of people who care very much about you. Suicide is not the answer.

Many times when I speak in a high school assembly the principal will tip me off to a student who has a very serious problem. At a high school in Georgia, I was told about a sixteen-year-old girl who wanted to commit suicide. The principal called her up to the counselor's office where I met with her for an hour.

"Honey, you're a beautiful girl," I said to her. "Why do you want to take your life?"

"I hate my parents," she answered. "They love my sister and hate me. I'm doing drugs, dating a man who's twenty and having sex." She shook her head and said, "I know it's wrong, but I don't care. Life isn't worth living."

"I want you to know something. I love you very much. Would you do one favor for me? Would you call this number collect when you get ready to take your life? If you do I promise I won't try to talk you out of suicide. I just want to choose the color of the casket, and blue's my favorite color."

She started giggling at my ridiculous humor.

"I can call you collect?"

"Anytime."

Ten days later, on a Friday afternoon in mid-May, she called.

"Mr. Morris, I'm getting ready to take my life."

"Where are you?"

She told me she was sitting in front of a National Guard Armory in a town about sixty miles north of Atlanta.

"I'm leaving right now," I said. "Please give me one hour."

I hopped in my car and drove as fast as I could to the town. I had no idea where the armory was, but somehow I managed to find it quickly. She was sitting on the curb, waiting. She got in the car, and we drove over to McDonald's.

For a while I told her some jokes and made her laugh. I told her about this fifteen-year-old boy who wanted a rifle worse than anything in the world. He pleaded with his mother who rebuffed him. "I told you I'd get you a rifle when you turn sixteen," she said.

Well, the day finally arrived, and his mother bought him the rifle and he immediately went out into the woods behind his house to hunt for a lion. He hunted all afternoon, until it got dark, but he didn't see anything. As he was climbing a hill he suddenly looked up and saw a lion staring down at him. The boy panicked. He threw down his rifle and ran back down the hill as fast as he could, but in his haste he tripped. Laying there on the ground, he heard the lion bounding towards him, and he knew that he was going to be eaten. Just then his mother's words echoed in his memory, "Son, when you're in trouble, pray." So, the boy quickly pressed his hands together and whispered, "Please let this be a Christian lion." Hearing a noise over his shoulder, he looked and the lion was right there. With his paws pressed together in prayer, the lion said, "Please bless this food to the nourishment of my body . . ."

She laughed, and then I told her about the time I was in another restaurant, and I asked the waitress if she had frog legs. The waitress replied, "No, I'm just walking this way because I broke my toe!"

"A mother hen was having trouble keeping her chicks in line," I continued, "and she declared, 'If your father could see you now, he'd turn over in his gravy.'"

After a few more jokes, her face had brightened up and I asked at last, "Honey, what's the problem?"

"I've tried to work things out with my mom, but it's not happening. Yesterday, I saw that man again, and he gave me drugs. I just feel so guilty."

We talked for nearly three hours about her problems. Finally, I drove her home. And we parked in her driveway.

I said, "I'd like to ask another favor."

I pulled some money out of my pocket and handed it to her.

"Will you go and buy something nice for yourself? Then buy a gift for your mother. Sunday is Mother's Day. I want you to give your mom that present and tell her you love her.

"I know you think your mom has failed you. But I'm sure she really does love you. Maybe she just doesn't know how to communicate her love. So you tell her you love her and that you've failed her, too. Say, 'Mom, I want to get to know you and love you.' If you will work at it, the two of you will learn to communicate."

The girl looked at me and then reached over and kissed me on the cheek. With her hand on the door just before jumping out of the car, she asked, "Mr. Morris, who are you? I can't talk to my principal, my teachers, or my parents. But I can talk to you, and I told you things today that I've never told anyone. Who are you?"

There was really only one way to answer her. "Honey," I said, "I'm just a big old ugly ex-con who cares."

That beautiful young girl did not take her life. She gave up drugs and the twenty-year-old man she was dating. And things gradually improved with her parents, because she learned to communicate and say, "I love you".

Suicide is not the answer.

I'm so thankful I have a burden for young people and for the wisdom to deal with their problems. I know they can mean it when they threaten suicide. I know they can take their lives, even though they really don't want to. Don't tell me a person must be insane to take his life. I once shared that feeling of desperation. There's not a doubt in my mind that I would have fulfilled my intention to commit suicide while I was in prison if I hadn't found hope. I know the feeling of those who want to die, and that has helped me communicate with kids.

Young people know they can share with me because I can keep a confidence. They know that I will do what I say, because my word is my bond. When I tell them I'll write, I write. When I tell them I'll come back, I do. When I give them my card and ask them to call collect, I accept their collect call. That's what they want - someone to understand them, someone to love and accept them as they are, someone to hug them and say, "There's hope, and I love you."

It's high time that we adults realize this. A teenager told me at her school one day she was planning to commit suicide. She said her father had raped her, and although he no longer lived with the family, she still suffered from this grievous emotional wound. I gave her my phone number and asked her to call me so that we could talk further. She did call me, and she also began writing. Her letters were filled with hopelessness.

"I am writing this letter four days after my graduation," she wrote, "and I feel terrible. I have so much pain and hurt eating at me inside that I am about to explode. You know, I still wish I were dead, but I haven't got the nerve to do it - not yet anyway. I just feel so empty and alone. I'm not happy with myself. I feel so cheap inside about my past. Even though it happened four years ago, the scars are still there. I've tried to put it aside, but something always brings it back. You know, I'm just downright tired of everything.

"Sometimes I wish I had a father who was different. I don't want my real father; I could never love him again. I have forgiven him for what he did to me, but that doesn't change what happened. I can never love him, and I wouldn't let myself even if I wanted to. I just wish I had an adopted father, someone who cares and won't reject me . . .

"I'm so alone. I hope I haven't bored you. Most people who supposedly care really don't . . . How many times I've come to the point of wanting to die! . . . Someone is always better than I am. I feel so rejected at times that if I just blew my head off, very few (I mean very few) people would notice . . . I'm fighting a losing battle. You know, it's pretty lonely . . ."

Could anything make a difference in the life of this desperate teenager? I had to find out. I was determined to become the adoptive father she so desperately wanted and needed. I asked her to tell me something she would really like to do. She wanted to attend a summer camp, so I arranged to sponsor her. With that experience her life began to change. She started singing in the choir in church and seemed hopeful for the first time since we had met.

She indicated that she wanted to come to Atlanta, where I lived, and attend a youth conference. She got to fly on a plane for the first time, and she was just thrilled with the experience. We got to spend some quality time together, and this made a big difference.

I asked if she planned to attend college and even offered to sponsor her. She said she wasn't ready for college yet. However, she did want to study to become a paramedic. So I sent her to paramedic school, and she later graduated.

Today this young woman who wanted to die is happily married and has a lovely family. She has a bright outlook for the future. Believing in herself and developing her potential made a difference in her life. Young people, please remember suicide is not the answer.

Race

The problem of the 20th and 21st century remains the problem of the color line. This line must, at last, be dissolved. Hardly an aspect of life has escaped this awful thing we call racism.

When I was growing up in South Carolina, many times I heard my father and other adults say that blacks were inferior to whites. They would say that blacks were ignorant, lazy, and smelled bad. Even today, many whites still hold the same beliefs their grandfathers did about blacks, because these beliefs are passed on from generation to generation.

I heard a story from a college professor of mine that illustrates this point. He was at a big international conference in a foreign country. As he talked to a friend of his at the head table, he noticed a well-dressed black man sitting alone at the far end of the table chowing down on a piece of chicken with real gusto.

The college professor said to his friend, "I feel sorry for that black man. He's sitting all by himself, and he probably can't speak any English. Someone really should go and talk to him."

After a few more minutes, the college professor decided that he would go talk to the black delegate. As he approached the black man was still eating, so the professor tapped him on the shoulder. The college professor smiled as he tried to communicate.

"Blah, blah, blah goot?" he said, motioning towards the chicken.

The black delegate stopped eating and looked around for a

moment before nodding and responding with, "Goot." Then the black man returned to his meal.

In a few minutes the evening speaker was called, and to the college professor's surprise and chagrin it was the black delegate. Not only did he speak English, but he had an Oxford accent and the most beautiful speaking voice the college professor had ever heard. He gave a wonderful speech that was met with a standing ovation. Stepping back from the podium, the keynote speaker headed towards the college professor, who had his head down until he was tapped on the shoulder. Sheepishly, he looked up.

"Blah, blah, blah goot?" the black man asked.

Sometimes our assumptions are innocent and well-intentioned, but this is where we are today. We still judge people by their skin color, and many whites still feel that those of another color are in some ways inferior. The sad truth is that many fathers have poisoned their childrens' minds with their own hatreds, and society echoes this racial ignorance. Children aren't born racist. They're taught. No wonder our children are confused when it comes to race and many become racists themselves.

On March 21, 1981, in Alabama two young white men, one twenty-six and one seventeen years old, were upset because a black man who had killed a white police officer was found not guilty in a jury trial earlier that day. As part of their Klu Klux Klan Unit 900's "revenge" they set out to kill a black man.

They found a nineteen-year-old black youth walking alone that night, ordered him into their car at gunpoint, drove to a neighboring county, and struck him with a tree limb more than 100 times. When he was no longer moving they looped a rope around his neck and - for good measure - cut his throat.

According to the seventeen-year-old's confession to the F.B.I. and his trial testimony, the two Klansmen then drove back to Mobile County to the home of the twenty-six-year-old's father, who was the second-highest Klan official in Alabama, to show off the trophy to unit members.

They tied thirteen knots in the rope around the black teenager's neck, looped the rope over a branch of a camphor tree on the avenue across the street from the father's home, and let the body swing. There is no question that the young man was trying to impress his father and would not otherwise have done the horrible crime.

On June 6, 1997, the twenty-six-year-old was put to death in the electric chair in Alabama. He was among the rarest breed of Alabama killers: a white sentenced to die for murdering a black. In fact, his execution was the first in the white-on-black murder category in Alabama since 1913.

How tragic! Yes, the sins of the fathers are visited on their children in many instances. The chain of hatreds that has been passed down from parent to child must be broken if we are ever to be free of racism. What our children know and believe, whether it is good or bad, they learned from watching and listening to their parents and those around them.

We must make every effort to be positive role models for our children, and raising our children must become a top priority in our lives. That means teaching children right from wrong, providing loving discipline, and encouraging respect for the dignity and humanity of others. It means teaching each child self-respect. It means being compassionate and caring as a parent and spending time with your children. When you treat a child as if he's worthless, he feels that he can never contribute anything worthwhile to society. Every child should feel that he's a valuable human being.

Too often these days the responsibility for raising the children is left to the mother. After a father deserts the family, you'll find that mother working several jobs if it's necessary. She will do anything and everything she can to support her children. A mother loves in a special way, and she will do whatever it takes to hold her family together. It's mothers that are the backbone of our society - not fathers. And I truly believe that a man is not really a man until he's in touch with the woman in him, and that's why mothers are so special.

But children need their fathers, as this story illustrates:

After I finished a speech in a high school in Alabama one day, a huge black kid built like Hercules came up to me. One of the students had already told me that he was the school's outstanding athlete and was going to a major college on a football scholarship.

In front of the entire student body, he said, "Mr. Morris, you're a great man. I've never had a father, and I was wondering if you would be my father."

Putting my arm around him, with tears in my eyes, I said, "Son, I'm honored you'd want me to be your father. However, I'm afraid I wouldn't do a very good job, because I live in Atlanta, Georgia, and I'm travelling most of the time. But I'll always be available to you. I will always be there for you. You can visit me, call me collect anytime, or write me. I'll help you any way I can. I love you, son, and I'm extremely proud of you."

I then gave him my card, and he gave me a big hug. All he wanted was to be loved and accepted. All he needed was a father's touch. Yes, fathers can make all the difference in the world in a teenager's life.

And I think black men are the ones that the black kids should be looking up to. They must become positive role models for future generations of black youth. Black fathers can provide strong leadership and can solve problems in the black community better than anyone else. Mothers cannot be expected to do it all by themselves - and they shouldn't have to.

But too many black fathers and teens have lost hope for the future. Often they feel that the system doesn't work for them or that it has a bias against them that keeps them in poverty. And as long as we ignore their concerns and needs, we will continue to see more violence and crime. Let's face it, we have created a criminal justice system that only focuses on the symptoms and not on the causes. Building more jails and locking up more young people isn't the answer. Our youth are our responsibility. I think we should spend more time and money training and educating them. They must be taught to achieve, to realize their potential and their talents. Of all the tragedies, I think unrealized potential is the worst.

Racism will not disappear just by focusing on race. Racism will disappear by focusing on achievement and finding a way for every citizen to be an achiever.

I'm convinced that two of the most important issues at the root of racism are education and economic opportunity. Unless we figure out a way to fix our worst schools and open the marketplace to minority businesses so that everyone can see the promise of a better life, the conditions will only worsen as far as racism is concerned.

When we improve our schools, make our neighborhoods safe, and significantly increase the number of minority-owned businesses we put the American dream within everyone's grasp. And it is imperative not that everyone succeed, but that everyone has the opportunity to succeed. The time has come to decide whether our nation will splinter along racial lines - causing us to become increasingly separate, unequal, and isolated - or else become the world's first truly multi-racial democracy. It's imperative that we understand the importance of ethnic and racial diversity to American success.

It is time for all of us to come together and fight for social and economic justice for all people regardless of color. I believe that we have improved in some cases. Minorities have been given more opportunities. But the situation as a whole has to be improved, because people are still judged by the color of their skin and not by the content of their heart. If we don't make it together, we'll fail separately.

And at present, we are not one nation under God, indivisible, with liberty and justice for all. We are a nation divided between the blacks and the whites. Let's face it, there is not enough respect between the races.

A recent study seemed to confirm the adage that Sunday morning in church-going America is when the nation's racial divide is the greatest. More than 70% of both blacks and whites say they worship where most church members are of the same race as themselves.

It doesn't have to be this way. Where we see differences, God does not. God is color-blind.

Racism has diminished all of the lives it has touched. I think it is high time for all of us, old and young, black and white, to come together.

God is not concerned whether we are black, white, or what color we are. The color of our blood is red.

This was a very difficult lesson for me to learn. I had blindly hated blacks all of my life until one day at Georgia State Penitentiary when the warden threw me into a cell with a black man. His name was

Marcus "Doc" Odomes. Through a long and painful process he and I learned to see one another as individuals. I think racism in America exists because the white community, as a whole, has made race a problem from generation to generation. So doing away with racism is ultimately the responsibility of the white community, and I told Doc I was sorry for having hated him. He apologized for hating me. And we became great friends.

You see, our hearts had changed, and once they did we began thinking and behaving differently. We stood up for one another, and when two white inmates came after me wanting to kill me, Doc didn't hesitate to put himself between me and my attackers. During the ensuing struggle, they stabbed him seven times. After the guards rushed him to the prison hospital, I cried as I looked at his blood. You know why? Because it was red, the same color as mine. Then and there I prayed for him.

Why can't we all learn to love one another like Doc and I learned in that prison cell? Why have we failed as a society in regards to integration? I don't believe that Americans are really interested in telling the truth or in hearing the truth about race. People don't want to change, because change can be difficult. You have to let go of the past and begin to think and behave differently, acting according to your convictions. Even now, I think blacks still feel the pain of slavery, and whites still feel the guilt.

Martin Luther King Jr. first challenged us as individuals and as a nation to act according to our convictions in regards to race more than thirty years ago. But back then we did not take up his challenge. I know I didn't.

On February 27, 1960, I witnessed the very first lunch counter sit-in protest at the Woolworth's in Greensboro, North Carolina. A college student at the time, my college buddies and I cursed those blacks and the few whites who demonstrated with them.

But that demonstration helped to spark the civil rights movement and Martin Luther King Jr.'s dream. What was his dream? He lived and died for equality, truth, peace, democracy, justice, non-violence, and love for all people - regardless of color. He taught that you can never right the wrong of violence with more violence and that no injustice can live forever.

His dream was a glorious one, and even now we are still struggling to realize it as a nation. Hopefully, we can learn to look past the color of the skin, and if we do we will find that we are more alike than different. And then we can begin again to try to communicate with one another, to learn from one another, to understand one another, and - finally - to love one another.

If we can learn to love one another, if each of us can sow just one seed of love into our lives, it may take some time, but the love will come back to us a thousand-fold. The law of the harvest says so.

But we must sow the seeds. We must be the ones who make the effort, because we can't wait on government any longer. The leadership and the commitment must come from each of us, our communities, our churches, City Hall, Boys' and Girls' Clubs, and corporations. And it only takes one person to make a real difference as this story illustrates:

Edwin Tucker, a close friend of mine, led a group of businessmen from Wilson, North Carolina, who wanted to do something for the underprivileged youth in their community. He knew that few if any of them had ever had the opportunity to go to a college football game, and he thought that it would be a treat for them. So, he contacted the local Boys' Club and told them what he wanted to do. He then bought a block of tickets for a football game at the University of North Carolina and arranged to have the children bused to and from the game.

One of those children who got to go to the Tar Heels game on that bright fall day was a thirteen-year-old black boy named Octavus Barnes. Octavus, whose mother and father were divorced, was reared by his grandmother in a housing project. He had never experienced anything like the pageantry or the excitement of being at a big-time college football game. He was thrilled, and he wanted more than anything to be on that field playing before thousands of cheering Carolina fans.

The next Monday he approached the director of the Boys' Club and asked him, "Do you think I could play for the University of North Carolina someday? It's the most beautiful place I've ever seen."

The director told him, "If you'll apply yourself and work as hard in the classroom as you do on the field you can. You can do anything you set your mind to."

That was all the young boy needed to hear. He starred at receiver on his high school football team and applied himself in the classroom, and he realized his dream of playing for the University of North Carolina.

On August 12, 1997, as he was preparing to leave his home in Wilson, North Carolina, to return to Chapel Hill for his senior year, he told his mother that he had learned from John Lotz, the assistant athletic director of North Carolina, the name of the man who had given him the ticket to his first college football game. Octavus told his mother that he could not return to college without thanking the man.

He went down to Edwin Tucker's furniture store and asked to see his benefactor. When Edwin stepped through the door of his office, the young man extended his hand and said, "Sir, I am Octavus Barnes, and I just wanted to thank you for giving me that ticket. You'll never know how much of an impact it has had on my life. Sir, I will graduate this December with a degree in sociology."

Edwin Tucker congratulated the young man on his success and told him that he was sending another group of inner city youths to the September 6th Tar Heel football game against the University of Indiana. He said that John Lotz had arranged for him to obtain 200 tickets. Octavus said that he'd like to speak to the group after the game.

On the day of the game, 200 youths and Octavus Barnes' mother rode on buses to Chapel Hill, North Carolina, to watch the Tar Heels take on the Hoosiers. The children were given $10 each to spend at the game.

Octavus Barnes started at receiver for the nationally-ranked Tar Heel football team. He played an outstanding game and scored a touchdown. After the game, as his mother and Edwin Tucker looked on, he spoke to the children.

"I can't tell you what it means to have all of you here. It certainly brings back memories. Ten years ago, Mr. Tucker gave me a ticket to a Carolina football game, and it had a tremendous impact on my life."

Octavus pointed to where he sat in the stands so long ago, and he told the children how deeply the game affected him. He related how the director of the Boys' Club told him to chase his dream of playing football in Chapel Hill and urged him to work hard on the field and in the classroom.

"I made a commitment that day to get better in football, to apply myself in the classroom, and to stay out of trouble," Octavus said. "I went home after school every day and studied, and then I went to the Boys' Club. The Boys' Club kept me out of trouble and on a straight and narrow path, and it helped me to reach my goal. I will graduate in December, and I owe my success to the Boys' Club and to my loving mother and grandmother, who supported me all the way."

After his speech, Octavus autographed posters of the Carolina football team for the children. And he thanked Edwin Tucker for helping him and for helping all of the kids that surrounded them that day.

"They're all worth it, aren't they?" Octavus asked, already knowing the answer.

If racism is to be eradicated, the leadership has to come from us as individuals. And we can all make a difference if we're willing to plant that one seed.

A young woman once complained to Mother Teresa, "What am I to do? I'm just one person, and there are so many people who need help! I can't help everyone!"

Mother Teresa's reply was simple and instructive, "Then, just help one person."

Little Things

Young people, you cannot compromise with sin. I've tried it, and I can tell you for a fact that it can't be done. You begin by taking just a single step down into the muck and mire of sin, and before you know it you are in over your head.

Take, for instance, cheating on a test. You try to justify the cheating by saying, "Well, last night I talked to my girlfriend on the phone so long I didn't have time to study. I won't cheat anymore."

But then you cheat again on the next test. And on the next one. And before you know it, it's time for the final exam. It counts for half your grade, and it will cover everything you were supposed to have studied all semester. Too late, you realize that you never really knew all of the material, because you cheated on every test. And even though you passed the tests, you'll fail the final exam and you'll fail the class. So, be aware of the little things, because they grow into big ones.

Let me give you the best illustration I could ever use to show you the importance of the little things in your life. Let me tell you about my most unforgettable character. His name was Sheephead.

I had begun to hear tales about Sheephead as soon as I arrived in prison. Inmates and guards spoke of a wild man who was reported to have killed seventeen inmates, and some said he had stabbed hundreds of prisoners during the thirty-odd years he had spent in prison. He had also killed one guard and permanently disabled another.

The story was widely circulated that Sheephead chopped an inmate to pieces with a meat cleaver and flushed the parts down the toilet. The guards thought the man had escaped - until they found his skull. It was too large to flush.

Locked in a wing of the prison to minimize the danger to himself as well as to other inmates, Sheephead became a living legend.

Three years passed before I met him. I was being taken to the outside hospital for surgery after severely injuring the little finger on my right hand in a fight.

A guard said, "Wait a minute. Another inmate is going with you."

The door opened, and there he stood, the man reputed to be the most violent inmate in the prison. I recognized him immediately, because his face did indeed resemble a sheep's head. Every facial bone had been broken in fights. I was frightened of the man.

When the guard shackled my right arm and ankle to Sheephead's left arm and ankle, I worked to steady my breathing so he wouldn't sense my fear.

"What if he tries to escape and both of us are shot?" I thought.

I worried as we were loaded into the prison van for the trip to Talmadge Memorial Hospital in Augusta, Georgia. We rode in silence for a while, and then I found the courage to speak.

"Is it all right if I talk to you?" I asked.

"Yeah," growled Sheephead.

"Are all the stories I've heard about you really true?"

"You ain't heard nothing yet," he boasted, and for 110 miles he poured out the story of his life.

He was from a poor family in south Georgia. As a sixteen-year-old boy he had broken into a store to steal a Pepsi and a pack of crackers. He was sentenced to one year in Georgia State Penitentiary. Inmates with a one-year sentence are usually paroled in six months and discharged in eight months.

"I had never been in a fight in my life until I came here," he said. "That first day in prison I was raped by an old inmate. My life was never the same after that. I became a homosexual and a drug addict, but I lived for the day I would be released."

Four months after arriving at the prison, the boy was working on an outside farm detail under the supervision of armed guards. Two old convicts forced him to take part in an escape plot: the men would grab a shotgun from one of the guards, and the teenager would seize the gun from the other guard. Fearing the convicts, the boy complied and grabbed the gun as told, but the two other men did not follow through. In self-defense, the boy shot both guards, killing one and paralyzing the other for life.

"When that guard died, I knew that I was through," Sheephead whispered.

For a few moments we rode along in silence before the story continued. After a murder trial, Sheephead was sentenced to die in the electric chair. After he had spent eight-and-a-half years on death row, the governor of Georgia commuted his sentence to life, and he was returned to the inmate population.

No longer frightened, I became fascinated by the old prisoner. As I listened to him and watched him talk, I began to realize that this sick old man was more like a lonely child than a notorious criminal.

When we returned to the prison, Sheephead was locked in a cell in the hospital ward where I worked. Hated by guards and inmates alike, he was a forgotten man. No one cared. He was dying of cancer, although his illness had not yet been diagnosed.

I visited Sheephead daily, often bringing him candy and a Pepsi. As we talked through the bars, I realized that he was so feeble-minded from being beaten in the head that he would kill an inmate if someone merely suggested the man was out to get him. I suspect this accounted for many of the prison killings.

Others saw Sheephead as a violent animal. But I saw him as a broken man who appeared to be 100, though he was only fifty. He loved me because I didn't look down on him. I gave him time and attention, and he returned the friendship by doing whatever I asked. One day, he told me he was planning to kill the doctor.

"He says I just want to go to the hospital to rest. I know I'm dying, but he won't do anything for me. I'm going to kill him," he said.

He showed me a knife, but didn't explain how he had obtained it. I begged him not to carry out the plan and promised to see that he received proper medical attention. He agreed. I pleaded his case with the hospital administrator, and tests soon confirmed that he had terminal cancer. As I looked at him, tears filled my eyes and I wondered, "Will that be me someday?"

Soon after that Sheephead died, after spending thirty-four years in prison. His unwanted body was buried in the prison graveyard. What began with stealing a Pepsi and a pack of crackers ended in a terrible waste of a life.

You know, the tragedy is not that Sheephead died, but that he never lived. So you can see, young people, how the little things can grow into big ones.

Love

I was at Georgia State Penitentiary for five years, and I never heard the word "love" mentioned. Before leaving Georgia State Penitentiary, I'd made a statement that all I wanted in life was a chance to share love.

Upon my release from prison, I was paroled to the Boys' Home in Orangeburg, South Carolina, where little unwanted, unloved, abused boys taught me the true meaning of love. Now I had my chance. I could become a loving, supportive father to dozens of boys who had no father. In addition, I would be paid a whopping six thousand dollars a year!

When I arrived at the Boys' Home, the boys were waiting for me. Large yellow ribbons were tied around the pecan trees, and a big sign announced, "Welcome home, Mr. Morris." I cried, realizing that here I would be loved and needed. It was one of the most touching moments of my life.

My responsibilities included coaching and counseling the boys who were ages eight to sixteen and from varied backgrounds. Some were orphans, some had been abused and neglected by their parents, some had been kicked out to roam the streets, and some were from broken homes. They were exactly what I needed. Being outcasts themselves, they wouldn't look down on me. I learned a great deal as those kids worked their way into my heart.

One unforgettable eight-year-old really won me over. Jerry had been abused by his parents. His vision was poor, and he spoke with difficulty. His mental ability also appeared limited, and the kids picked on him constantly. Once, Jerry and several others attended a large summer camp. When I stopped by to check on them, I noticed that all the kids from the other places were eating snacks, but my boys had no money for such treats. I bought them each a candy bar and a soft drink and left some money in an account for each boy. As I started to leave, little Jerry came running up to me.

"Mr. Harold, I know why you bought that candy and pop," he said.

"Why?" I responded.

"Because you love us," he said, wrapping his arms around my legs.

I turned my face so that he couldn't see the tears. That small boy - so physically and mentally limited that he could hardly express himself - was the only boy who showed gratitude. He gave more love than all the others! I have never forgotten Jerry or the lesson I learned from him: never judge a person by what he appears to be; it's the heart that counts. And this little boy, though handicapped, taught me the importance of sharing love and reaching out to others who are less fortunate.

One of my most memorable Sundays was Mother's Day in 1978, shortly after my release from prison. It was special because I was thinking so much about my own mother. For the first time in ten years, I'd be spending Mother's Day with her. After the service, I planned to make the 80-mile drive to her home for dinner that night.

But the day was also special because of Toby, one of the boys who sat next to me. Toby was thirteen and disliked by most of the other kids, because he was starving for attention. He'd have to rank among the greatest liars I ever met, but his fibbing was all done for attention.

Toby was all arms and legs and absolutely pathetic on the athletic field. He tried to make up for it with big talk and bragging. The other kids resented his mouth and tried to pick fights, but he'd always back off when he was provoked. He was too gentle to be tough. There was a sweetness about him, and he was not afraid to say, "I love you," or "I care". He just needed somebody to love and care for him, too.

One day Toby told me that he never knew his father and that his mother didn't care about him.

"Why wouldn't they care about me?" he asked with tears in his eyes.

"I don't know your parents or why they gave you up," I responded. "But I doubt it had anything to do with you. Parents sometimes act very childish. They want a child but later decide they can't be good parents."

Then I told him that I understood his hurt, "Toby, for nearly ten years I felt no one loved me. While I was in prison, I felt all alone and that nobody really cared."

It hurt me as much as it did him that it was primarily the attractive kids who were invited to the homes of prospective adoptive parents.

So one weekend I told him, "Toby, I'm signing you out today. We're going to the beach. You're going to be my buddy this weekend."

At the beach, Toby had the time of his life. I gave him money for rides and let him eat all the hot dogs and junk food he wanted. He acted like a boy turned loose in a toy store. After that weekend, he followed me everywhere.

And so he sat next to me in the fifth row that Mother's Day Sunday. The pastor presented awards and gifts to the oldest and youngest mothers in the congregation, and then he spoke about how mothers mirror God's love for us. In light of my reunion with my own mother, it was a very emotional message for me.

As I looked around the church, I saw mothers sitting with children in their laps and husbands with their arms draped proudly around the shoulders of their wives. Then I looked at the disadvantaged boys and couldn't help thinking how the pastor's message was being received by their little ears, because they had no mothers.

At the end of the service, Toby got up without saying a word to me and walked down the aisle. The pastor leaned down, and Toby whispered something in his ear. Then Toby turned around, and I could see his lips quivering and tears streaming down his cheeks as he faced the silent congregation.

With a shaking voice the pastor said, "Ladies and gentlemen, little Toby from the Boys' Home has come to us with a very special prayer request. He hasn't seen his mother in more than five years, but he says he loves her very much and prays for her everyday. Toby wants to know if we'll pray for his mother - that she's safe and that one day she will love him."

As the pastor led in prayer, the entire congregation was gripped with emotion. When Toby came back and sat next to me, my eyes were flooded with tears. I leaned over, put my arm around his shoulders, and drew his body closer.

"Toby, I can't take the place of your mother," I said, "but I love you and will be a father to you if you let me."

He put his hand on my leg and said, "I love you, Mr. Morris."

I looked him in the eye.

"I love you, too, son," I responded.

It wasn't his fault that his father and mother had deserted him. He needed love, and just as people had reached out and loved me, I could now reach out and love Toby and others like him.

Of course, you don't win them all, and I had my share of failures, too. The most painful involved a blond-haired, blue-eyed boy named Danny. He was nine years old and was everything I could hope for in a son. If boys are made out of snips, snails, and puppy dog tails, little Danny got double of everything. I'd never seen a kid as competitive and tough at his age. He'd fight if necessary, yet he knew how to laugh. He said hip things, walked with a swagger, was built solid as a pit bull terrier, and had confidence that wouldn't quit. He had a smart little mouth, and when I'd call, "Danny!" he'd answer, "That's my name, don't wear it out."

Perhaps because he reminded me of myself at his age, I loved him more than all the other boys. I would have given anything to raise him as my son, love him, educate him, and try to help him become a winner in life.

Endurance was another quality I appreciated, and Danny would never quit. One day I read in the paper about a track meet, so I made special arrangements for the boys from the home to participate in those races. I explained the events to the kids and coached them for a week. On Saturday morning, we hopped into an old van and drove forty miles to Columbia, South Carolina. On the way over there I gave them a little speech.

"If you enter an event, you must finish," I said. "That's all I ask of you. I don't expect you to win, but I do expect you to compete to the best of your ability and cross the finish line. The kids you're competing against are well trained. They're the best in the state. They're already winners, or they wouldn't be here. But, you've been allowed to compete, and you wanted to go - so no half efforts. You finish, and I promise that after the meet I'll feed you all the hamburgers you can eat."

Several thousand people were there to watch the track and field events. All ten kids I brought finished their events, though some of them walked across the finish line. It was pitiful looking at some of them and the way they were dressed. They were anything but athletic, and people laughed at them. I ignored the laughs and worked on the infield, coaching the boys and giving them Pepsi-colas and hot dogs to keep their spirits up.

The last event of the day was the mile run in which Danny was competing. None of the boys had won any awards, but I felt Danny had a chance. There were twenty other competitors in that race, two of whom were rated as the top runners in the state. One owned the state record for his age group. As Danny headed for the starting line, I told him, "All you've got to do is finish third. You'll get a medal and qualify for the National Junior Olympics. Now listen to me. It's hot, and you must run four laps around this track. I'll stay near you here in the infield and help you pace yourself. Just listen to me."

The gun sounded, and Danny quickly took the lead and held it through the second lap. The two top runners caught him, and racing as three they lapped the other athletes by the final lap. The boy that held the state record took a one hundred yard lead and finished first. Danny and the other top runner were neck and neck at the finish line, but Danny took second by a breath.

I ran to the finish line whooping like a wild Indian and grabbed Danny. I lifted him up on my shoulders and ran him around the track. This was more fun than all the athletic awards I'd won in high school! Danny, an untrained, uncoached cast off had finished second! I was crying with joy as I looked up and saw his blond hair waving in the air and his smile about ready to burst.

When Danny accepted his medal, he took one look at the prize and turned to me. "One day I'll win the Olympic gold medal," he said brightly. Since he'd qualified for the National Junior Olympics, I suggested that we register immediately.

"I'll pay your fee," I said.

He shook his head, "I can't enter."

"What do you mean?"

"I don't want to be away from the home. My mother might come to get me, and I have to be there."

I loved Danny so much and wanted to do whatever I could to help him develop his potential. And I wanted to spare him the heartache of holding onto a dream that I was certain would never come true. Danny's mother had given him up several years before, and I'd never heard of a mother reclaiming her child after that long.

What I really wanted to do was adopt him, but I was prevented from doing that because I'd been to prison and was unmarried. So I figured out an alternative. I went to my brother in Pawley's Island, South Carolina, and I explained the situation. He agreed to adopt Danny, but when I discussed the plan with Danny he objected.

"My mother might come back," he said.

I was disappointed he would pass up the advantages a stable family could offer him. Not wanting to concede defeat to a nine-year-old boy, I invited him to spend a week with my brother's family that summer. My brother had a son two years older than Danny, and together the youngsters had a great time. On the drive back to the Boys' Home, I asked Danny what he thought of my family.

"They're cool."

"Do you like my nephew?"

"He's a little mean, but I straightened him out."

"Well, how would you like to live with them?"

"No thanks."

"But you just said you liked them. They'd be good to you."

"I tried a family once, and I'll never do that again. Nobody cares."

"Listen to me, son. I care. And I'd like to adopt you. You could stay with my brother for now. Once I get married, you can come live with me, and I'll love and educate you. My family will support and stand by you. You can count on me. I'll be loyal to you. I'll give you the life you've never known. I really love you."

Then, without thinking about the potential consequences of what I was saying, I added, "I know this is hard for you to accept, but your mother is never coming back to get you. She doesn't care, or else she'd have returned by now. You've got to give up that dream, son."

Danny looked at me with sudden fury in his eyes. "I hate you!" he sputtered. "You're just like all the others! You don't care! You don't love me! You don't understand! My mother cares about me. She had to make a decision about keeping me or my baby sister, and she gave me away. But she loves me, and one day she's coming back."

"Son, I'm sorry. I didn't mean-"

"I hate you!" he yelled.

"Son, I'm sorry, I'm sorry," I said, with tears in my eyes.

I'd have given anything if I could take back those words, but Danny never forgave me. From that point until the day I left the home, he hardly said ten words to me. No matter what I tried to do, he refused my friendship.

My impulsive response ruined our relationship. But I learned a significant truth: no one can take the place of parents in a child's heart. No matter what happens, a child loves his parents, especially his mother, and he wants to be loved by them. I should have remembered that from my own experiences.

Later, when I visited the Boys' Home during a break from college, I was surprised to learn that Danny's mother finally did return for him. His daddy, whom he never knew, had been killed in a motorcycle accident. There was a will, and his mother needed the boy to collect some insurance money. So she came and got him, and they moved to Texas. After several years I found out he'd dropped out of school and was hanging out on the street. Knowing his toughness, I figured that would happen. It would have been impossible for him to have stayed out of trouble in that environment without proper guidance. It breaks my heart to think he could be in prison now, especially knowing I could have given him the support he needed to make it. I'd love to see him again; I hate to think I might have to visit a prison to do that.

Young people, you may not have much in common with little

orphan boys like Toby or Jerry or Danny. But we're all fragile and need to be handled with love.

I believe the word love is the most misused word in our vocabulary. I think one of the saddest things in life is to grow old and be unwanted and unloved.

I'm so thankful there were people who cared for me. They reached out to me when I was a nobody - just convict number 62345. They showed me love. But for every one of me, there are thousands upon thousands who are never loved and end up in nameless cemeteries, like Sheephead Kelly did. And for every little Toby of the world there are thousands of orphan children who never see the face of love, a smile, a kind word, open arms, or an open home.

Children's lives are like twigs. They grow in the direction they are bent. If they are shown love, they grow in love. They become balanced, happy individuals who then, in turn, reach out to others in love.

But if they are abused, ignored, or cast aside, they'll grow in that direction, too. They'll end up hard and bitter. Some of them will end up in prison. Some will end up in a grave without anybody to even claim their bodies. And every last one of us is the same. We, too, grow in the direction we're bent.

Young people, please, won't you tell someone that you love them? Someone needs to hear it as much as you need to say it. You should tell your parents you love them. Now, I realize they will think you're on drugs. Why not go to school tomorrow and tell your teachers that you love them? Tell someone less attractive than you at school that they are special and that you care about them. Now is the time to tell others that you love them.

When I think of wanting to be loved, I'm reminded of the story of a little girl who was orphaned when her parents were killed in an auto accident. She was placed in an orphanage, but she was unattractive and she was teased mercilessly. She had great trouble making friends with the other children. After months of trying, she gave up and kept to herself. One day the director of the orphanage looked out his office window and saw the little girl walking by herself towards the front gate.

Thinking she was trying to run away, the director followed her at a distance so that she could not see him. He watched as she walked through the front gate of the orphanage and down the street to a tree with a branch that stuck out over the sidewalk. She placed a note into the branch and then turned around and walked back to the orphanage.

Later, the director left the orphanage and retrieved the note from the tree. It read, "To anyone who finds this, I love you."

The adolescent years can be years of great selfishness, when young people think only of themselves and would never reach out to someone like a lonely little girl. Reach out to someone who can give you nothing in return or to someone who is unlovable in the eyes of the rest of the world. I believe that we should reach out to others with arms of love. Help little orphan boys like Toby and Jerry and Danny.

Closing

Whatever you do, young people, never forget the things I've talked about. And, in closing, I would like to give you some examples to pattern your life after. You see, I'm not who you want to be in life.

The first example is a twelve-year-old boy who came to the fence at Georgia State Penitentiary and told me that he loved me. When the world had turned its back on me he said, "I believe in you. You're not a murderer." No one believed in me but that young boy.

He told me his name was Jimmy Hale, that his father was a state trooper, and that his mother worked as a nurse at the prison hospital. "We live on the prison reservation," he said, pointing to the white house where he lived. I could see the house from my cell.

He came to the prison fence to see me almost every day. He always wore T-shirts with slogans on them, such as, "I'm a winner! God don't sponsor no losers!" I laughed at his shirts but not at the seriousness with which he shared his faith.

Jimmy always had a basketball in his hands. His goal was to be the greatest basketball player in the whole world, and he was obviously a gifted athlete. We tossed the ball back and forth across the fence. Being a former all-state basketball player, I suggested leg exercises to build his strength and gave him pointers to improve his dribbling. I watched him as he practiced up and down the road and around the guard tower, switching from his left hand to his right and dribbling between his legs.

We developed a strong friendship in spite of the wire barrier. I instructed him about sports and tried to encourage him.

One day, he asked me if I would go to his high school and speak. It was about twenty miles from the prison. I thought he was going to bust me out of the joint.

I said, "How am I going to do that?"

He and his father went to the warden and pleaded their case. Finally, the warden gave in, and I went to his high school to speak. That young boy got up and introduced me and what he said, I'll never forget.

He said, "Students, I want you to know that I care about you. This old man ain't much to look at, but he's my friend and he's taught me a great deal. And I care very much about you, and some of you are wrecking your lives and you know it. You're committing immoral sex acts. You're using alcohol and other drugs. You're going down the same road he went down a long time ago. Please listen to this man. Because forty-five minutes from now he will leave here. He will go back to Georgia State Penitentiary. That door will slam. He will die there. It's real."

The friendship of that little boy helped to make the black days bearable. But I was not prepared for the sad news that he brought me one day. His family had purchased a house in town and planned to move very soon.

"I've brought you something," he said, handing the gift through the fence.

It was a wooden cross he had made using two small branches. He had shellacked them and added a string so that I could hang the cross in my cell.

"I made it myself," he said. "I won't ever forget you, and I want to thank you for teaching me everything."

I said, "I'll never forget you either, Jimmy."

He had become my whole life. Standing there, I didn't let him see me cry. But after he left I wept.

Then one day his mother, who was a nurse in the prison, came to see me with a special request.

She said, "Tonight his basketball team is in the state finals. The game is going to be on the radio, and he wants you to listen."

Oh, I couldn't wait for the game to get started. He was wearing number 30. My old number. There were five seconds left in the game, his team was down by one, and his team had the ball. They called time-out. They set up one last shot. He took the shot, and made it. He was chosen the outstanding player. He scored 27 points, and they interviewed him on the radio.

In the tense silence that followed, I heard the radio announcer, "We're here with Jimmy Hale whose last second shot won the game. Jimmy, you had a big game with 27 points, and you certainly didn't play like a freshman but you had to be a little nervous when you took that last shot."

"No, sir," Jimmy answered. "I had a good teacher."

That young boy came to that prison to see me the day before I left on parole. Except he was not little anymore. He was a senior in high school, and he could dunk a basketball. He hugged my neck, and he said, "I want to thank you for being the brother I never had."

I said, "I want to thank you for the impact you've had on my life and for loving me."

When you're looking for someone to pattern your life after, young people, I hope you will choose a twelve-year-old boy who had the courage to take a stand with his life - a young boy who dared to be different, who had the courage to stand up to his peer group and say, "Hey, I'm not going to follow you. You need to follow me."

He's the greatest example of positive peer pressure I have ever known. Today, twenty years later, we both live in the Atlanta, Georgia, area. Jimmy has been a state trooper for nearly twenty years and has a lovely wife and three wonderful children. I am godfather to his daughter, Hannah. He remains one of my closest friends, and I'm so thankful that he came into my life.

After all these years, Jimmy is still helping people. On September 1, 1997, he pulled over a car for speeding. The nervous driver was hurrying to the hospital with his pregnant wife, and Jimmy let him off with a warning. Later, Jimmy saw the same black man he had pulled over, William Cody, standing by his car on the side of the road and waving frantically. Jimmy stopped and delivered the baby in the backseat of Cody's car. Later that week the Atlanta Journal/ Constitution ran a picture of Jimmy visiting with five-day-old Kiyah Kaitlan Cody and her mother, Tonya, in the Cody home.

The next example is a black man named Marcus "Doc" Odomes, a man I first met at Georgia State Penitentiary.

After the prison rioted, the warden threw both of us into an eight-by-ten foot cell, and the door was slammed shut. In order to success-fully integrate the prison, the warden wanted to show that a black and a white inmate could live together. Inmates and guards were laying odds on which of us would kill the other.

Both of us were all-state athletes before entering prison, and we were used by the warden to recruit other inmates to play in the first integrated basketball game in the history of the prison. This game was the catalyst for the successful integration of the prison.

There were only inches of space between the beds in our eight-by-ten foot cell. There we sat, staring at each other.

"You don't like me, do you?" he asked.

"No," I said. "I hate your guts."

He looked at me, and he said, "Why do you hate me?"

I thought I would have had fifty reasons to give him. I couldn't think of one.

"'C-cause you're black," I stammered.

"That's right," he said. "You hate me because of the color of my skin. I don't hate you because you're white. I hate you because you'd be sorry in any color."

To make a long story longer, that man became my closest friend as we spent more than three years in that cell. We shared everything we had. Every time you saw one, you saw the other. The other inmates even called us "Salt and Pepper".

One day two white inmates came to our cell to kill me. Doc fought them in order to save my life. He was stabbed several times and taken to the prison hospital to die.

After they took him away, I cried as I looked at his blood. You know why? Because it was red, the same color as mine.

In the prison hospital, I told him that I loved him and that I owed him my life and would take his place if I could.

"I won't ever forget you," I said. "I won't let anyone forget you. I'll spend the rest of my life trying to teach others what you have taught me."

He squeezed my hand, and in a low, soft, pained voice he said, "I love you, Super Honky. You're a true friend."

Through his life he issued a challenge to me that will go with me to my grave; he challenged me to share what he and I learned in that cell with others. You see, he helped me become free not only from my physical prison, but from the shackles of sin and despair. He shared love with me when I had no one else, taught me how to be colorblind, stood with me when I needed a friend, taught me about faith, and - finally - he was willing to give his life that I might live. His life challenged mine. I shall never forget him. He will forever live in my memory.

In the summer of 1997, I returned to the prison graveyard, Pissant Hill. As I stood at Pissant Hill in the driving rain, I said, "You were right, Doc. I'm unshackled. I'm free. Freer than I've ever been in my life."

If ever there were young people to say no to all these things that I have talked about, I hope it will be you - this generation. You can make a difference.

I hope that you will remember the importance of making the right choices in your life. And I hope that you will never forget this: you always reap what you sow in life.

FOR GENERAL ORDERING

ALSO AVAILABLE BY HAROLD MORRIS:

The Law of the Harvest, taken from the novel *Unshackled,* is an inspirational and instructional guide for parents and teenagers. Unforgettable characters fill each chapter, and their stories - whether uplifting or tragic - bear out the same eternal truth: you always reap what you sow in life.

After sixteen years of speaking to millions of teenagers all over the world, Harold Morris gives parents and teens the benefit of his experiences in a colorful narrative that goes right to the heart of the problems today's teens face.

Harold Morris writes, "What did I sow into my life? I associated with the wrong kinds of people, I drank, I did drugs, I had immoral sex, and I was proud to call myself a racist. What did I reap? Two life sentences at Georgia State Penitentiary for armed robbery and murder, and I almost died there."

Twice Pardoned, the award winning video by Harold Morris, is a 33 minute presentation in which he speaks to 12,000 teenagers about the law of the harvest - a simple truth that applies to the physical as well as the spiritual universe: you always reap what you sow. In this gripping narrative, he discusses wrong association and peer pressure, alcohol, drugs, sex and dating, suicide, race, and the importance of love. He vividly illustrates the crucial importance of making the right choices early in life.

TO ORDER: *Unshackled*: US $24.99/CAN $32.99
The Law of the Harvest: US $6.99/CAN $9.99
Twice Pardoned video: US $19.99/CAN $27.99
OR, all three of the above in one package for
US $44.99/CAN $62.99 (a savings of 22%)

Please call 1-888-457-2315 or send your order with a check or money order to: **Nantucket Publishing**
602 S.W. Ward Blvd.
Wilson, N.C. 27893

Please include US $3.99/CAN $6.99 for each individual item (US $4.99/ CAN $8.99 for the 3 part package) for shipping and handling; VISA and Mastercard welcome. Sorry, no COD's.

(Continued on the following page.)

FOR TRADE BOOKSELLERS

Nantucket Publishing is the exclusive distributor to the trade for products by Harold Morris. To order:

By mail: **Nantucket Publishing**   By phone: **1-800-244-2421**
                602 S.W. Ward Blvd.
                Wilson, N.C. 27893   By fax: **1-252-291-3408**

ATTENTION SCHOOLS:

Unshackled, ***The Law of the Harvest***, and the **Twice Pardoned** video can be purchased at quantity discounts for educational use. To learn more about discount pricing and to order, call **1-800-244-2421** between 9:00AM and 5:00PM EST Monday - Friday.

Visit us on the web at: www.unshackled.com